Instructor's Edition

BUILDING VOCABULARY SKILLS

Donald J. Goodman

MUSKEGON COMMUNITY COLLEGE

Carole Mohr

TOWNSEND PRESS   Marlton, NJ 08053

Copyright © 1990, 1995 by Townsend Press, Inc.
Printed in the United States of America
ISBN 0-944210-79-1

Send book orders and requests for desk copies or supplements to:
Townsend Press
1038 Industrial Drive
Berlin, NJ 08009

For even faster service, call us at our toll-free number:
1-800-772-6410

Or FAX your request to:
1-609-753-0649

ISBN 0-944210-79-1

Contents

Note: For ease of reference, the title of the passage that concludes each chapter appears in parentheses.

UNIT FOUR

UNIT FIVE

Appendixes

Preface

The problem is all too familiar: *students just don't know enough words*. Reading, writing, and content teachers agree that many students' vocabularies are inadequate to the demands of courses. Weak vocabularies limit students' understanding of what they read and the clarity and depth of what they write.

The purpose of the Townsend Press vocabulary series is to provide a solid, workable answer to the vocabulary problem. The series consists of three books, each of which *teaches* 300 important words or word parts. Within each book are 30 chapters, with 10 words or word parts in each chapter. Here are the distinctive features of BUILDING VOCABULARY SKILLS and the other books in the series.

1   An intensive words-in-context approach. Studies show that students learn words best by seeing them repeatedly in different contexts, not through rote memorization. BUILDING VOCABULARY SKILLS gives students an intensive in-context experience by presenting each word in seven different contexts. Each chapter takes students through a productive sequence of steps:

- Students first see a word in a preview.
- They then infer the meaning of the word by considering two sentences in which it appears.
- Based on their inferences, students select and confirm each word's meaning in a matching test. They are then in a solid position to further deepen their knowledge of a word.
- Finally, they strengthen their understanding of a word by applying it three times: in two sentence practices and in a passage practice.

Each encounter with a word brings it closer to becoming part of the student's permanent word bank.

2   Abundant practice. In addition to the extensive practice in each chapter, there are *four unit tests* at the end of each six-chapter unit. These tests reinforce students' knowledge of every word in every chapter. Further, there are added tests in the *Test Bank* and the *computer disks* that accompany the book. All this practice means that students learn in the surest possible way: by working closely and repeatedly with each word.

3   Controlled feedback. Students receive feedback on two of the practices in each vocabulary chapter. A limited answer key at the back of the book lets them see how they did with the opening preview of words. The key also provides answers for the first sentence check in the chapter. The key enables students to take an active role in their own learning. And they are likely to use the answer key in an honest and positive way if they know they may be tested on the many activities and selections for which answers are not provided. (Answers not in the book are in the Instructor's Edition. They can, of course, be copied and passed out at the teacher's discretion.)

4   Focus on essential words. A good deal of time and research went into selecting the 300 words and word parts featured in the book. Word frequency lists were consulted, along with lists in a wide number of vocabulary books. In addition, the authors and editors each prepared their own lists. A computer was used to help in the consolidation of the many word lists. A long process of group discussion then led to final decisions about the words and word parts that would be more helpful for students on a basic reading level.

5   Appealing content. Dull practice materials work against learning. On the other hand, meaningful, lively, and at times even funny sentences and passages can spark students' attention and thus encourage their grasp of the material. For this reason, a great deal of effort was put into creating sentences and passages with both widespread appeal *and* solid context support. We have tried throughout to make the practice materials truly enjoyable for teachers and students alike. Look, for example, at the passage on page 8 that closes the first chapter of this book.

6   Clarity of format. The book has been designed so that its very format contributes to the learning process. All ten words of a chapter appear on a single page, and each practice begins and ends on one page. In particular, each chapter has a two-page spread (turn, for example, to pages 6-7) so that students can refer to the ten words in context on one side while working on the matching test and sentence check on the other side. And a second color has been used within the book to help make the content as visually appealing as possible.

7 Supplementary materials.

a A combined *Instructor's Manual and Test Bank* is available at no charge to instructors using the book. It can be obtained by writing to the Reading Editor, Townsend Press, Pavilions at Greentree—408, Marlton, NJ 08053. This booklet contains pre- and post-tests for all five units in the text as well as teaching guidelines, suggested syllabi, an answer key, and a set of mastery tests for each chapter.

b A *comprehensive series of computer disks* also accompanies the book. These disks provide up to four tests for each vocabulary chapter in the book. The disks are self-booting and contain a number of other user- and instructor-friendly features, including brief explanations of answers, a sound option, frequent mention of the user's first name, a running score at the bottom of the screen, and a record-keeping file.

Probably in no other area of reading instruction is the computer more useful than in reinforcing vocabulary. This vocabulary program takes full advantage of the computer's unique capabilities and motivational appeal. Here's how the program works:

- Students are tested on the ten words in a chapter, with each word in a sentence context different from any in the book itself.
- After students answer each question, they receive immediate feedback: The computer tells if a student is right or wrong and *why*, frequently using the student's first name and providing a running score.
- When the test is over, the computer supplies a test score and—this especially is what is unique about this program—a chance to retest on the specific words the student got wrong. For example, if a student misses four items on a test, the retest provides *four different sentences* that test just those four words. Students then receive a score for this special retest. What is so valuable about this, of course, is that the computer gives students added practice in the words they most need to review.
- In addition, the computer offers a *second*, more challenging test in which students must identify the meanings of the chapter words without benefit of context. This test is a final check that students have really learned the words. And, again, there is the option of a retest, tailor-made to recheck only those words missed on the first definition test.

By the end of this program, students' knowledge of each word in the chapter will have been carefully reinforced. And this reinforcement will be the more effective for having occurred in an electronic medium that especially engages today's students.

A demo disk will be sent to any teacher requesting it. The full set of disks, with unlimited copying privileges, will be available at no charge to departments that have adopted the book.

8 Realistic pricing. We wanted a book that would offer the highest possible quality at the best possible price. We are delighted that Townsend Press has committed to sell this book to students at a price under ten dollars. While the book is comprehensive enough to serve as a primary text, its modest price also makes it an inexpensive supplement.

9 One in a sequence of books. BUILDING VOCABULARY SKILLS is one of seven books in the Townsend Press Vocabulary Series. GROUNDWORK FOR A BETTER VOCABULARY is the basic book in the series. It is followed by the three main books in the series: BUILDING VOCABULARY SKILLS (also a basic text), IMPROVING VOCABULARY SKILLS (an intermediate text), and ADVANCING VOCABULARY SKILLS (a more advanced text); there are also short versions of these three books. Suggested grade levels for the three main books are included in the *Instructor's Manual.* Together, the books will help create a vocabulary foundation that will make any student a better reader, writer, and thinker.

Acknowledgments

Our thanks go to the talented group of writers and editors at Townsend Press who have worked closely with us on the book: John Langan, Joan Dunayer, Jane Mackay, and Beth Johnson Ruth. We also acknowledge the extraordinary computer programming efforts of Terry Hutchison. Inspiration for the cover came from an idea by Janet M. Goldstein, and the cover itself owes thanks to the artistry of Larry Didona. Finally, we are grateful for the design, editing, and proofreading skills of Janet M. Goldstein.

Donald J. Goodman   *Carole Mohr*

Introduction

WHY VOCABULARY DEVELOPMENT COUNTS

You have probably often heard it said, "Building vocabulary is important." Maybe you've politely nodded in agreement and then forgotten the matter. But it would be fair for you to ask, "Why *is* vocabulary development important? Provide some evidence." Here are four compelling kinds of evidence.

1   Common sense tells you what many research studies have shown as well: vocabulary is a basic part of reading comprehension. Simply put, if you don't know enough words, you are going to have trouble understanding what you read. An occasional word may not stop you, but if there are too many words you don't know, comprehension will suffer. The *content* of textbooks is often challenge enough; you don't want to work as well on understanding the *words* that make up that content.

2   Vocabulary is a major part of almost every standardized test, including reading achievement tests, college entrance exams, and armed forces and vocational placement tests. Test authors know that vocabulary is a key measure of both one's learning and one's ability to learn. So they have a separate vocabulary section as well as a reading comprehension section. The more words you know, then, the better you are likely to do on such important tests.

3   Studies have made clear that students with strong vocabularies are more successful in school. And one widely known study found that a good vocabulary, more than any other factor, was common to people enjoying successful careers in life. Words are in fact the tools not just of better reading, but of writing, speaking, listening, and thinking as well. The more words you have at your command, the more effective your communication can be, and the more influence you can have on the people around you.

4   In the world of the 1990s, a good vocabulary will count more than ever. Far fewer people will work on farms or in factories. Far more will be in jobs that provide services or process information. More than ever, words will be the tools of our trade: words we use in reading, writing, listening, and speaking. Furthermore, experts say that workers of the 90s will be called on to change jobs and learn new skills at an ever-increasing pace. The keys to survival and success will thus be the abilities to communicate skillfully and learn quickly. A solid vocabulary is essential for both of these skills.

The evidence is overwhelming, then, that building vocabulary is crucial. The question thus becomes, "What is the best way of going about it?"

WORDS IN CONTEXT: THE KEY TO VOCABULARY DEVELOPMENT

Memorizing lists of words is a traditional method of vocabulary development. But a person is likely to forget such memorized lists quickly. Studies show that to master a word (or a word part), you must see and use it in various contexts. By working actively and repeatedly with a word, you greatly increase the chance of really learning it.

The following activity will make clear how the book is organized and how it uses a words-in-context approach. Answer the questions or fill in the missing words in the spaces provided.

Contents

Turn to the table of contents on pages iii-iv.

- How many chapters are in the book? ___*30*___
- Most chapters present vocabulary words. How many chapters present word parts? ___*4*___
- Three short sections follow the chapters. The first provides a limited answer key; the second gives helpful information on using _____*a dictionary*_____; and the third is an index of the 300 words and word parts in the book.

Vocabulary Chapters

Turn to Chapter 1 on pages 5-9. This chapter, like all the others, consists of six parts:

- The *first part*, on page 5, is titled _____*Previewing the Words*_____

This preview introduces you to the ten words covered in the chapter. After you try filling in the blanks, you are asked to check the ___*answers*___ at the back and to fill in any empty blanks.

- The *second part* of the chapter, on page 6, is titled _____*Ten Words in Context*_____

The left-hand column lists the ten words. Under each word is its ___*pronunciation*___ (in parentheses) and its part of speech (*noun, verb,* or *adjective*). For example, we are told that *acknowledge,* the first word on page 6, is a verb.

Using the pronunciation guide requires only a bit of information: Short vowels have no special mark, while long vowels are indicated with a line above the vowel. (Note that long vowels have the sound of their own name.) What is the first word in the list with a long vowel? _____*anecdote*_____ . Symbols that sound like "uh"—like the "uh" a speaker makes when hesitating—are symbolized by the schwa (ə), which looks like an upside down *e*. What is the first word in the list with a schwa? _____*alternative*_____ . Finally, an accent mark (') tells which syllable to emphasize when pronouncing a word. What is the first word in the list with an accent on the second syllable? ___*acknowledge*___ A brief guide to the dictionary on page 167 gives further information on pronouncing words.

To the right of each word are two sentences that help you understand its meaning. In each sentence, the *context* —the words surrounding the boldfaced word—provides clues you can use to figure out the definition. For example, look at the first sentence for the word *acknowledge.*

Andrea was annoyed when Hal used one of her jokes in his class speech without **acknowledging** that the joke was hers.

Based on the context, what is the meaning of *acknowledging*?

    a. hiding   b. wishing   ⓒ admitting   d. denying

A second sentence also helps you pin down the meaning:

> Even when the votes were counted, Senator Rice refused to **acknowledge** that he had lost.

By looking closely at each pair of sentences, you can decide on the meaning of a word. (In the example above, *acknowledging* clearly means *admitting*.) As you figure out each meaning, you are working actively with the word. You are creating the groundwork you need to understand *and* to remember the word. Getting involved with the word and developing a feel for it, based upon its use in context, is the key to word mastery.

It is with good reason, then, that the directions at the top of page 6 tell you to look _____*closely*_____ and _____*carefully*_____ at the context. Doing so deepens your sense of the word and prepares you for the next activity.

• The ***third part*** of the chapter, on page 7, is titled __*Matching Words and Definitions*__.

According to research, it is not enough to see a word in context. At a certain point, it is important as well to see the meaning of a word. The matching test provides that meaning, but it also makes you look for and think about that meaning. In other words, it continues the active learning that is your surest route to learning and remembering a word.

Note the caution that follows the test. Do not proceed any further until you are sure that you know the correct meaning of each word.

• The ***fourth part*** of the chapter (also on page 7) is titled _____*Sentence Check 1*_____.

Here are ten sentences that give you an opportunity to apply your understanding of the ten words. After inserting the words, check your answers in the limited key at the back of the book. Be sure to use the answer key as a learning tool only. Doing so will help you to master the words and to prepare for the last two activities and the unit tests, for which answers are not provided.

• The ***fifth part*** of the chapter, on page 8, is titled _____*Sentence Check 2*_____, and the ***sixth part*** is titled _____*Final Check*_____.

Both practices test you on all ten words, giving you a chance to deepen your mastery. In the second activity, you have the context of an entire passage in which you can practice and apply the words.

At the bottom of the last page of this chapter is a box where you can enter your score for the final two checks. These scores should also be entered into the vocabulary performance chart located on the inside back page of the book. To get your score, take 10% off for each item wrong, as shown in the following chart:

> 0 wrong = 100%
> 1 wrong = 90%
> 2 wrong = 80%
> 3 wrong = 70%
> 4 wrong = 60%
> 5 wrong = 50%
> and so on.

Word Parts Chapters

In all, there are 260 words in the chapters and 40 word parts. *Word parts*, also known as *prefixes*, *suffixes*, and *roots*, are building blocks used in many common English words. Learning word parts can help you to spell and pronounce words, to unlock the meanings of unfamiliar words, and to remember new words.

Each of the four word parts chapters follows the same sequence as the vocabulary chapters do. Keep the following guideline in mind as well. To find the meaning of a word part, you should do two things.

1   First decide on the meaning of each boldfaced word in "Ten Word Parts in Context." If you don't know a meaning, use context clues to find it. For example, consider the two sentences for the word part *ex*:

> "Inhale as you lower your head," called out the exercise instructor, "and **exhale** as you do the sit-up."

> "My uncle isn't a very good businessperson—he once tried to **export** rice to China and vodka to Russia."

You can conclude that *exhale* means the opposite of *inhale* ("to breathe in"); thus *exhale* means "to breathe out." You can also determine that *export* means "to send goods out of a country to sell them."

2   Then decide on the meaning each pair of boldfaced words has in common. This will also be the meaning of the word part they share. In the case of the two sentences above, both words include the idea of something going out. Thus *ex* must mean "out" or "from."

You now know, in a nutshell, how to proceed with the words in each chapter. Make sure that you do each page very carefully. *Remember, as you work through the activities, you are learning the words.*

How many times in all will you use each word? If you look, you'll see that each chapter gives you the opportunity to work with each word seven times. Each "impression" adds to the likelihood that the word will become part of your active vocabulary. You will have further opportunities to use the word in the four unit tests that follow each chapter and on the computer disks that are available with the book.

Information on the computer disks and the other two books in the Townsend Press vocabulary series can be obtained by writing to the address on the back cover.

FINAL THOUGHTS

The facts are in. A strong vocabulary is a source of power. Words can make you a better reader, writer, speaker, thinker, and learner. They can dramatically increase your chances of success in school and in your job.

But words will not come automatically. They must be learned in a program of regular study. If you commit yourself to learning words, and you work actively and honestly with the chapters in this book, you will not only enrich your vocabulary—you will enrich your life as well.

Unit One

Previewing the Words

Find out how many of the ten words in this chapter you already know. Try to complete each sentence with the most suitable word from the list below. Use each word once.

Leave a sentence blank rather than guessing at an answer. Your purpose here is just to get a sense of the ten words and what you may know about them.

acknowledge	alternative	anecdote	appropriate	avert
candid	compel	comply	concise	drastic

1. People do not always support _____*drastic*_____ changes in fashion, such as extreme shifts in hem lines.

2. Magazine articles often begin with an _____*anecdote*_____ in order to gain the reader's interest.

3. Though Rita had asked Jack for his _____*candid*_____ opinion, she was still hurt when he criticized her paper.

4. Our boss expects us to _____*comply*_____ with his instructions without asking questions or pointing out problems.

5. People often find it difficult to _____*acknowledge*_____ their errors. They hate to admit they were wrong.

6. When you go on a job interview, it is _____*appropriate*_____ to dress as you would if you had the position you're interviewing for.

7. Dale's poor grades left him with two _____*alternative*_____s—to work fewer hours at his part-time job or to drop a class.

8. My history teacher would often _____*compel*_____ us to do useless work, such as memorizing the date each state entered the union.

9. Answers to essay questions should be _____*concise*_____. Often students waste test time by writing wordy answers that don't say much.

10. When English sailors learned they could _____*avert*_____ the disease of scurvy by eating citrus fruits, they began keeping limes on board. Thus English sailors became known as "limeys."

Now check your answers by turning to page 163. Fix any mistakes and fill in any blank spaces by writing in the correct answers. By doing so, you will complete this introduction to the ten words.

You're now ready to strengthen your knowledge of the words you already know and to master the words you're only half sure of, or don't know at all. Turn to the next page.

Ten Words in Context

Figure out the meanings of the following ten words by looking *closely and carefully* at the context in which the words appear. Doing so will prepare you for the matching test and the practices on the two pages that follow.

1 **acknowledge**
(ak-nol'-ij)
-verb

   a. Andrea was annoyed when Hal used one of her jokes in his class speech without **acknowledging** that the joke was hers.

   b. Even when the votes were counted, Senator Rice refused to **acknowledge** he had lost.

2 **alternative**
(ôl-tûr'-nə-tiv)
-noun

   a. The teacher stated the **alternatives** to Tim—retake the test or get a D for the course.

   b. When her dog clearly began to suffer from cancer, Inez felt she had no **alternative**. It was necessary to have him put to sleep.

3 **anecdote**
(an'-ik-dōt')
-noun

   a. Dad told the children an **anecdote** about getting his tie caught in a file cabinet at work just as the boss walked in.

   b. I once heard the following **anecdote** about a stagehand's revenge on a bossy actor: the stagehand added wheels to a table used in a play; when the actor leaped onto the table during the play's most dramatic scene, he rolled straight off into the wings.

4 **appropriate**
(ə-prō'-prē-it)
-adjective

   a. Chuck has little sense of what is socially **appropriate**. For example, he went to his sister's wedding in jogging shoes.

   b. In a church it is considered **appropriate** for a man to take his hat off, but in a synagogue it is considered proper for a man to cover his head.

5 **avert**
(ə-vûrt')
-verb

   a. Nancy **averted** an unpleasant meeting with her ex-boyfriend by leaving the store before he saw her.

   b. To **avert** an accident with the car in front of his, Larry quickly cut hard to the right and ran into a stop sign.

6 **candid**
(kan'-did)
-adjective

   a. A child is a striking combination of boldfaced liar ("I didn't eat the cookie") and painfully **candid** reporter ("Gee, you've gotten really fat").

   b. Many people admire David's open, **candid** nature; others consider him too outspoken.

7 **compel**
(kəm-pel')
-verb

   a. It is a sad sight to see the crack of a whip **compel** a grand cat like the lion to leap through hoops for a crowd's amusement.

   b. You can **compel** a weaker person to obey, but you can never force someone to feel respect.

8 **comply**
(kəm-plī')
-verb

   a. If someone with an iron pipe demands your wallet, it is safer to **comply** than to resist.

   b. My husband is so used to being boss at work that he is annoyed when I don't **comply** with his every request at home.

9 **concise**
(kon-sīs')
-adjective

   a. Journalists tend to write very **concise** prose because a newspaper column offers limited space.

   b. Unlike many politicians, our mayor is **concise**—his speeches are short but say much.

10 **drastic**
(dras'-tik)
-adjective

   a. The new president of Super Steel Products took **drastic** steps, closing two factories and laying off 300 employees.

   b. "This time I will let you off with just an hour after school," the principal said. "But if it happens again, the punishment will be more **drastic**."

Matching Words and Definitions

Check your understanding of the ten words by matching each word with its definition. Look back at the sentences in "Ten Words in Context" as needed to decide on the meaning of each word.

_e_	1. **acknowledge**	a.	to do as commanded or asked
_c_	2. **alternative**	b.	proper; suitable to the situation
_h_	3. **anecdote**	c.	a choice
_b_	4. **appropriate**	d.	extreme; harsh or intense
_j_	5. **avert**	e.	to confess or admit
_g_	6. **candid**	f.	to force
_f_	7. **compel**	g.	very honest
_a_	8. **comply**	h.	a short story of an event
_i_	9. **concise**	i.	communicating much in a few clear words
_d_	10. **drastic**	j.	to prevent

CAUTION: Do not go any further until you are sure the above answers are correct. If you have studied the "Ten Words in Context," you will know how to match each word. Then you can use the matches to help you in the following practices. Your goal is to reach a point where you don't need to check definitions at all.

➤ *Sentence Check 1*

Complete each sentence below with the most suitable word from the box. Use each word once.

acknowledge	alternative	anecdote	appropriate	avert
candid	compel	comply	concise	drastic

1. Because Frank seems so ____*candid*____, everyone believes him even when he tells a lie.

2. The drummer told interesting ____*anecdote*____s about famous rock singers he had played for.

3. People often take ____*drastic*____ steps in anger, extreme actions that they later regret.

4. When he saw no way to ____*avert*____ the crash, the pilot jumped out of the plane.

5. In traditional wedding ceremonies, the clergy person is often wordy, while the bride and groom are very ____*concise*____.

6. Many Americans do not fully ____*comply*____ with the tax rules of this country.

7. A couple of older boys tried to ____*compel*____ some first graders to hand over their lunch money.

8. After high school, Kenny felt his ____*alternative*____s were either to join the military or to get a job. Then, when he had saved enough money, he could go to college.

9. When the real ax-murderer confessed, the police had to ____*acknowledge*____ that the wrong man had been jailed.

10. In most American schools, it is not ____*appropriate*____ for students to call their teachers by their first names.

Now check your answers to these questions by turning to page 163. Going over the answers carefully will help you prepare for the next two checks, for which answers are not given.

➤ Sentence Check 2

Complete each sentence below with two words from the following list. Use each word once.

acknowledge	alternative	anecdote	appropriate	avert
candid	compel	comply	concise	drastic

1-2. The sale sign was huge but ___*concise*___ —it said only, "___*Drastic*___ price cuts."

3-4. In colonial America, it was thought ___*appropriate*___ for wives to ___*comply*___ with all their husbands' commands.

5-6. "The poor economic situation leaves me no ___*alternative*___ ," said the company president. "It ___*compel*___s me to lay off some of our workers."

7-8. Our business instructor told an ___*anecdote*___ about a company that ___*avert*___(e)d failure by sharing ownership with all its workers.

9-10. "I *acknowledge* that you have a perfect right to do whatever you like with your hair," said the teenage girl's mother. "But, to be ___*candid*___ , I don't find green curls attractive."

➤ Final Check: Taking Exams

Here is a final opportunity for you to strengthen your knowledge of the ten words. First read the following passage carefully. Then fill in each blank with a word from the box at the top of this page. (Context clues will help you figure out which word goes in which blank.) Use each word once.

There are five test-taking methods to consider when faced with exams. The first is to impress your teachers with very clever answers. For example, you might respond to any question beginning with the word "why" with a simple, (1)___*concise*___ "Why not?" This is not recommended, however, unless you know an instructor has great respect for humor. A second method is simply to refuse to take an exam. You might try writing something like, "This is a free country, so you can't (2)___*compel*___ me to take this test. Besides, I partied all last night." This method should not be used unless you are in (3)___*drastic*___ need, as it involves a great deal of risk. It is (4)___*appropriate*___ only if you have shown yourself to be very brilliant throughout the course and you are the teacher's pet. Otherwise, you can expect your teacher simply to refuse to pass you. A third way of dealing with a test is to (5)___*candid*___ly admit helplessness. According to one (6)___*anecdote*___ , a student openly (7)___*acknowledge*___(e)d ignorance by writing, "God only knows the answer to this question." Unfortunately, the instructor's response was, "God gets an A. You get an F." So maybe we'd better move on to the fourth method. This is to cheat. Do this only if you are hopeless and your teacher is both deaf and blind. Thus, if you want to (8)___*avert*___ failure, you usually have no (9)___*alternative*___ —you must (10)___*comply*___ with school rules. The final method for dealing with college exams, then, is clear: learn the material.

SCORES: Sentence Check 2 _____%   Final Check _____%

Enter your scores above and in the vocabulary performance chart on the inside back cover of the book.

Previewing the Words

Find out how many of the ten words in this chapter you already know. Try to complete each sentence with the most suitable word from the list below. Use each word once.

Leave a sentence blank rather than guessing at an answer. Your purpose here is just to get a sense of the ten words and what you may know about them.

dialogue	erratic	extensive	forfeit	fortify
illuminate	isolate	refuge	reminisce	urban

1. Just as the cockroach annoys _____*urban*_____ dwellers, the mosquito pesters people in the country and suburbs.

2. Tina's test scores are _____*erratic*_____—sometimes she scores very high, other times very low.

3. Babies need milk to _____*fortify*_____ their bones.

4. My grandmother likes to _____*reminisce*_____ about her childhood in Ireland.

5. The author's _____*dialogue*_____ was always sharp and bare: "You love me?" "Uh-huh." "Good."

6. Jackie did _____*extensive*_____ research for her paper by reading many books and articles.

7. If Phil drives carelessly and damages his parents' car, he will _____*forfeit*_____ the right to drive it any more.

8. During the power failure, Leslie used a battery-operated lamp to _____*illuminate*_____ the living room.

9. Some people _____*isolate*_____ themselves when they are unhappy. Others seek the company of friends and family.

10. My wife and I first met when we took _____*refuge*_____ in the same doorway during a sudden rain.

Now check your answers by turning to page 163. Fix any mistakes and fill in any blank spaces by writing in the correct answers. By doing so, you will complete this introduction to the ten words.

You're now ready to strengthen your knowledge of the words you already know and to master the words you're only half sure of, or don't know at all. Turn to the next page.

Ten Words in Context

Figure out the meanings of the following ten words by looking *closely and carefully* at the context in which the words appear. Doing so will prepare you for the matching test and the practices on the two pages that follow.

1 **dialogue**
(dī'-ə-log')
-noun

   a. The movie got an R rating because its **dialogue** includes violent and sexual language.

   b. Lois had trouble writing convincing **dialogue**. When the characters in her novel spoke to each other, they didn't sound realistic.

2 **erratic**
(i-rat'-ik)
-adjective

   a. My son's eating habits are **erratic.** One day he'll barely eat, and the next he'll eat enough for three.

   b. The driver ahead of me was **erratic**—he kept changing his speed and his lane.

3 **extensive**
(ek-sten'-siv)
-adjective

   a. John dislikes mowing grass, so he has only a small yard instead of an **extensive** lawn.

   b. To save the wounded police officer, doctors performed **extensive** surgery that lasted for hours.

4 **forfeit**
(fôr'-fit)
-verb

   a. "By cheating on your history test," said the principal, "you have **forfeited** your right to graduate this term."

   b. Some people work so non-stop that they accomplish much but **forfeit** their health.

5 **fortify**
(fôr'-tə-fī')
-verb

   a. The night before running a marathon, Elsa **fortifies** herself by eating a large plate of pasta.

   b. The builders planned to **fortify** the old tower with steel beams.

6 **illuminate**
(i-lōō'-mə-nāt')
-verb

   a. Before electricity, streets were **illuminated** by gaslight.

   b. On Halloween, we made our trick-or-treat rounds with a flashlight to **illuminate** the way.

7 **isolate**
(ī'-sə-lāt')
-verb

   a. I thought I would enjoy **isolating** myself at the vacation cabin, but I soon felt lonely.

   b. Freddy was such a troublemaker that the teacher put his desk in a far corner to **isolate** him from the other students.

8 **refuge**
(ref'-yōōj)
-noun

   a. A motorcycle offers no **refuge** in bad weather.

   b. In *The Wizard of Oz*, Dorothy doesn't reach the storm cellar in time to take **refuge** from the tornado.

9 **reminisce**
(rem'-ə-nis')
-verb

   a. On their wedding anniversary, Lenny and Jean **reminisced** about their first date.

   b. My father showed me his trophy and **reminisced** about his years as a star basketball player.

10 **urban**
(ur'-bən)
-adjective

   a. Skyscrapers make for tightly packed **urban** populations. For example, some 35,000 people work in the twin towers of the World Trade Center in New York City.

   b. Gladys likes **urban** living because she grew up in the city, but Ben, who grew up on a farm, prefers country life.

Matching Words and Definitions

Check your understanding of the ten words by matching each word with its definition. Look back at the sentences in "Ten Words in Context" as needed to decide on the meaning of each word.

_e_	1. **dialogue**	a.	to light up
_j_	2. **erratic**	b.	to lose through some fault or be forced to give up by way of penalty
_g_	3. **extensive**	c.	shelter; protection
_b_	4. **forfeit**	d.	of or in a city
_h_	5. **fortify**	e.	a passage or the whole of conversation in a poem, narration, or drama
_a_	6. **illuminate**	f.	to separate from others
_f_	7. **isolate**	g.	large in space or amount
_c_	8. **refuge**	h.	to strengthen
_i_	9. **reminisce**	i.	to remember and talk about the past
_d_	10. **urban**	j.	not consistent

CAUTION: Do not go any further until you are sure the above answers are correct. If you have studied the "Ten Words in Context," you will know how to match each word. Then you can use the matches to help you in the following practices. Your goal is to reach a point where you don't need to check definitions at all.

➤ Sentence Check 1

Complete each sentence below with the most suitable word from the box. Use each word once.

dialogue	erratic	extensive	forfeit	fortify
illuminate	isolate	refuge	reminisce	urban

1. The skater's _____erratic_____ performances showed she was too inconsistent to hire for the ice show.

2. In London during World War II, bomb shelters provided _____refuge_____ from air attacks.

3. Vitamins and minerals _____fortify_____ the body against disease.

4. Politicians who take bribes and are caught _____forfeit_____ their good names.

5. Criminals are put in prison to _____isolate_____ them from the rest of society.

6. The night before graduation, Gary and I _____reminisce_____(e)d about our four years together.

7. The pioneers used candles to _____illuminate_____ book pages at night.

8. Woody Allen's movies often show a funny contrast between spoken _____dialogue_____ and facial expressions.

9. Before his parents visit him, Don gives his apartment a(n) _____extensive_____ cleaning—dusting or scrubbing every surface.

10. There's a big difference between a(n) _____urban_____ sky and a country sky. In the country, there are no bright lights to overpower the starlight.

Now check your answers to these questions by turning to page 163. Going over the answers carefully will help you prepare for the next two checks, for which answers are not given.

➤ Sentence Check 2

Complete each sentence below with two words from the following list. Use each word once.

dialogue	erratic	extensive	forfeit	fortify
illuminate	isolate	refuge	reminisce	urban

1-2. The loud celebrating on the Fourth of July is so _____*extensive*_____ in my neighborhood that the only place I find _____*refuge*_____ from the noise is in my basement.

3-4. Curt _____*reminisce*_____(e)d for hours, revealing that his life had been very _____*erratic*_____. At some points in his life, he was very busy, married, and well off. At other times, he lived alone and was out of work.

5-6. Cities could reduce _____*urban*_____ crime if they would _____*illuminate*_____ streets and playgrounds with brighter lights, since criminals work in the shadows.

7-8. To keep the opposing army from trying to _____*isolate*_____ his weaker force from the rest of the unit, the general decided to _____*fortify*_____ his defenses.

9-10. In a _____*dialogue*_____ between the hero and the Devil, the Devil tries to get the hero to_____*forfeit*_____ his soul in exchange for fame and wealth.

➤ Final Check: Nate the Woodsman

Here is a final opportunity for you to strengthen your knowledge of the ten words. First read the following passage carefully. Then fill in each blank with a word from the box at the top of this page. (Context clues will help you figure out which word goes in which blank.) Use each word once.

Nate had spent most of his 70 years in the woods. (1)_____*Urban*_____ life was not for him. He preferred to (2)_____*isolate*_____ himself from others and find (3)_____*refuge*_____ in nature from the crowds and noise of the city. He was more than willing to (4)_____*forfeit*_____ such advantages as flush toilets and electric blankets for the joy of watching a sunrise (5)_____*illuminate*_____ the frozen pines.

Living so alone as he did made him (6)_____*erratic*_____. For example, one minute he'd be tight-lipped, and the next he'd (7)_____*reminisce*_____ at length about his youth. His knowledge of nature was (8)_____*extensive*_____, and so I learned much from him through the years.

One event shows how wise he was about the woods and how miserly he could be with words. One evening Nate, my cousin Arthur, and I were crossing a meadow. Arthur's interest in some little white mushrooms that grew there led to this (9)_____*dialogue*_____:

"These mushrooms look so good," said Arthur. "Did you ever use them, Nate?"

"Yep," said Nate. "My ma used to cook 'em up."

"Great!" said Arthur. Nate's words seemed to (10)_____*fortify*_____ Arthur's desire for those mushrooms. He gathered about a hundred of them. "How'd she fix them?" he asked Nate.

"Cooked 'em up with sugar water."

"Really? And then you ate them that way?"

"Ate 'em?" Nate was horrified. "You crazy? We used to put 'em in a bowl on the table to kill flies!"

SCORES: Sentence Check 2 _____% Final Check _____%

Enter your scores above and in the vocabulary performance chart on the inside back cover of the book.

Previewing the Words

Find out how many of the ten words in this chapter you already know. Try to complete each sentence with the most suitable word from the list below. Use each word once.

Leave a sentence blank rather than guessing at an answer. Your purpose here is just to get a sense of the ten words and what you may know about them.

delete	impartial	integrity	legitimate	lenient
menace	morale	naive	overt	undermine

1. Is it _____*legitimate*_____ for a boss to tell a secretary to make and serve coffee? Or is it improper?

2. The team's _____*morale*_____ was high: they were in good spirits and thought they would win the game.

3. Ron's fast, zig-zag driving makes him a _____*menace*_____ on the road.

4. Parents who do not lie, cheat, or steal show their children the value of _____*integrity*_____.

5. Tammy's late hours, bad eating habits, and chain smoking have begun to _____*undermine*_____ her health.

6. All children like _____*lenient*_____ babysitters who allow bedtime to be postponed an hour or two.

7. Jeremy _____*delete*_____d one section of his essay after deciding it was merely repetitious.

8. The _____*naive*_____ person may not survive in the inner city. It's best to be aware of all the city's dangers and how to guard against them.

9. Can a judge who has had a bitter divorce be truly _____*impartial*_____ in a divorce trial? Or may such a judge be biased against the husband or wife in the trial?

10. Embarrassed by John's public show of affection, Kim asked him to be less _____*overt*_____ about his feelings when others were around.

Now check your answers by turning to page 163. Fix any mistakes and fill in any blank spaces by writing in the correct answers. By doing so, you will complete this introduction to the ten words.

You're now ready to strengthen your knowledge of the words you already know and to master the words you're only half sure of, or don't know at all. Turn to the next page.

Ten Words in Context

Figure out the meanings of the following ten words by looking *closely and carefully* at the context in which the words appear. Doing so will prepare you for the matching test and the practices on the two pages that follow.

1 **delete**
(di-lēt')
-*verb*

  a. I accidentally **deleted** several paragraphs of my research paper from the computer. It took ten minutes to retype them.

  b. The invitation list is too long. Unless we **delete** a few names, the party will be too crowded.

2 **impartial**
(im-par'-shəl)
-*adjective*

  a. Too much pre-trial publicity makes it difficult for lawyers to find **impartial** jurors, people who have no bias about the trial.

  b. "I'm an **impartial** judge of character," Dolores joked. "I distrust all people equally, without prejudice."

3 **integrity**
(in-teg'-rə-tē)
-*noun*

  a. Marsha trusted Tom with the key to the cash register because she knew he had **integrity.**

  b. I thought our senator had great **integrity,** so I was shocked to hear she took a bribe.

4 **legitimate**
(le-jit'-ə-mit)
-*adjective*

  a. "A need to see the final episode in your favorite soap opera," said the teacher, "is not a **legitimate** excuse for missing class."

  b. Any company that guarantees to make all investors millionaires can't possibly be **legitimate.**

5 **lenient**
(lē'-nē-ənt)
-*adjective*

  a. Ms. Hall is very **lenient** about late papers. If you hand one in even a week late, she doesn't lower your grade.

  b. Mom wouldn't let us feed our poodle during dinner. But Dad, more **lenient,** would look the other way when we slipped the dog something under the table.

6 **menace**
(men'-is)
-*noun*

  a. Acid rain is the biggest **menace** to the survival of fresh-water fish.

  b. Smokey the Bear urges campers to be careful with fire, a great **menace** to forests.

7 **morale**
(mə-ral')
-*noun*

  a. Art class was good for Tyrone's **morale.** Each time the teacher praised his drawings, his confidence and enthusiasm increased.

  b. The workers' **morale** was so low that they constantly complained about the job. Only going home could cheer them up.

8 **naive**
(no-ēv')
-*adjective*

  a. Though young, Rhoda is not **naive.** Being on her own for so long has made her streetwise.

  b. Having had little experience with salespeople, my young daughter is so **naive** about them that she believes everything they tell her.

9 **overt**
(ō-vurt')
-*adjective*

  a. Sometimes **overt** racism is easier to deal with than the hidden kind. You can better fight what is out in the open.

  b. Martha's love of books was **overt**—books spilled over the shelves in every room of her apartment.

10 **undermine**
(un'-dər-mīn')
-*verb*

  a. Leroy tried to **undermine** the coach's authority by making jokes about him behind his back.

  b. Numerous floods had **undermined** the house's foundations to the extent that the house was no longer safe.

Matching Words and Definitions

Check your understanding of the ten words by matching each word with its definition. Look back at the sentences in "Ten Words in Context" as needed to decide on the meaning of each word.

_e_	1. **delete**	a. fair; not biased; without prejudice
_a_	2. **impartial**	b. a threat
_j_	3. **integrity**	c. in accordance with law and custom; lawful or proper
_c_	4. **legitimate**	d. general mood in regard to confidence and enthusiasm; spirit
_h_	5. **lenient**	e. to cross out or erase
_b_	6. **menace**	f. to gradually weaken or damage
_d_	7. **morale**	g. obvious; not hidden
_i_	8. **naive**	h. not strict or harsh in disciplining and/or punishing; merciful
_g_	9. **overt**	i. lacking worldly experience; unsuspecting; unsophisticated
_f_	10. **undermine**	j. honesty

CAUTION: Do not go any further until you are sure the above answers are correct. If you have studied the "Ten Words in Context," you will know how to match each word. Then you can use the matches to help you in the following practices. Your goal is to reach a point where you don't need to check definitions at all.

➤ Sentence Check 1

Complete each sentence below with the most suitable word from the box. Use each word once.

delete	impartial	integrity	legitimate	lenient
menace	morale	naive	overt	undermine

1. When my brother and I argued, my mother remained_____*impartial*_____—she didn't want to favor either of us.

2. Alison's repeated criticisms _____*undermine*_____d her sister's confidence.

3. Drugs have become a terrible _____*menace*_____ to the well-being of American children.

4. Toby's _____*morale*_____ was low after his operation, but he cheered up once he was allowed to get out of bed.

5. It isn't considered _____*legitimate*_____ for a 20-year-old man to date a 13-year-old girl. However, if each were ten years older, it would be perfectly proper.

6. My father is so _____*naive*_____ about business deals that he has been tricked by cheaters more than once.

7. Leon typed "_____*delete*_____" into the computer, followed by the name of the document he wanted to erase.

8. Mrs. Dean's dislike for the mayor was _____*overt*_____. She stood right up in front of the crowd and said exactly what she thought of him.

9. "The boss is _____*lenient*_____ about an employee's first mistake," Sherry's co-worker warned, "but he's strict about a second one."

10. Mark Twain once joked that he had even more _____*integrity*_____ than George Washington. "Washington could not lie," he said. "I can, but I won't."

Now check your answers to these questions by turning to page 163. Going over the answers carefully will help you prepare for the next two checks, for which answers are not given.

➤ Sentence Check 2

Complete each sentence below with two words from the following list. Use each word once.

delete	impartial	integrity	legitimate	lenient
menace	morale	naive	overt	undermine

1-2. Nick's interest in Janice's money is _____ *overt* _____ enough for all her friends to notice. But Janice is

so_____ *naive* _____ that she has no idea about the real reason for Nick's attention.

3-4. The staff's _____ *morale* _____ quickly fell when they learned that some of the company's earnings were

put into a business that was not _____ *legitimate* _____ and that was being investigated by the police.

5-6. To give her essay _____ *integrity* _____, Isabel _____ *delete* _____d some statements that were not entirely

true.

7-8. Donald is a real _____ *menace* _____ in the classroom. It's not uncommon for him to _____ *undermine* _____

classroom order by snapping little spitballs at other students.

9-10. My parents should be _____ *impartial* _____, but they're much more _____ *lenient* _____ with my sisters

than with me. They often get off with a scolding, while I'm usually grounded for one or more days.

➤ Final Check: Who's on Trial?

Here is a final opportunity for you to strengthen your knowledge of the ten words. First read the following passage carefully. Then fill in each blank with a word from the box at the top of this page. (Context clues will help you figure out which word goes in which blank.) Use each word once.

"I must be really (1)_____ *naive* _____ about our justice system," Karen said as we left the

courtroom to get lunch. "I truly believed that if I pressed charges against that man for attacking me, he

would have a trial with a jury that would be (2)_____ *impartial* _____ enough to fairly consider all the

evidence, which would be brought out by reasonable questioning. That man is the criminal, but I felt as if I

were the one on trial. I'm ready to give up."

After sitting at the trial all morning, I could understand why Karen's (3)_____ *morale* _____ was so

low. The opposing lawyer's attempts to embarrass her and (4)_____ *undermine* _____ her image before the

jury were so (5)_____ *overt* _____ that nobody in the courtroom could miss them. He seemed to have no

(6)_____ *integrity* _____ at all. His misleading questions about her sex life and manner of dressing were

clearly meant to give the false impression that it had been her own actions that were not

(7)_____ *legitimate* _____ — that Karen "asked" to be attacked by behaving improperly. Her lawyer had

succeeded in having certain remarks (8)_____ *delete* _____d from the record, but the damage had been

done. The jury had already heard things like "short skirts" and "sleep with your boyfriend." They might

jump to conclusions instead of considering the evidence. I just hoped they would find that man guilty. I

also prayed that the judge would not be (9)_____ *lenient* _____, but would see what a

(10)_____ *menace* _____ to society this man was and sentence him to many years in prison.

> **SCORES:**   Sentence Check 2 _____%   Final Check _____%

Enter your scores above and in the vocabulary performance chart on the inside back cover of the book.

Previewing the Words

Find out how many of the ten words in this chapter you already know. Try to complete each sentence with the most suitable word from the list below. Use each word once.

Leave a sentence blank rather than guessing at an answer. Your purpose here is just to get a sense of the ten words and what you may know about them.

agenda	antidote	apathy	bland	propaganda
prospects	radical	reinforce	relevant	ruthless

1. If Kay is promoted, her _____*prospects*_____ for getting a raise will be good. More responsibility usually means more money.

2. The flat landscape was completely _____*bland*_____. There weren't even trees or flowers to provide interest.

3. The mother searched for an _____*antidote*_____ to reverse the effects of the poison her baby had swallowed.

4. "Of course, I favor _____*radical*_____ action," Andy said. "Extreme changes are needed to eliminate unjust laws."

5. The military dictatorship used _____*propaganda*_____ in booklets, speeches, and films to spread its lies.

6. To prevent the old building from collapsing, construction workers will _____*reinforce*_____ it with steel beams.

7. The meeting's _____*agenda*_____ was mailed to the committee members so they could prepare for the issues that would be discussed.

8. Soldiers in all wars have committed _____*ruthless*_____ acts of violence against innocent civilians.

9. When you do a research paper, you need to find _____*relevant*_____ evidence—evidence that relates to the points you are trying to make.

10. The neighbors' _____*apathy*_____ for a senior-citizen center became very clear when not one of them showed up at the meeting about the center.

Now check your answers by turning to page 163. Fix any mistakes and fill in any blank spaces by writing in the correct answers. By doing so, you will complete this introduction to the ten words.

You're now ready to strengthen your knowledge of the words you already know and to master the words you're only half sure of, or don't know at all. Turn to the next page.

Ten Words in Context

Figure out the meanings of the following ten words by looking *closely and carefully* at the context in which the words appear. Doing so will prepare you for the matching test and the practices on the two pages that follow.

1 **agenda**
(ə-jen'-də)
-noun

   a. There are two items on the **agenda** for today's office meeting: the company's new product and the Christmas party.

   b. Items on Ralph's daily **agenda** include driving his granddaughter to school, working at the soup kitchen, and walking his dog after dinner.

2 **antidote**
(an'-ti-dōt')
-noun

   a. Because there was no **antidote** for the snake's poison, the cat that was bitten died.

   b. For me, a good **antidote** to feeling low is to bake a batch of brownies.

3 **apathy**
(ap'-ə-thē)
-noun

   a. Student **apathy** turned to intense interest when the psychology teacher discussed Freud's views on sex.

   b. Voter **apathy** was high, so the turnout on election day was very low.

4 **bland**
(bland)
-adjective

   a. The addition of a bright red scarf changed Linda's grey outfit from **bland** to striking.

   b. Mexicans, accustomed to hot and spicy foods, often find American dishes **bland** by comparison.

5 **propaganda**
(prop'-ə-gan'-də)
-noun

   a. A common way of trying to convince people to accept ideas is the use of **propaganda**—passing out information that promotes those ideas.

   b. The political candidates ran TV ads made up largely of **propaganda** directed against their opponents.

6 **prospects**
(pros'-pekts)
-noun

   a. The movie's **prospects** for doing well at the box office were harmed by several bad reviews in the newspapers and on TV.

   b. What are my **prospects** of finding a hotel room in this town during Super Bowl weekend?

7 **radical**
(rad'-i-kəl)
-adjective

   a. I won't vote for the **radical** candidate—his beliefs are too extreme for me.

   b. Most students tried to change school policy through peaceful compromise, but a **radical** group wanted to take over the president's office by force.

8 **reinforce**
(rē'-in-fôrs')
-verb

   a. Jonathan's wisecrack **reinforced** the teacher's opinion that he was interested only in fooling around.

   b. Some pantyhose are **reinforced** at the heels and toes with extra layers of material, so they won't rip.

9 **relevant**
(rel'-ə-vənt)
-adjective

   a. History is always **relevant** to our lives because it shows us what results can follow certain actions.

   b. "The weather is not **relevant** to this conversation," Yvonne's mother said. "Don't change the subject when I bring up your speeding tickets."

10 **ruthless**
(rooth'-lis)
-adjective

   a. My English teacher is a **ruthless** grader of essay exams. He shows no mercy for weak reasoning or faulty grammar.

   b. Barry is so **ruthless** that he would step on co-workers to advance himself.

Matching Words and Definitions

Check your understanding of the ten words by matching each word with its definition. Look back at the sentences in "Ten Words in Context" as needed to decide on the meaning of each word.

_d_	1. **agenda**	a.	chances of success
_i_	2. **antidote**	b.	lack of interest and concern
_b_	3. **apathy**	c.	to strengthen; add support to
_f_	4. **bland**	d.	a list of things to be done; schedule
_j_	5. **propaganda**	e.	lacking pity; merciless
_a_	6. **prospects**	f.	dull; not interesting or exciting
_h_	7. **radical**	g.	related to the matter at hand; to the point
_c_	8. **reinforce**	h.	favoring extreme changes, especially in politics and government
_g_	9. **relevant**	i.	something that reduces the effects of a poison; anything that relieves a harmful situation
_e_	10. **ruthless**	j.	the systematic spread of ideas to further a cause or to oppose a person or thing; the ideas spread to support or oppose a cause

CAUTION: Do not go any further until you are sure the above answers are correct. If you have studied the "Ten Words in Context," you will know how to match each word. Then you can use the matches to help you in the following practices. Your goal is to reach a point where you don't need to check definitions at all.

➤ *Sentence Check 1*

Complete each sentence below with the most suitable word from the box. Use each word once.

agenda	antidote	apathy	bland	propaganda
prospects	radical	reinforce	relevant	ruthless

1. There are _____*ruthless*_____ drivers who make no effort to avoid hitting animals on the road.

2. Carlos' personality is so unexciting, so _____*bland*_____, that people tend not to notice him.

3. Your statement isn't _____*relevant*_____—it has nothing to do with our conversation.

4. Victoria will _____*reinforce*_____ the plant by tying its thin stem to a strong stick.

5. My sister's _____*prospects*_____ of passing Accounting I aren't good. She hasn't studied all term.

6. All medicine cabinets should contain a general _____*antidote*_____ for accidental poisoning.

7. Every morning Lin writes out her _____*agenda*_____, jotting down what she needs to accomplish that day.

8. Because Todd wants to do away with all private ownership of guns, many people consider his views too _____*radical*_____.

9. Sidewalk litter is a sign of _____*apathy*_____, showing that people don't care about a clean environment.

10. Advertisements are an important part of the _____*propaganda*_____ used by companies to persuade us to buy their products.

Now check your answers to these questions by turning to page 163. Going over the answers carefully will help you prepare for the next two checks, for which answers are not given.

➤Sentence Check 2

Complete each sentence below with two words from the following list. Use each word once.

agenda	antidote	apathy	bland	propaganda
prospects	radical	reinforce	relevant	ruthless

1-2. Working at top speed, the doctors injected the poisoned woman with a powerful _____*antidote*_____. Everyone in the emergency room seemed anxious and tense except the woman's husband, so we wondered at his apparent _____*apathy*_____.

3-4. The mayor's _____*agenda*_____ for his new term includes canceling city services for poor children. He knows this action seems cruel, but he says he must be _____*ruthless*_____ in order to balance the budget.

5-6. Professor Turner's lectures would not seem so _____*bland*_____ to students if he wouldn't speak in such a dull tone of voice and if he included information that seemed _____*relevant*_____ to their lives.

7-8. Louise, a _____*radical*_____ feminist, used to avoid associating with most men. Now, however, she's learned to direct her anger only at those who she feels spread _____*propaganda*_____ harmful to women.

9-10. If Henry starts exercising, his _____*prospects*_____ for getting into shape will be very good. His desire to exercise was _____*reinforce*_____(e)d by the fact that he gained ten pounds last year.

➤Final Check: Students and Politics

Here is a final opportunity for you to strengthen your knowledge of the ten words. First read the following passage carefully. Then fill in each blank with a word from the box at the top of this page. (Context clues will help you figure out which word goes in which blank.) Use each word once.

During the 1960's, many young people were attracted to (1)_____*radical*_____ political groups. The groups' (2)_____*agenda*_____ included ending the war in Vietnam, feeding the hungry, and doing away with all forms of social prejudice. University students demanded courses more (3)_____*relevant*_____ to the times: women's studies, Afro-American literature, and world religions. These activists hoped to serve as a(n) (4)_____*antidote*_____ to the "traditional" thinking of the 1950's they considered so harmful. The music and literature of the day helped spread the movement's anti-war, pro-love and often pro-drug (5)_____*propaganda*_____. Many small newspapers that sprang up helped to (6)_____*reinforce*_____ these messages.

Some who were politically active in the 60's are concerned by the (7)_____*apathy*_____ of young people today, who don't seem to care about their world. The middle-aged activitists fear that today's students are, at best, so lacking in spirit as to be (8)_____*bland*_____ and harmless. At worst, they are so money-hungry and (9)_____*ruthless*_____ that they couldn't care less about people who are poverty-stricken. But others believe that the (10)_____*prospects*_____ for social progress are better than they might seem. Students, they say, will soon again take the lead in pushing for social change.

SCORES: Sentence Check 2 _____ %   Final Check _____ %

Enter your scores above and in the vocabulary performance chart on the inside back cover of the book.

5

Previewing the Words

Find out how many of the ten words in this chapter you already know. Try to complete each sentence with the most suitable word from the list below. Use each word once.

Leave a sentence blank rather than guessing at an answer. Your purpose here is just to get a sense of the ten words and what you may know about them.

endorse	erode	gruesome	hypocrite	idealistic
illusion	impact	imply	novice	obstacle

1. The magician created the _____*illusion*_____ that his assistant was floating upside down in midair.

2. Wind and rain _____*erode*_____ rocks, making them smoother and rounder.

3. Anita was a complete _____*novice*_____ when she came to work at the bank, but now she has enough experience to train new tellers.

4. The TV minister was a _____*hypocrite*_____—he earned a fortune talking about how noble it is to be poor.

5. The newspaper described the _____*gruesome*_____ murder. The killer stabbed the victim dozens of times.

6. To be a radio announcer, Marla will have to overcome the _____*obstacle*_____ of her strong regional accent.

7. "I have a dream," said Martin Luther King, proud to be _____*idealistic*_____ and to have a vision of how to achieve a better world.

8. The senator refused to _____*endorse*_____ any candidate who didn't share his views on the minimum wage.

9. When the two cars crashed into each other, the _____*impact*_____ was so great that one driver was thrown from his car.

10. People often _____*imply*_____ the question "Would you like to go out with me tonight?" by asking only, "Do you have plans for tonight?"

Now check your answers by turning to page 163. Fix any mistakes and fill in any blank spaces by writing in the correct answers. By doing so, you will complete this introduction to the ten words.

You're now ready to strengthen your knowledge of the words you already know and to master the words you're only half sure of, or don't know at all. Turn to the next page.

Ten Words in Context

Figure out the meanings of the following ten words by looking *closely and carefully* at the context in which the words appear. Doing so will prepare you for the matching test and the practices on the two pages that follow.

1 **endorse**
(en-dôrs')
-*verb*

    a. "If you **endorse** the new shopping mall," said the speaker, "you're supporting a large increase in neighborhood traffic."

    b. Some athletes earn more money **endorsing** such products as cereal and sneakers than they do playing their sport.

2 **erode**
(i-rōd')
-*verb*

    a. As water **eroded** the topsoil, the tree roots beneath it became more and more visible.

    b. The nation's confidence in its leader was **eroded** by his increasingly wild accusations against his enemies.

3 **gruesome**
(grōō'-səm)
-*adjective*

    a. The automobile accident was so **gruesome** that I had to look away from the horrible sight.

    b. Connie's sunburned skin was **gruesome**—cracked and purplish red in some places, swollen and yellowish in others.

4 **hypocrite**
(hip'-ə-krit')
-*noun*

    a. Dominic is such a **hypocrite**. He cheats his customers while complaining to them about how hard it is to be an honest, struggling salesman.

    b. Maybe the worst **hypocrites** are those who preach love and then attack anyone of a different culture or faith.

5 **idealistic**
(i-dē'-ə-lis'-tik)
-*adjective*

    a. Very **idealistic** people are drawn to work in which they feel they can make the world a better place.

    b. My sister is too **idealistic** ever to marry for wealth or fame—she would marry only for love.

6 **illusion**
(i-lōō'-zhən)
-*noun*

    a. Rena's belief that she and Jon had a strong relationship turned out to be an **illusion**. He had been dating other women without telling her.

    b. It is only an **illusion** that the sun sets and rises. It is really the earth that is turning away from and then towards the sun.

7 **impact**
(im'-pakt)
-*noun*

    a. When birds accidentally fly into windows, the **impact** often kills them.

    b. That boxer punches with such force that the **impact** of his uppercut can knock out most opponents.

8 **imply**
(im-plī')
-*verb*

    a. To Sherlock Holmes, the clues **implied** that the murderer was an elderly man who carried a cane.

    b. When my friend asked me, "Do you feel all right?" she **implied** that I did not look well.

9 **novice**
(nov'-is)
-*noun*

    a. Since Roger has never played tennis, he will have to join the class for **novices.**

    b. "Don't buy an expensive camera for a **novice**," said the saleswoman. "Let your son first get some experience with a cheap camera."

10 **obstacle**
(ob'-stə-kəl)
-*noun*

    a. I'd better clean my apartment soon. There are too many **obstacles** on the floor between my bed and the refrigerator.

    b. The major **obstacle** to Hal's getting a promotion is his laziness.

Matching Words and Definitions

Check your understanding of the ten words by matching each word with its definition. Look back at the sentences in "Ten Words in Context" as needed to decide on the meaning of each word.

_e_	1. **endorse**	a.	to express indirectly; suggest
_i_	2. **erode**	b.	a barrier; something that interferes
_f_	3. **gruesome**	c.	one who claims to be something he or she is not; an insincere person
_c_	4. **hypocrite**	d.	a mistaken view of reality; an image leading to a false impression
_j_	5. **idealistic**	e.	to support; express approval of; to state in an ad that one supports a product or service, usually for a fee
_d_	6. **illusion**	f.	horrible; shocking; frightful
_h_	7. **impact**	g.	a beginner; someone new to a field or activity
_a_	8. **imply**	h.	the force of one thing striking another
_g_	9. **novice**	i.	to gradually wear (something) away
_b_	10. **obstacle**	j.	characterized by an emphasis on ideals and principles over practical considerations

CAUTION: Do not go any further until you are sure the above answers are correct. If you have studied the "Ten Words in Context," you will know how to match each word. Then you can use the matches to help you in the following practices. Your goal is to reach a point where you don't need to check definitions at all.

➤ Sentence Check 1

Complete each sentence below with the most suitable word from the box. Use each word once.

endorse	erode	gruesome	hypocrite	idealistic
illusion	impact	imply	novice	obstacle

1. The horror movie became too ___gruesome___ when the monster started eating people.

2. Year after year, the waves continue to ___erode___ the beach, wearing it away by constantly beating against it.

3. Poems often ___imply___ an idea. That is, they hint at the idea rather than state it directly.

4. I was such a(n) ___novice___ at computers that I didn't even know how to insert a disk.

5. Karen is the least ___idealistic___ person I know. She is guided only by a desire to get ahead.

6. Don't be such a(n) ___hypocrite___! If you don't like Arlene, then you shouldn't pretend that you do.

7. An actress hired to ___endorse___ meat products on TV was fired when it was learned she rarely ate meat herself.

8. Ballet dancers sometimes break their toes when they land with too great a(n) ___impact___ after a leap.

9. I can never drive straight into our driveway because there are always ___obstacle___s there— tricycles, garbage cans, or toys.

10. When the moon is low in the sky, it looks much larger than when it appears overhead. This difference in size, however, is only a(n) ___illusion___.

Now check your answers to these questions by turning to page 163. Going over the answers carefully will help you prepare for the next two checks, for which answers are not given.

➤ Sentence Check 2

Complete each sentence below with two words from the following list. Use each word once.

endorse	erode	gruesome	hypocrite	idealistic
illusion	impact	imply	novice	obstacle

1-2. "Just because I let them meet in the church basement," said Reverend Lucas, "does not ___*imply*___ that I ___*endorse*___ everything the group stands for."

3-4. When the first soldier to fly in an airplane took off in 1908, he had no ___*illusion*___ about the danger, but he never expected to die from the ___*impact*___ of crashing into a cemetery wall.

5-6. The first Peace Corps volunteers may have been ___*idealistic*___, but they were tough about their dreams. No ___*obstacle*___ would keep them from working for a better world.

7-8. Because she was just out of college, Faye was a(n) ___*novice*___ at interviewing job applicants. Nevertheless, she could see that Perry was a(n) ___*hypocrite*___ who boasted about job skills he didn't have.

9-10. Ten years in the soil had ___*erode*___d the body down to a mere skeleton. But when a gardener's shovel uncovered the ___*gruesome*___ remains of the murder victim, she could still be identified by a golden locket around her neck.

➤ Final Check: Night Nurse

Here is a final opportunity for you to strengthen your knowledge of the ten words. First read the following passage carefully. Then fill in each blank with a word from the box at the top of this page. (Context clues will help you figure out which word goes in which blank.) Use each word once.

I'm no (1)___*hypocrite*___, so I'll admit I sometimes wish I'd never taken the job of nurse on the midnight shift. No one in my family would (2)___*endorse*___ my decision, and maybe they were right. I had no (3)___*illusion*___ about the difficulty of the work. I knew the emergency room would be tough, but I wasn't going to let that be an (4)___*obstacle*___. Still, I guess I did start out more (5)___*idealistic*___ about helping the world than I am now, ten months later. I don't mean to (6)___*imply*___ that I've soured on nursing, because I haven't. But when I rushed that first stretcher off the ambulance—as a mere (7)___*novice*___ at the job—disappointment hadn't started to (8)___*erode*___ my hopeful outlook yet.

The work is at one of the city's biggest hospitals. More often than not, each shift brings a series of bloody, (9)___*gruesome*___ cases. There are shootings and stabbings, and I often see skull fractures showing the (10)___*impact*___ of baseball bats on human heads.

The other day, when I went to buy some shoes for work, the clerk asked me, "What kind of soles would you like?"

Before I could stop myself, I answered, "Some that won't slip in blood."

SCORES: Sentence Check 2 _____ % Final Check _____ %	

Enter your scores above and in the vocabulary performance chart on the inside back cover of the book.

Previewing the Word Parts

Common word parts—also known as *prefixes, suffixes, and roots*—are used in forming many words in English. This page will introduce you to ten common word parts.

Try to match each word part on the left with its definition on the right. Use the words in parentheses as hints to help you guess the meanings. If you can't decide on an answer, leave the space blank. Your purpose here is just to get a sense of the ten word parts and what you may know about them. (You'll have another chance to try this exercise after considering the word parts in context.)

	Word Parts	Definitions
d	1. **auto-** (autobiography, autograph)	a. many
e	2. **ex-** (exclude, exit)	b. not
j	3. **-ful** (beautiful, faithful)	c. one
a	4. **multi-** (multiply, multipurpose)	d. self
h	5. **pre-** (predict, precaution)	e. out, from
f	6. **re-** (repeat, rewrite)	f. again
i	7. **super-** (superstar, supervise)	g. see
b	8. **un-** (unfair, untie)	h. before
c	9. **uni-** (uniform, united)	i. greater, above
g	10. **vis, vid** (vision, video)	j. full of

Now go on to "Ten Word Parts in Context" on the next page. Working through this chapter will help you to strengthen your knowledge of the word parts you already know and to master the word parts you're only half sure of, or don't know at all.

Keep in mind that learning word parts can pay several dividends. Word parts can help with the spelling and pronunciation of many words. They can also help you to unlock the meanings of unfamiliar words.

Ten Word Parts in Context

Figure out the meanings of the following ten word parts by looking *closely and carefully* at the context in which they appear. Doing so will prepare you for the matching test and the practices on the two pages that follow.

1 **auto-**   a. In restaurants called **automats,** you serve yourself by putting coins in slots and removing food from behind small glass doors.

          b. It is possible to hypnotize yourself through a process called **autohypnosis.**

2 **ex-**   a. "Inhale as you lower your head," called out the exercise instructor, "and **exhale** as you do the sit-up."

          b. My uncle isn't a very good businessman. He once tried to **export** rice to China and vodka to Russia.

3 **-ful**   a. Even though the movie and meal were pretty bad, I had a **delightful** evening because the company was so good.

          b. Many children, **fearful** of the dark, feel comforted by a night light.

4 **multi-**   a. Belle is **multilingual**—she speaks English, French, and Chinese.

          b. Ours is a **multiracial** neighborhood. In fact, the area attracts people who want their children to grow up among many races.

5 **pre-**   a. People who believe in fate think our lives are mainly **predetermined** and that we therefore can't do much to change things.

          b. I like to get to the theater in time to see the **previews** of coming movies.

6 **re-**   a. **Reheated** coffee tastes like raw mud.

          b. My aunt bought a house that was in poor condition, fixed it up, and then **resold** it for a profit.

7 **super-**   a. When you're a **superstar** like Michael Jackson, it's impossible to have privacy in public.

          b. The **superintendent** of schools has called a meeting of all the principals to discuss the growing drug problem.

8 **un-**   a. Our history teacher has an **unusual** approach to teaching. He often wears costumes and lectures as one of the historical people we're learning about.

          b. When I am involved in a good novel, I am totally **unaware** of the world around me.

9 **uni-**   a. The company combined crayons, paints and paper into one **unit** and sold it as a children's art kit.

          b. The dancers in the chorus line kicked their legs up and down in perfect **unison.**

10 **vis, vid**   a. Myra's **vision** is perfect. She wears contact lenses only to change the color of her eyes.

          b. My husband made a **videotape** of our baby's birth.

Matching Word Parts and Definitions

Check your understanding of the ten word parts by matching each with its definition. See also the suggestions on page 4.

_d_	1. **auto-**	a.	many
_e_	2. **ex-**	b.	not
_j_	3. **-ful**	c.	one
_a_	4. **multi-**	d.	self
_h_	5. **pre-**	e.	out, from
_f_	6. **re-**	f.	again
_i_	7. **super-**	g.	see
_b_	8. **un-**	h.	before
_c_	9. **uni-**	i.	greater, above
_g_	10. **vis, vid**	j.	full of

CAUTION: Do not go any further until you are sure the above answers are correct. If you have studied the "Ten Word Parts in Context," you will know how to match each word part. Then you can use the matches to help you in the following practices. Your goal is to reach a point where you don't need to check definitions at all.

➤ Sentence Check 1

Complete each partial word in the following sentences with a word part from the box. Use each word part only once. You may want to check off each word part as you use it.

auto-	ex-	-ful	multi-	pre-
re-	super-	un-	uni-	vis

1. After the earthquake, the city was (...*built*) _____*rebuilt*_____ a few miles away, in a safer location.

2. Bees and butterflies can see certain colors that are not (...*ible*) _____*visible*_____ to the human eye.

3. It is difficult for small neighborhood stores to compete with (...*markets*) _*supermarkets*_ .

4. Jurors must not (...*judge*) _____*prejudge*_____ a case. They must listen to all the evidence before coming to a conclusion.

5. I find it (*rest*...) _____*restful*_____ to vacation at home, where I can relax and catch up on reading and movies.

6. The legendary (...*corn*) _____*unicorn*_____, a horselike animal with one horn, is often shown as having a lion's tail and a goat's beard.

7. My grandfather used to (...*tract*) _____*extract*_____ my loose baby teeth by tying each to a string and then yanking the string.

8. In her (...*biography*) _____*autobiography*_____, *Blackberry Winter*, Margaret Mead writes about her childhood, her three marriages, and her career.

9. My bedroom is really a (...*purpose*) _*multipurpose*_ room. I read, watch TV, eat snacks, talk on the phone, do push-ups, daydream and sleep there.

10. Anyone who bumps into a stonefish is really (...*lucky*) _____*unlucky*_____, for it has thirteen poisonous spines sticking out of its body.

Now check your answers to these questions by turning to page 163. Going over the answers carefully will help you prepare for the next two checks, for which answers are not given.

➤ Sentence Check 2

Complete each word in the sentences below with a word part from the following list. Use each word part once.

auto-	ex-	-ful	multi-	pre-
re-	super-	un-	uni-	vis

1-2. The magician held up a small, (. . .*folded*) ____*unfolded*____ red cloth so that we could see all of it. Then, in a flash, he had a (*hand*. . .) ____*handful*____ of flowers.

3-4. Students caught drinking anywhere on the school grounds are (. . . *pelled*) ____*expelled*____ from school (. . . *matically*)____*automatically*____ .

5-6. Unless we learn to be more accepting of each other, I cannot (*en*. . .*ion*) ____*envision*____ a time when this family will be peaceful and (. . .*fied*) ____*unified*____ .

7-8. I painted the company president's office last week, but my (. . .*visor*) ____*supervisor*____ said I now have to (. . .*paint*) ____*repaint*____ it in a different color.

9-10. A psychic (. . .*dicted*) ____*predicted*____ a growth in my financial situation. She was right: my debts have (. . .*plied*) ____*multiplied*____ .

➤ Final Check: Theo's Perfect Car

Here is a final opportunity for you to strengthen your knowledge of the ten word parts. First read the following passage carefully. Then complete each partial word in the parentheses below with a word part from the box at the top of this page. (Context clues will help you figure out which word part goes in which blank.) Use each word part once.

My young son Theo wants to be an (. . . *mobile*) (1)____*automobile*____ designer some day. In the meanwhile, he feels he can (. . .*pare*) (2)____*prepare*____ for that day by working on his design of a (. . . *ior*) (3)____*superior*____ car.

So far, this great car of his runs on air. Theo says that means future gas stations will need only air pumps, for both the tank and the tires. In addition, his car has the ability to become (*in*. . . *ible*) (4)____*invisible*____ . (Theo feels it would be (*help* . . .) (5)____*helpful*____ for a car to disappear whenever the driver is chased by bad guys.) The car will also have trays for candy instead of ashes and an (. . . *tended*) (6)____*extended*____ trunk, to hold lots of luggage, toys, and plastic bags for people who get carsick. The dashboard will have buttons for many odd functions, including turning the wheel sideways into a tight parking spot. The tires will be (. . . *colored*) (7)____*multicolored*____, with circles of red, yellow, purple, and blue.

I tell Theo that his car is imaginative and (. . . *que*) (8)____*unique*____ —surely there is none other like it in the world. But then I (. . . *mind*) (9)____*remind*____ him that if he doesn't do his math homework, it's (. . . *likely*) (10)____*unlikely*____ that General Motors will hire him as a designer.

SCORES:	Sentence Check 2 _____%	Final Check _____%

Enter your scores above and in the vocabulary performance chart on the inside back cover of the book.

UNIT ONE: *Test 1*

PART A
Choose the word that best completes each sentence and write it in the space provided.

1. **anecdote
   integrity
   antidote
   obstacle**

   Certain hunters dip their arrows in the poison from a tiny frog— a deadly poison

   for which there is no ____*antidote*____.

2. **fortify
   undermine
   reinforce
   illuminate**

   Smoking and drinking ____*undermine*____ your health.

3. **avert
   erode
   compel
   endorse**

   In river rafting, to ____*avert*____ disaster, you must steer clear of rocks.

4. **bland
   extensive
   impartial
   concise**

   Damage to the old car was so ____*extensive*____ that repairs would have cost more

   than the car did.

5. **drastic
   erratic
   naive
   concise**

   The other speaker rambled on for an hour, but Greg was ____*concise*____. Ten

   minutes and he was done.

6. **bland
   overt
   legitimate
   gruesome**

   A salt-free diet need not be ____*bland*____. Throw in a few hot peppers, and

   your dish will have zing.

7. **comply
   undermine
   endorse
   isolate**

   The nurses asked our union to ____*endorse*____ their strike by signing a letter

   of support.

8. **alternative
   agenda
   impact
   morale**

   After I failed my first two algebra quizzes, I decided the sensible *alternative*

   to flunking was to get some tutoring.

9. **erratic
   candid
   gruesome
   relevant**

   Although the movie is titled *Tears of Blood*, it isn't ____*gruesome*____ —it contains

   no violence or gore.

10. **hypocrite
    novice
    menace
    refuge**

    When Jimmy practiced saying dirty words in first grade, he was only a

    ____*novice*____ , but by sixth grade he was an expert.

11. **erratic**
    idealistic
    ruthless
    urban

    One advantage of _____*urban*_____ living is the city's wealth of live entertain-

    ment, including plays and concerts.

12. **drastic**
    radical
    candid
    lenient

    When my boyfriend agreed with me that my new perm looked terrible, I regretted

    that he's always so _____*candid*_____.

13. **propaganda**
    dialogue
    agenda
    apathy

    The _____*agenda*_____ of our Humor Club meetings usually consists of swapping

    funny stories and then playing a practical joke on some unlucky non-member.

PART B

Circle **C** if the italicized word is used **correctly**. Circle **I** if the word is used **incorrectly**.

C (I) 14.   The tornado *reinforced* the house, ripping off the roof.

(C) I 15.   Alaskan wolves are no *menace* to humans—they don't attack people.

(C) I 16.   The newly fallen snow was so bright under the moonlight that it *illuminated* the entire street.

C (I) 17.   In 17th-century Massachusetts, one *lenient* jury hanged a dog accused of being a witch.

C (I) 18.   *Impartial* employers often pre-judge overweight job applicants as likely to be lazy.

C (I) 19.   The candidate was happy to see his support from factory workers finally start to *erode.*

(C) I 20.   Since he wanted to borrow the car that night, Harry decided to *comply* with his mother's request to clean his room.

C (I) 21.   The businessman was well-loved for his *ruthless* treatment of his employees and his partners.

(C) I 22.   The *impact* of the baseball I caught was so great that my hand stung even though I was wearing a mitt.

(C) I 23.   New York City's Wall Street is named for a wall built to be an *obstacle* to Indians who might want to enter what was then a small city.

C (I) 24.   To *forfeit* my health, I take plenty of vitamins, eat well, and get enough sleep.

(C) I 25.   To some extent, stars are an *illusion.* Because starlight takes thousands of years to reach us, many of the stars we see no longer exist.

SCORE: (Number correct) _____	x 4 = _____ %

Enter your scores above and in the vocabulary performance chart on the inside back cover of the book.

UNIT ONE: *Test 2*

PART A

Complete each sentence with a word from the box. Use each word once.

acknowledge	deleted	dialogue	drastic
fortify	hypocrite	integrity	isolates
morale	propaganda	prospects	refuge
reminisce			

1. High stone walls and a ring of water were used to _____*fortify*_____ castles against attack.

2. Since Lee is shy, his _____*prospects*_____ as an insurance salesman seem poor.

3. In the 1870's one man took _____*drastic*_____ action when his wife refused to serve him breakfast: he divorced her.

4. Americans _____*acknowledge*_____ a great fear of cancer. When surveyed, most report that they fear the disease more than any other.

5. The state park, where no hunting is permitted, serves as a _____*refuge*_____ for wildlife that might otherwise be killed.

6. A large part of war is _____*propaganda*_____—spreading information that makes the enemy look bad.

7. _____*Morale*_____ is so low in my office that no one even feels up to discussing how depressed we all are.

8. When the R-rated movie was shown on TV, all curse words were _____*deleted*_____. As a result, nearly every sentence had gaps.

9. People who work alone in toll booths must often feel their job _____*isolates*_____ them too much, especially late at night.

10. Westerns are shown throughout the world. Still, it's odd to think of cowboys speaking their

    _____*dialogue*_____ in German, French, or Japanese.

11. Dominic has _____*integrity*_____. When he accidentally backed into a parked car and smashed one of its lights, he was honest enough to leave a note with his name and number.

12. The woman was a _____*hypocrite*_____—she gave speeches about the evils of drugs but was arrested three times for drunk driving.

13. I listened to my grandparents _____*reminisce*_____ about all the crazy fads they've seen come and go, including T-shirts that gave off a smell of chocolate, garlic, or fish when scratched.

PART B
Circle **C** if the italicized word is used **correctly.** Circle **I** if the word is used **incorrectly.**

C (I) 14. It is always *appropriate* to drink and drive.

(C) I 15. On most American beaches, it's not *legitimate* to go topless.

C (I) 16. Meg is so *idealistic* that the happiest moment of her life is the day her parents bought her a Rolls Royce convertible.

C (I) 17. My little sister is so *naive* about baseball that she knows the names and records of dozens of players.

(C) I 18. Ray is *overt* in his feelings for Julie. He paid for a billboard on Main Street that reads, "Julie, I love you. Ray."

(C) I 19. Our school will soon begin a *drastic* change in its dress code. For the first time, all students will have to wear uniforms to school.

C (I) 20. Winston Churchill had such a good memory he could *imply* an entire Shakespearean play word for word.

C (I) 21. Because I've been scatter-brained lately, I decided to *compel* a list of things I needed to do.

(C) I 22. "What you do in your private life certainly is *relevant* to our team," yelled the coach, "especially if you do it until four in the morning."

C (I) 23. When his team won the basketball game, Doug showed such *apathy* that he jumped up and down shouting "Yeah!" until he sprained his ankle.

(C) I 24. Cesar's moodiness makes his work *erratic.* One week he's a top salesman, and the next week he can't seem to sell a thing.

(C) I 25. In 5th-century France and Spain, a doctor was required to leave a cash deposit before caring for a patient. If the patient lived, the doctor got his money back. If the patient died, the doctor *forfeited* the deposit.

SCORE: (Number correct) _____ x 4 = _____ %

Enter your scores above and in the vocabulary performance chart on the inside back cover of the book.

UNIT ONE: Test 3

Complete each sentence in a way that clearly shows you understand the meaning of the boldfaced word. Take a minute to plan your answer before you write.

Example: If you receive a wedding invitation, it is **appropriate** _to respond by the date requested._

1. One well-known product **endorsed** by a well-known person is _____ (Answers will vary.) _____

2. Two things that can **illuminate** a room are _____

3. The driver **averted** a crash by _____

4. One **obstacle** to professional success is _____

5. A sign of high **morale** on a team is _____

6. The judge was so **lenient** that _____

7. Being a **novice** as a waiter, Artie _____

8. The following remark could **undermine** someone's confidence: _____

9. I know that my father has **integrity** because _____

10. When it comes to taxes, Dinah is so **radical** that she believes _____

PART B

After each boldfaced word are a *synonym* (a word that means the same as the boldfaced word), an *antonym* (a word that means the opposite of the boldfaced word), and a word that is neither. Mark the antonym with an *A*.

	Example:	**delete**	*A* restore	_____ erase	_____ insult

11. **isolate**   *A* include   _____ freeze   _____ separate

12. **concise**   _____ old   *A* wordy   _____ brief

13. **impartial**   _____ fair   *A* prejudiced   _____ small

14. **gruesome**   _____ horrible   _____ powerful   *A* lovely

15. **apathy**   _____ illness   _____ unconcern   *A* caring

PART C

Use five of the following ten words in sentences. Make it clear that you know the meaning of the word you use. Feel free to use the past tense or plural form of a word.

agenda	compel	drastic	erode	erratic
illusion	legitimate	menace	prospects	urban

16. _____ *(Answers will vary.)* _____

   _____

17. _____

   _____

18. _____

   _____

19. _____

   _____

20. _____

SCORE: (Number correct) _____ x 5 = _____ %

Enter your scores above and in the vocabulary performance chart on the inside back cover of the book.

UNIT ONE: Test 4 (Word Parts)

PART A

Listed in the left-hand column below are ten common word parts, along with words in which the parts are used. In each blank, write in the letter of the correct definition on the right

Word Parts   **Definitions**

_i_ 1. **auto-**   autobiography, auto   a. before

_j_ 2. **ex-**   exhale, exit   b. see

_c_ 3. **-ful**   beautiful, colorful   c. full of

_d_ 4. **multi-**   multiply, multipurpose   d. many

_a_ 5. **pre-**   preheat, precaution   e. one

_h_ 6. **re-**   repaint, reboil   f. not

_g_ 7. **super-**   superstar, superior   g. greater, above

_f_ 8. **un-**   unhappy, unpopular   h. again

_e_ 9. **uni-**   uniform, united   i. self

_b_ 10. **vis, vid**   vision, video   j. out, from

PART B

Find the word part that correctly completes each word. Then write the full word in the blank space. Not every word part will be used.

auto-	ex-	ful-	multi-	pre-
re-	super-	un-	uni-	vis

11. If the tail of a certain lizard is cut off, the tail will (. . .*grow*) _____*regrow*_____ to full size.

12. According to surveys, Americans consider lack of (. . .*ion*) _____*vision*_____ the worst physical handicap.

13. In some early marriages, bride and groom "tied the knot" by having their sleeves tied together, as a symbol

    of their (. . .*on*) _____*union*_____.

14. Bacteria never die—they just keep (. . . *plying*) _____*multiplying*_____. One splits into two, two split into four, and so on.

15. My girlfriend says my problem is not that my income is too low but that my (. . . *penses*) _____*expenses*_____ are too high.

PART C
Use your knowledge of word parts to determine the meaning of the boldfaced words. Circle the letter of each meaning.

16. In our garden, weeds are **plentiful.**

a. lacking   (b) numerous   c. spread out

17. Factories are increasingly **automated.**

(a) self-running   b. high-speed   c. complicated

18. The teacher thinks Alice's essays are **superlative.**

a. wordy   b. poor   (c) of the highest quality

19. I opened the suitcase and found my china clown **unbroken.**

a. broken in half   b. broken to bits   (c) not broken

20. My decision to get a job was **premature.**

(a) made before the right time   b. made at exactly the right time   c. made after the right time

---

SCORE: (Number correct) _____ x 5 = _____ %

Enter your scores above and in the vocabulary performance chart on the inside back cover of the book.

Previewing the Words

Find out how many of the ten words in this chapter you already know. Try to complete each sentence with the most suitable word from the list below. Use each word once.

Leave a sentence blank rather than guessing at an answer. Your purpose here is just to get a sense of the ten words and what you may know about them.

concede	conservative	contrary	denounce	deter
disclose	scapegoat	superficial	sustain	transition

1. _____*Contrary*_____ to popular belief, gorillas aren't violent; they are gentle vegetarians.

2. Under oath in court, the senator was finally willing to _____*concede*_____ that he had taken bribes.

3. Making the _____*transition*_____ from a small junior high school to a large high school can be very difficult for shy students.

4. The conversation at the party was _____*superficial*_____. No one said anything deeper than "Boy, it's cold outside."

5. Jesse is very _____*conservative*_____ in his eating habits. He eats only meat and potatoes, refusing to try anything new.

6. Although the runner was still moving fast, he couldn't _____*sustain*_____ the speed at which he had begun the race.

7. Throughout the heated campaign, the two political candidates continued to _____*denounce*_____ each other as ineffective and dishonest.

8. The fact that only one person in ten is accepted into that nursing program didn't _____*deter*_____ Elena from applying.

9. Senator Jacobs refused to _____*disclose*_____ his dealings with the South American dictator, claiming his business affairs were private.

10. When Dad was furious about the holes in the garden, I was afraid to confess I had been digging for

    buried treasure. So I blamed my dog Speck for the mess, making him the _____*scapegoat*_____.

Now check your answers by turning to page 164. Fix any mistakes and fill in any blank spaces by writing in the correct answers. By doing so, you will complete this introduction to the ten words.

You're now ready to strengthen your knowledge of the words you already know and to master the words you're only half sure of, or don't know at all. Turn to the next page.

Ten Words in Context

Figure out the meanings of the following ten words by looking *closely and carefully* at the context in which the words appear. Doing so will prepare you for the matching test and the practices on the two pages that follow.

1 **concede**
(kən-sēd')
-*verb*

   a. Our aunt hates to admit an error. She will never **concede** that she might be wrong.

   b. After pretending it was easy learning to use the new computer, Ross had to **concede** he was struggling and ask for help.

2 **conservative**
(kən-sûr'-və-tiv)
-*adjective*

   a. My **conservative** relatives were shocked when I broke with tradition and wore a rose-colored wedding gown.

   b. When the mayor suggested a new method of recycling garbage, a **conservative** member of the audience called out, "What we've done in the past is good enough. Why change things?"

3 **contrary**
(kon'-trer-ē)
-*adjective*

   a. Claire's father insists she share his views. He doesn't allow her to express an opinion **contrary** to his.

   b. Dale and her husband have **contrary** ideas on how to spend a vacation. He wants to sleep on the beach for a week, but she prefers visiting museums.

4 **denounce**
(di-nouns')
-*verb*

   a. During the Nazi rule, anyone in Germany who publicly **denounced** Hitler—as cruel or mad—risked imprisonment, torture, and death.

   b. When Eugene said he saw me steal from another student's locker, I **denounced** him as a liar.

5 **deter**
(di-tûr')
-*verb*

   a. No one is sure how much the threat of execution **deters** murder.

   b. Beth's parents disapproved of her dating someone from a different culture, but their prejudice didn't **deter** her—she still dated Po-Yen.

6 **disclose**
(dis-klōz')
-*verb*

   a. When I applied for financial aid, I had to **disclose** my annual income. But it embarrassed me to reveal this information.

   b. The police don't like to **disclose** all the facts of a murder to the newspapers. That way, there will be some information which only the murderer would know.

7 **scapegoat**
(skāp'-gōt')
-*noun*

   a. Several girls put dye into their high school swimming pool. In need of a **scapegoat,** they then blamed another student who knew nothing about the prank.

   b. Because the manager wanted a **scapegoat** for his own mistake, he fired an innocent employee.

8 **superficial**
(soo'-pər-fish'-əl)
-*adjective*

   a. Sal and Anita are interested only in appearances. They are so **superficial** that it's impossible to have a deep friendship with them.

   b. My teacher said my essay on divorce was too **superficial,** that I didn't go into the subject with enough depth.

9 **sustain**
(sə-stān')
-*verb*

   a. My diets usually last three days at the most. I can't **sustain** my willpower any longer than that.

   b. The singer can **sustain** a high note for almost a minute.

10 **transition**
(tran-zish'-ən)
-*noun*

   a. Mark's parents were amazed at how easily he made the **transition** from full-time student to full-time employee.

   b. "The **transition** from being childless to being a parent is drastic," said the new father. "Last week, only two quiet people lived at home. Suddenly, we have a third, noisy resident."

Matching Words and Definitions

Check your understanding of the ten words by matching each word with its definition. Look back at the sentences in "Ten Words in Context" as needed to decide on the meaning of each word.

_e_	1. **concede**	a.	lacking depth or meaning; insignificant
_j_	2. **conservative**	b.	conflicting; totally different; opposite
_b_	3. **contrary**	c.	a change from one activity, condition, or location to another
_h_	4. **denounce**	d.	someone blamed for the mistakes of others
_f_	5. **deter**	e.	to admit to something
_g_	6. **disclose**	f.	to prevent or discourage
_d_	7. **scapegoat**	g.	to reveal; make known
_a_	8. **superficial**	h.	to openly condemn; express disapproval of
_i_	9. **sustain**	i.	to keep something going; continue
_c_	10. **transition**	j.	tending to resist change; favoring traditional values and views

CAUTION: Do not go any further until you are sure the above answers are correct. If you have studied the "Ten Words in Context," you will know how to match each word. Then you can use the matches to help you in the following practices. Your goal is to reach a point where you don't need to check definitions at all.

➤ *Sentence Check 1*

Complete each sentence below with the most suitable word from the box. Use each word once.

concede	conservative	contrary	denounce	deter
disclose	scapegoat	superficial	sustain	transition

1. The teenagers who smashed the window made an innocent bystander a ____*scapegoat*____, claiming he had thrown the rock.

2. To ____*sustain*____ a high grade point average throughout college requires much studying.

3. We turned on the TV and heard a speaker ____*denounce*____ all nuclear arms as "suicidal."

4. Even after Stuart listed scientific facts that support his theory, the teacher refused to ____*concede*____ that Stuart might be right.

5. A childhood stutter didn't ____*deter*____ Leon. He overcame his speech handicap and reached his goal of being a radio announcer.

6. I try to judge people by their character, not by something as ____*superficial*____ as physical appearance.

7. Knowing my passion for chocolate, my mother refused to ____*disclose*____ the location of the bite-size Hershey bars, which she was saving for company.

8. The ____*transition*____ from her own apartment to a nursing home has been difficult for my grandmother.

9. Though Geena and Tom are happily married, they cast ____*contrary*____ votes in almost every election—she's a Republican and he's a Democrat.

10. When Dawn brought home a boyfriend with purple hair and an earring, her ____*conservative*____ parents—who prefer everything old-fashioned and traditional—nearly fainted.

Now check your answers to these questions by turning to page 164. Going over the answers carefully will help you prepare for the next two checks, for which answers are not given.

➤ Sentence Check 2

Complete each sentence below with two words from the following list. Use each word once.

concede	conservative	contrary	denounce	deter
disclose	scapegoat	superficial	sustain	transition

1-2. Starting with the _____*transition*_____ from home to college, some students neglect high school friendships which they had vowed always to _____*sustain*_____.

3-4. If Stan were not so _____*superficial*_____ , Ellen's lack of money wouldn't _____*deter*_____ him from becoming her friend.

5-6. Mary Ann's parents always _____*denounce*_____ her, although she is rarely at fault. She has become the _____*scapegoat*_____ for the entire family.

7-8. Mayor Jones was _____*conservative*_____—he preferred traditional solutions. So it was hard for him to _____*concede*_____ that some of the broad-minded ideas of his opponent might work.

9-10. Once Sandy _____*disclose*_____(e)d her true values in the course of our conversation, I realized they were quite _____*contrary*_____ to what I had supposed. She was a different type of person than I had thought.

➤ Final Check: Relating to Parents

Here is a final opportunity for you to strengthen your knowledge of the ten words. First read the following passage carefully. Then fill in each blank with a word from the box at the top of this page. (Context clues will help you figure out which word goes in which blank.) Use each word once.

When I was a kid, my parents were everything to me—the smartest, most interesting, most loving people in the world. But when I turned 13, they seemed suddenly (1)_____*contrary*_____ to what they had been. Now they were mean and strict, and so (2)_____*conservative*_____ that they disliked every new thing that entered my life. They hated my hair, my music, my friends. Sometimes it seemed they even hated me.

Now that I'm making the (3)_____*transition*_____ from my teen years to adulthood, I have to (4)_____*concede*_____ that my parents aren't so bad. Perhaps, at times, I even made them (5)_____*scapegoat*_____s for problems I had caused myself. Now I'd like to have really deep talks with them, not just the (6)_____*superficial*_____ chats we've had lately. But it's hard for us to (7)_____*sustain*_____ a conversation about anything but unimportant subjects. Instead, I'd like to (8)_____*disclose*_____ my plans and dreams to them, but I'm afraid they'll (9)_____*denounce*_____ my ideas as foolish or wrong. It's hard not to let my fears (10)_____*deter*_____ me from seeking a better relationship with my parents, but I think it's worth a try.

SCORES: Sentence Check 2 _____% Final Check _____%

Enter your scores above and in the vocabulary performance chart on the inside back cover of the book.

Previewing the Words

Find out how many of the ten words in this chapter you already know. Try to complete each sentence with the most suitable word from the list below. Use each word once.

Leave a sentence blank rather than guessing at an answer. Your purpose here is just to get a sense of the ten words and what you may know about them.

compensate	conceive	derive	diversity	inhibit
moderate	supplement	surpass	tentative	verify

1. Nobody can _____*surpass*_____ Meryl Streep in acting ability; she's the best.

2. Make a _____*tentative*_____ career choice and then investigate what it involves. If it doesn't interest you, then look for another possible career.

3. The Meyers' new German shepherd will _____*inhibit*_____ neighborhood children from playing on their lawn.

4. The insurance company had to _____*compensate*_____ Ernie for the loss of a finger while on a construction job.

5. I _____*derive*_____ satisfaction from keeping my budget down with cheap but delicious foods such as beans and grains.

6. If your pets aren't eating enough, you can _____*supplement*_____ their diet with a high-nutrition food.

7. The Sneakers Galore store has sneakers in all price categories: budget, _____*moderate*_____ and expensive.

8. Shirley Dowd won the election by only ten votes, so her opponent demanded that the election board

   _____*verify*_____ the results with a recount.

9. Looking at the size of some dinosaur bones helps me _____*conceive*_____ of just how enormous dinosaurs were.

10. Students love the _____*diversity*_____ of the menu at the nearby diner. No matter what they feel like eating, they can find it there.

Now check your answers by turning to page 164. Fix any mistakes and fill in any blank spaces by writing in the correct answers. By doing so, you will complete this introduction to the ten words.

You're now ready to strengthen your knowledge of the words you already know and to master the words you're only half sure of, or don't know at all. Turn to the next page.

Ten Words in Context

Figure out the meanings of the following ten words by looking *closely and carefully* at the context in which the words appear. Doing so will prepare you for the matching test and the practices on the two pages that follow.

1 **compensate**
(kom'-pən-sāt')
-*verb*

   a. Some companies still don't **compensate** women for their work as much as they pay men who do the same or similar work.

   b. When an oil rig explosion killed Sam, the company **compensated** his widow with $100,000. However, nothing could really repay her for his loss.

2 **conceive**
(kən-sēv')
-*verb*

   a. When studying Australia in school, I **conceived** of an interesting class project—each student could write to an Australian pen pal.

   b. Most people in the 1800s could not have imagined such things as TV and heart transplants. What will the next century bring that we cannot yet **conceive** of?

3 **derive**
(di-rīv')
-*verb*

   a. We **derive** plastics from oil. As a result, when oil prices go up, so do the prices of plastic products.

   b. Sarah **derived** pleasure from visiting and reading to old people after school. She enjoyed their company and felt she was doing something worthwhile.

4 **diversity**
(di-vûr'-si-tē)
-*noun*

   a. There's a great **diversity** of breakfast cereals at the supermarket. There are so many different kinds that they take up half an aisle.

   b. "One thing I'm looking for in a college," Sandra told her counselor, "is **diversity**. I want to meet many different kinds of people."

5 **inhibit**
(in-hib'-it)
-*verb*

   a. Steve wanted to drive fast in his new car, but the fact that he had already gotten two speeding tickets **inhibited** him.

   b. Many people believe exercise makes one eat more, but I find exercise **inhibits** my urge to snack.

6 **moderate**
(mod'-ər-it)
-*adjective*

   a. The trail was neither flat nor extremely steep—it was **moderate,** for the average hiker.

   b. The prices at this restaurant aren't dirt cheap, but they are **moderate**. So we should be able to have a nice dinner without spending too much.

7 **supplement**
(sup'-lə-mənt)
-*verb*

   a. Many people use vitamins to **supplement** their diet.

   b. At busy times of the year, the department store **supplements** its sales staff with temporary workers.

8 **surpass**
(sər-pas')
-*verb*

   a. You can reach and even **surpass** many of your highest goals.

   b. Denise failed by just inches to **surpass** Rhonda's record leap of five feet in the high jump.

9 **tentative**
(ten'-tə-tiv)
-*adjective*

   a. Our wedding date is **tentative.** We have to be sure Ben's parents are free that weekend before we finalize the date.

   b. Class membership was **tentative** because many students were still dropping and adding courses.

10 **verify**
(ver'-ə-fī')
-*verb*

   a. Race officials **verified** who the winner was by checking a photo of the horses at the finish line.

   b. We'd love to come to the party, but I have to check my calender to **verify** that we're free that evening.

Matching Words and Definitions

Check your understanding of the ten words by matching each word with its definition. Look back at the sentences in "Ten Words in Context" as needed to decide on the meaning of each word.

_b_ 1. **compensate**   a. variety

_i_ 2. **conceive of**   b. to make suitable payment to; pay; repay

_f_ 3. **derive**   c. to do better than; go beyond in achievement or quality

_a_ 4. **diversity**   d. to test or check the truth or accuracy of something; prove

_j_ 5. **inhibit**   e. to add to, especially to make up for a lack

_h_ 6. **moderate**   f. to receive from a source; get

_e_ 7. **supplement**   g. not definite or final

_c_ 8. **surpass**   h. medium; average; not extreme in quality, degree or amount

_g_ 9. **tentative**   i. to think up; imagine; develop in the mind

_d_ 10. **verify**   j. to hold back; prevent

> *CAUTION*: Do not go any further until you are sure the above answers are correct. If you have studied the "Ten Words in Context," you will know how to match each word. Then you can use the matches to help you in the following practices. Your goal is to reach a point where you don't need to check definitions at all.

➤ Sentence Check 1

Complete each sentence below with the most suitable word from the box. Use each word once.

compensate	conceive	derive	diversity	inhibit
moderate	supplement	surpass	tentative	verify

1. The Mississippi River _____*derive*_____s its name from Indian words meaning "big river."

2. To _____*verify*_____ that his checkbook balance was correct, Craig added the numbers again.

3. If you aren't very hungry, then take only a _____*moderate*_____ helping of food.

4. The exact cast of the movie remains _____*tentative*_____ until it is known whether or not Paul Newman is available.

5. Babe Ruth's record number of home runs in a single baseball season was _____*surpass*_____(e)d by Roger Maris.

6. The Motor Bureau now _____*supplement*_____s the driver's manual with an attached publication on the new driving laws.

7. Even with her relatives, shy Yoko didn't feel free to be herself. Their noisy talk _____*inhibit*_____(e)d her.

8. Artists feel frustrated when what they _____*conceive*_____ in their minds fails to appear on the painted canvas.

9. "Hearing a _____*diversity*_____ of opinions is fine," said Lynn. "But it would be nice if everyone in this family could agree once in a while."

10. When my uncle helped me pay for college, he said I could _____*compensate*_____ him by helping someone else pay for college when I can afford to.

Now check your answers to these questions by turning to page 164. Going over the answers carefully will help you prepare for the next two checks, for which answers are not given.

➤ Sentence Check 2

Complete each sentence below with two words from the following list. Use each word once.

compensate	conceive	derive	diversity	inhibit
moderate	supplement	surpass	tentative	verify

1-2. I cannot _____*conceive*_____ of being in a relationship with a woman who would _____*inhibit*_____ my personal growth.

3-4. I have _____*tentative*_____ plans to meet Cesar at the Midtown Theatre at eight, but first I must _____*verify*_____ the show time and call him back.

5-6. By mistake, the textbook left out some important information, so the publishing company decided to _____*compensate*_____ readers—it _____*supplement*_____(e)d the text with a free booklet containing the missing information.

7-8. I _____*derive*_____ great pleasure from having my paintings in an art show, but nothing can _____*surpass*_____ the joy I get in actually doing the painting.

9-10. City College offers a wide _____*diversity*_____ of courses and majors at a _____*moderate*_____ price. Many students don't realize they have an unusually wide choice of courses at a lower cost than at many other colleges.

➤ Final Check: Job Choices

Here is a final opportunity for you to strengthen your knowledge of the ten words. First read the following passage carefully. Then fill in each blank with a word from the box at the top of this page. (Context clues will help you figure out which word goes in which blank.) Use each word once.

After job-hunting for two months, Jessica had to decide whether to work for a fashion magazine or a clothing store. She already had (1)_____*tentative*_____ job offers from both employers. They would make the offers definite after they were able to (2)_____*verify*_____ the information on her job application.

In the meanwhile, Jessica thought about the good and bad points of the two jobs. Both offered the (3)_____*diversity*_____ that Jessica liked; she hated doing the same thing every day. Both had good benefits, such as sick leave and vacation time. However, the two companies would not (4)_____*compensate*_____ her equally. At the clothing store, Jessica would start out at a (5)_____*moderate*_____ salary level. With her many expenses, she might even have to find a part-time job in the evenings to (6)_____*supplement*_____ this salary. But there were other, better points. Working for the store, Jessica would be free to put her many ideas into practice right away. Her manager said he would encourage, not (7)_____*inhibit*_____, attempts to move up in the company. In fact, she would probably move into a new position in about six months. At the fashion magazine, Jessica's starting salary would far (8)_____*surpass*_____ that of the store—she wouldn't have to worry about money at all. But the possibilities for promotions and raises were not so sure. Jessica could (9)_____*conceive*_____ of learning a lot from either job and felt she could (10)_____*derive*_____ much satisfaction from either one. This would not be an easy decision.

SCORES: Sentence Check 2 _____% Final Check _____%

Enter your scores above and in the vocabulary performance chart on the inside back cover of the book.

Previewing the Words

Find out how many of the ten words in this chapter you already know. Try to complete each sentence with the most suitable word from the list below. Use each word once.

Leave a sentence blank rather than guessing at an answer. Your purpose here is just to get a sense of the ten words and what you may know about them.

alter	ample	blunt	chronic	chronological
optimist	pretense	prolong	refrain	remorse

1. Maureen can be _____*blunt*_____ to the point of cruelty. She once told Randy she'd never date him because he's so short.

2. Someone called me under the _____*pretense*_____ of doing a telephone survey, but he really wanted to sell me storm windows.

3. Rose, always an _____*optimist*_____, expected her lost luggage to be returned by some handsome, helpful stranger.

4. The criminal who seemed truly sorry for his crime received a shorter jail term than his partner, who showed no _____*remorse*_____.

5. Gerry arranged her photos in _____*chronological*_____ order, from infancy to adulthood.

6. To play the part of an old man, the teen needed to _____*alter*_____ his appearance with a white wig and wrinkle lines.

7. Darrell is such a(n) _____*chronic*_____ liar that he can't get through the day without telling a falsehood.

8. "I know you've been waiting to meet my boyfriend for a long time," Ebony said, "so I won't _____*prolong*_____ the suspense. Here he is."

9. "Please _____*refrain*_____ from smoking on the bus," the driver said. "You may smoke at our next rest stop."

10. I like to buy sweaters and jeans that fit with _____*ample*_____ room, so that if they shrink, they'll still be loose enough.

Now check your answers by turning to page 164. Fix any mistakes and fill in any blank spaces by writing in the correct answers. By doing so, you will complete this introduction to the ten words.

You're now ready to strengthen your knowledge of the words you already know and to master the words you're only half sure of, or don't know at all. Turn to the next page.

Ten Words in Context

Figure out the meanings of the following ten words by looking *closely and carefully* at the context in which the words appear. Doing so will prepare you for the matching test and the practices on the two pages that follow.

1 **alter**
(ôl'-tər)
-verb

  a. Written words can be rewritten, but spoken words cannot be **altered.**

  b. Fern's dramatic weight loss and new hairstyle so **altered** her appearance that we barely recognized her.

2 **ample**
(am'-pəl)
-adjective

  a. My compact car has **ample** room. Even Mario, who is six feet tall, never feels cramped in it.

  b. My parents believe that the most important requirement of any celebration is that there be **ample** food, so that no one will be hungry.

3 **blunt**
(blunt)
-adjective

  a. "I'll be **blunt**," Phyllis said, as plainspoken as ever. "You're a jerk."

  b. My best friend is so **blunt** that he never softens the truth. He always states his opinion in a painfully straightforward way.

4 **chronic**
(kron'-ik)
-adjective

  a. Bernard's need to be the center of attention is **chronic.** He will speak loudly, wear a jacket so bright it could glow in the dark, or do whatever else is necessary to keep all eyes focused on him.

  b. Leon has been chain-smoking for so long that he has developed a **chronic** cough, heard daily by everyone in the office.

5 **chronological**
(kron'-ə-loj'-i-kəl)
-adjective

  a. I would have followed the movie better if it had presented events in **chronological** order, instead of jumping back and forth in time.

  b. In your resume, list your jobs in reverse **chronological** order—begin with the most recent job and go backward.

6 **optimist**
(op'-tə-mist)
-noun

  a. Jerry is a true **optimist.** While her friends get out their umbrellas, she puts on suntan lotion.

  b. Alonso is such an **optimist** that when he lost his job, he said only, "I bet I'll find a better one now."

7 **pretense**
(prē'-tens)
-noun

  a. The robber entered people's houses under the **pretense** of being a repairman.

  b. I asked several questions about Alan's illness, under the **pretense** of being concerned. In truth, I've never even liked Alan.

8 **prolong**
(prə-lông')
-verb

  a. Pulling off a bandage always hurts, but pulling it off slowly **prolongs** the pain.

  b. My registration for fall classes was **prolonged** because I forgot my course card and had to stand in two extra lines.

9 **refrain**
(ri-frān')
-verb

  a. I **refrained** from saying what I really thought about Anne's haircut because I didn't want to hurt her feelings.

  b. Since she's on a diet, Stella **refrained** from eating a second piece of carrot cake.

10 **remorse**
(ri-môrs')
-noun

  a. Russell's mother was filled with **remorse** after she hit him. She always regrets her outbursts of temper.

  b. Feeling **remorse** over breaking his sister's Sony Walkman, Chet apologized and promised to buy her a new one.

Matching Words and Definitions

Check your understanding of the ten words by matching each word with its definition. Look back at the sentences in "Ten Words in Context" as needed to decide on the meaning of each word.

_d_	1. **alter**	a.	continuing; lasting a long time; constant
_f_	2. **ample**	b.	a false show or claim
_i_	3. **blunt**	c.	someone who expects a good outcome
_a_	4. **chronic**	d.	to change
_h_	5. **chronological**	e.	to hold oneself back from doing something
_c_	6. **optimist**	f.	more than enough; plenty
_b_	7. **pretense**	g.	a feeling of regret and guilt
_j_	8. **prolong**	h.	in the time order in which events happened
_e_	9. **refrain**	i.	rudely brief and straightforward
_g_	10. **remorse**	j.	to make something last longer

CAUTION: Do not go any further until you are sure the above answers are correct. If you have studied the "Ten Words in Context," you will know how to match each word. Then you can use the matches to help you in the following practices. Your goal is to reach a point where you don't need to check definitions at all.

➤ Sentence Check 1

Complete each sentence below with the most suitable word from the box. Use each word once.

alter	ample	blunt	chronic	chronological
optimist	pretense	prolong	refrain	remorse

1. I couldn't _____refrain_____ from laughing when Laurie bent over to pick up her pencil and split her tight jeans.

2. My father always expects the worst, but my mother is a(n) _____optimist_____.

3. I used to dislike my neighbor, but learning he drove meals to elderly shut-ins _____alter_____(e)d my opinion of him.

4. The record store will _____prolong_____ its "One Day Only" sale to two days, since a storm kept people away the first day.

5. Dana's mother left a(n) _____ample_____ hem when she made the dress so she could lengthen the skirt as Dana grew.

6. Immediately after calling her sister an idiot, Lydia felt _____remorse_____. So she hugged her sister and said, "I didn't mean that."

7. If the teacher had been _____blunt_____, she would have told Kevin his essay was terrible. Instead, she politely said, "It could use much more work."

8. A story in which early events are hidden until the end is often more dramatic than one told in strict _____chronological_____ order.

9. Although Pilar's back pain was _____chronic_____, having lasted for five years, she refused to undergo surgery.

10. With the _____pretense_____ of being attracted to Paula, Dick asked her to dance; but his real reason was to make his ex-girlfriend jealous.

Now check your answers to these questions by turning to page 164. Going over the answers carefully will help you prepare for the next two checks, for which answers are not given.

➤ Sentence Check 2

Complete each sentence below with two words from the following list. Use each word once.

alter	ample	blunt	chronic	chronological
optimist	pretense	prolong	refrain	remorse

1-2. Although her marriage was unhappy, Nell chose to _____*prolong*_____ it. An _____*optimist*_____, she kept thinking her relationship with her husband would improve.

3-4. Sylvester can't _____*refrain*_____ from sniffling and blowing his nose because he suffers all summer from _____*chronic*_____ hay fever.

5-6. The murderer told what happened in simple _____*chronological*_____ order, without showing any _____*remorse*_____: "First I loaded the gun, and then I drove to the mall. Next, I started shooting people."

7-8. _____*Blunt*_____ criticism is rarely the best way to _____*alter*_____ someone's behavior. Gentle suggestions tend to bring about more change.

9-10. Dressed in shabby clothes, Darren made a _____*pretense*_____ of being poor. Few people knew he had _____*ample*_____ money to live well.

➤ Final Check: No Joking

Here is a final opportunity for you to strengthen your knowledge of the ten words. First read the following passage carefully. Then fill in each blank with a word from the box at the top of this page. (Context clues will help you figure out which word goes in which blank.) Use each word once.

My poor mother is the worst joke teller I've ever met. She has a (1)_____*chronic*_____ inability to remember stories and punchlines—she's been like that for years. She begins a story in (2)_____*chronological*_____ order and then interrupts herself to say, "No, wait a minute. That's not the way it goes." In this way, she manages to (3)_____*prolong*_____ jokes, making them more long than funny. Still, she can't (4)_____*refrain*_____ from trying to tell them. And she has (5)_____*ample*_____ opportunity to try when our family gets together. My uncle loves to see her embarrass herself, so he makes a (6)_____*pretense*_____ of thinking she is funny. My father is more (7)_____*blunt*_____; he tells Mother outright that she has ruined the joke. After each failure, she is filled with (8)_____*remorse*_____ and swears she'll never tell another. But I don't believe she'll ever (9)_____*alter*_____ her behavior. An (10)_____*optimist*_____, she always believes her next joke will be her best.

SCORES:	Sentence Check 2 _____%	Final Check _____%

Enter your scores above and in the vocabulary performance chart on the inside back cover of the book.

Previewing the Words

Find out how many of the ten words in this chapter you already know. Try to complete each sentence with the most suitable word from the list below. Use each word once.

Leave a sentence blank rather than guessing at an answer. Your purpose here is just to get a sense of the ten words and what you may know about them.

acute	anonymous	apprehensive	arrogant	bestow
donor	phobia	prominent	prudent	recipient

1. The supermarket puts sale items in _____*prominent*_____ places so they can be easily seen.

2. It is more _____*prudent*_____ to carry traveler's checks than to carry a large amount of cash.

3. A rich _____*donor*_____ gave the statue of the famous artist to the city, to place in a park.

4. Kim's embarrassment at being overdressed was so _____*acute*_____ that she left the party soon after arriving.

5. As the _____*recipient*_____ of a full scholarship, Bernard didn't even have to pay for his college texts.

6. Many folk songs are _____*anonymous*_____, their composers' names having been lost long before the songs were ever published.

7. A good teacher knows when to _____*bestow*_____ praise on a student and when to give helpful criticism.

8. After winning his company's Salesman of the Year award twice, Vinnie became overconfident and

   _____*arrogant*_____ among the other salespeople.

9. The frightened puppy huddled in the corner of the shelter cage. But Margo felt sure he would become

   less _____*apprehensive*_____ after she took him home and he got used to her.

10. My brother has an extreme fear of the dark. Because of this _____*phobia*_____, at age 30 he still sleeps with a night light on.

Now check your answers by turning to page 164. Fix any mistakes and fill in any blank spaces by writing in the correct answers. By doing so, you will complete this introduction to the ten words.

You're now ready to strengthen your knowledge of the words you already know and to master the words you're only half sure of, or don't know at all. Turn to the next page.

Ten Words in Context

Figure out the meanings of the following ten words by looking *closely and carefully* at the context in which the words appear. Doing so will prepare you for the matching test and the practices on the two pages that follow.

1 **acute**
(ə-kyōōt')
-*adjective*

   a. Gil joked, "This painting looks like something my two-year-old son would do." Then he felt **acute** regret when he learned the artist was standing behind him.

   b. My headache pains were so **acute** that they felt like needles in my head.

2 **anonymous**
(ə-non'-ə-məs)
-*adjective*

   a. Many **anonymous** works are very famous. For example, the author of the well-known Christmas carol "God Rest Ye, Merry Gentlemen" is unknown.

   b. Laura tore up an **anonymous** note saying her husband was seeing another woman. "If the writer was too ashamed to sign the note," said Laura, "why should I believe it?"

3 **apprehensive**
(ap'-ri-hen'-siv)
-*adjective*

   a. Ginny was **apprehensive** as she approached the cow, not knowing if it would try to bite or kick her.

   b. It is natural to be **apprehensive** when making a major purchase such as a computer or a car. Only the very wealthy can afford not to be at all nervous at such times.

4 **arrogant**
(ar'-ə-gənt)
-*adjective*

   a. Having been a very spoiled child, Becky turned out to be a very **arrogant** grownup.

   b. One of the most **arrogant** people I know paid the state extra money to get a custom license plate that reads: "IMBEST."

5 **bestow**
(bi-stō')
-*verb*

   a. The Manhattan School of Music **bestowed** an honorary degree on a famous musician who had never gone to college.

   b. At the science fair, the judges **bestowed** first prize on Vincent's experiment showing that dogs are colorblind.

6 **donor**
(dō'-nər)
-*noun*

   a. Every **donor** to the fund for a new children's hospital will be listed in one of the fund-raising bulletins.

   b. The man's twin sister was the **donor** of his new kidney.

7 **phobia**
(fō'-bē-ə)
-*noun*

   a. Terry has joined a group that helps people with **phobias** because she wants to overcome her extreme fear of even the smallest spiders.

   b. Ned's fear of flying is so severe that he won't even step onto an airplane. But he says he's in no rush to cure his **phobia** since driving is cheaper anyway.

8 **prominent**
(prom'-ə-nənt)
-*adjective*

   a. Crystal's long black hair is so **prominent** that it's the first thing you notice about her.

   b. The most **prominent** balloon in the parade was of Big Bird because it was so large and such a bright yellow.

9 **prudent**
(prōōd'-ənt)
-*adjective*

   a. Sidney has learned the hard way that it's not **prudent** to tease our ill-tempered dog.

   b. **Prudent** as always, Meg thought carefully before finally deciding which of the used cars would be the best buy.

10 **recipient**
(ri-sip'-ē-ənt)
-*noun*

   a. Katherine Hepburn was the **recipient** of an Academy Award for her role in *On Golden Pond* in 1981, almost fifty years after her first Academy Award.

   b. Doug was the annoyed **recipient** of fourteen pieces of junk mail on the same day.

Matching Words and Definitions

Check your understanding of the ten words by matching each word with its definition. Look back at the sentences in "Ten Words in Context" as needed to decide on the meaning of each word.

_e_	1. **acute**	a. a person who gives, contributes, or donates
_i_	2. **anonymous**	b. frightened; uneasy; anxious
_b_	3. **apprehensive**	c. a continuing, abnormally extreme fear of a particular situation or thing
_f_	4. **arrogant**	d. cautious; careful; wise
_j_	5. **bestow**	e. severe; sharp
_a_	6. **donor**	f. filled with self-importance; overly proud and vain
_c_	7. **phobia**	g. very noticeable; obvious
_g_	8. **prominent**	h. a person who receives
_d_	9. **prudent**	i. written or given by an unknown or unidentified person
_h_	10. **recipient**	j. to give as an honor or a gift

CAUTION: Do not go any further until you are sure the above answers are correct. If you have studied the "Ten Words in Context," you will know how to match each word. Then you can use the matches to help you in the following practices. Your goal is to reach a point where you don't need to check definitions at all.

➤Sentence Check 1

Complete each sentence below with the most suitable word from the box. Use each word once.

acute	anonymous	apprehensive	arrogant	bestow
donor	phobia	prominent	prudent	recipient

1. Because of her _____phobia_____, Martha will walk up twenty floors to avoid taking an elevator.

2. The unsigned letter to the editor was not published because it was the newspaper's policy never to print _____anonymous_____ letters.

3. A final exam causes Phil such _____acute_____ anxiety that he has trouble falling asleep the night before taking one.

4. The rich and powerful are sometimes _____arrogant_____—they can mistake always getting their own way for always being right.

5. Carla was so popular that each year she was the _____recipient_____ of dozens of Valentines.

6. When he retires, the professor will _____bestow_____ his art collection on the school.

7. "Your decision to wait to marry until after graduation seems _____prudent_____ to me," Larry's father said, pleased his son was acting so wisely.

8. Cliff became more and more _____apprehensive_____ about the driving test for his license. He was afraid he'd forget to signal, fail to park correctly, or even get into an accident.

9. Because the new tax laws limit certain deductions, there are fewer _____donor_____s of art to museums.

10. The bank robber purposely moved with a(n) _____prominent_____ limp so that witnesses would be sure to notice his "handicap" and put police on someone else's trail.

Now check your answers to these questions by turning to page 164. Going over the answers carefully will help you prepare for the next two checks, for which answers are not given.

➤ Sentence Check 2

Complete each sentence below with two words from the following list. Use each word once.

acute	anonymous	apprehensive	arrogant	bestow
donor	phobia	prominent	prudent	recipient

1-2. The millionaire was so _____*arrogant*_____ that he refused to be a major _____*donor*_____ to the new town library unless it was named for him.

3-4. It's _____*prudent*_____ to keep medication on hand if anyone in the family is subject to _____*acute*_____ asthma attacks.

5-6. When Joey is very _____*apprehensive*_____, such as when he has to give a speech in class, his stutter becomes especially _____*prominent*_____.

7-8. The famous actress was sometimes the _____*recipient*_____ of _____*anonymous*_____ letters from fans too shy to sign their names.

9-10. Martha felt her therapist had _____*bestow*_____ed upon her the greatest of gifts: freedom from fear of open spaces. Before her treatment, Martha's _____*phobia*_____ had kept her a prisoner in her own home.

➤ Final Check: Museum Pet

Here is a final opportunity for you to strengthen your knowledge of the ten words. First read the following passage carefully. Then fill in each blank with a word from the box at the top of this page. (Context clues will help you figure out which word goes in which blank.) Use each word once.

"I've got great news!" the museum director shouted as he ran into the employees' lunchroom. "Someone wants to (1)_____*bestow*_____ five million dollars on the museum."

"Who?" one staff member asked excitedly.

"I don't know. He wishes his gift to remain (2)_____*anonymous*_____. There's just one catch," he added. The employees' smiles faded, and they began to look (3)_____*apprehensive*_____.

"It seems our mystery (4)_____*donor*_____ has a strange (5)_____*phobia*_____: he's terribly afraid of cats." Everyone turned to look at Willard, who had been the museum pet since he'd wandered in as a tiny kitten more than five years ago. As usual, the big orange cat was stretched out in a (6)_____*prominent*_____ spot near the lunchroom entrance. He continued licking himself, not aware that he was the (7)_____*recipient*_____ of everyone's attention.

"I'm afraid Willard will have to go," the director said sadly. "This contributor isn't just a little afraid of cats; his fear is really (8)_____*acute*_____. Apparently, he panicked when he saw Willard the last time he came. We can't risk frightening him again. It just wouldn't be (9)_____*prudent*_____—remember, he might give us more money in the future."

"I think it's pretty (10)_____*arrogant*_____ of this contributor, whoever he is, to ask us to give up poor old Willard for him, even if he does want to give us the money," one employee said angrily.

"I know you'll miss Willard," the director said, "but I'll be glad to have him come live at my house. You can all visit him whenever you like." And so Willard found a new home, where he still lives happily. The museum used the five million dollars to build a new addition, which was known as the Willard Wing.

> **SCORES:** Sentence Check 2 _____% Final Check _____%

Previewing the Words

Find out how many of the ten words in this chapter you already know. Try to complete each sentence with the most suitable word from the list below. Use each word once.

Leave a sentence blank rather than guessing at an answer. Your purpose here is just to get a sense of the ten words and what you may know about them.

absurd	adhere	affluent	alienate	assess
compile	contempt	defect	doctrine	dogmatic

1. Angie used bubble gum to make the poster of Prince _____*adhere*_____ to her bedroom wall.

2. My parents were _____*dogmatic*_____—they made their rules clear and never listened to our point of view.

3. Because Harris shows his emotions so openly, it is easy to _____*assess*_____ his moods.

4. The salesman said, "If there is any _____*defect*_____ in the stereo system, you may return it for a full refund."

5. The married senator should have known that his affairs with women would _____*alienate*_____ him from voters.

6. The _____*doctrine*_____ of the divine right of kings was based on the belief that a king's power came from God.

7. The lawyer tried to overcome his _____*contempt*_____ for the child abuser in order to defend him well in court.

8. A law against suicide is _____*absurd*_____. People who succeed cannot be punished; those who fail aren't guilty.

9. The teacher asked students to _____*compile*_____ information on their family histories by interviewing parents and grandparents.

10. Lottery winners have learned that being _____*affluent*_____ is not so easy. Many mismanage their winnings and end up without lottery money until the next year's payment.

Now check your answers by turning to page 164. Fix any mistakes and fill in any blank spaces by writing in the correct answers. By doing so, you will complete this introduction to the ten words.

You're now ready to strengthen your knowledge of the words you already know and to master the words you're only half sure of, or don't know at all. Turn to the next page.

Ten Words in Context

Figure out the meanings of the following ten words by looking *closely and carefully* at the context in which the words appear. Doing so will prepare you for the matching test and the practices on the two pages that follow.

1 **absurd**
(ab-surd')
-adjective

   a. When six-foot Randy came to the costume party in only diapers, he looked so **absurd** that everyone burst into laughter.

   b. It seemed **absurd** to Helen that she had more cooking experience than the teacher of her cooking class.

2 **adhere**
(ad-hēr')
-verb

   a. Beware of sitting on a hot car seat in shorts—your thighs may **adhere** to the plastic.

   b. The bandage **adhered** so strongly to my skin that pulling it off hurt more than the original sore.

3 **affluent**
(af'-lōō-ənt)
-adjective

   a. Some people live an **affluent** lifestyle by overcharging on their credit cards—a bad habit that can lead to a mountain of debts.

   b. Should our tax rules benefit the **affluent** more than the poor?

4 **alienate**
(āl'-yən-āt')
-verb

   a. The teacher often insulted Maria. His rude behavior began to **alienate** the other students, who had once thought of him as a friend.

   b. Bill and Joanne thought their marriage could survive when they worked in different cities. But being apart so much eventually **alienated** them from each other.

5 **assess**
(ə-ses')
-verb

   a. It is harder for teachers to **assess** answers to essay questions than to grade multiple-choice items.

   b. After the fire, insurance representatives came to **assess** the damage.

6 **compile**
(kəm-pīl')
-verb

   a. Before writing her essay, Sharon **compiled** a list of the points she wanted to make.

   b. It took hours to **compile** the names of all of the friends and family who would be invited to the wedding.

7 **contempt**
(kən-tempt')
-noun

   a. Vera pitied the beggar, but her boyfriend felt only **contempt**, saying, "He's too lazy to get a job."

   b. Molly expressed her **contempt** for Art's clumsy dancing by leaving him in the middle of the dance floor.

8 **defect**
(dē'-fekt')
-noun

   a. The only **defect** in the actor's good looks was that his ears stuck out. Careful camera angles and a longer haircut hid the problem.

   b. "Check these peaches for **defects**, Tom," said the grocer to his new employee. "Remove any with dark spots or other imperfections."

9 **doctrine**
(dok'-trin)
-noun

   a. Dr. Martin Luther King, Jr., followed a **doctrine** of fighting for social change without violence.

   b. Many sincerely practice their faith without understanding all its **doctrines.** The fine points of principle do not interest everyone.

10 **dogmatic**
(dôg-mat'-ik)
-adjective

   a The boss's **dogmatic** style bothered me. He listened to only one person's opinions— his own.

   b. A **dogmatic** teacher demands that students accept what is taught without question. Rather than insisting on their own views, teachers should encourage students to express opinions.

Matching Words and Definitions

Check your understanding of the ten words by matching each word with its definition. Look back at the sentences in "Ten Words in Context" as needed to decide on the meaning of each word.

_h_ 1. **absurd**   a. disrespect; a feeling that a person or thing is inferior and undesirable

_d_ 2. **adhere**   b. to evaluate; decide on the quality or value of

_g_ 3. **affluent**   c. opinionated; stating an opinion as if it were a fact

_f_ 4. **alienate**   d. to stick firmly

_b_ 5. **assess**   e. a fault; imperfection

_i_ 6. **compile**   f. to cause to become unfriendly or emotionally separated

_a_ 7. **contempt**   g. wealthy

_e_ 8. **defect**   h. ridiculous; opposed to common sense

_j_ 9. **doctrine**   i. to gather together in an organized form, such as a list or pile

_c_ 10. **dogmatic**   j. the principle or principles taught to a religious, political, or other group

CAUTION: Do not go any further until you are sure the above answers are correct. If you have studied the "Ten Words in Context," you will know how to match each word. Then you can use the matches to help you in the following practices. Your goal is to reach a point where you don't need to check definitions at all.

➤Sentence Check 1

Complete each sentence below with the most suitable word from the box. Use each word once.

absurd	adhere	affluent	alienate	assess
compile	contempt	defect	doctrine	dogmatic

1. You cannot always _____assess_____ a student's progress by his or her grades.

2. Many of the houses in _____affluent_____ neighborhoods have burglar alarms.

3. Margo's parents' constant arguments began to _____alienate_____ her from them.

4. When Jerry cheated on the final, and then bragged about it as well, Eva felt _____contempt_____ for him.

5. Filling out a tax form is easier if you first _____compile_____ all the information you will need.

6. If you study the _____doctrine_____s of several religions, you may be surprised by the similarity of some of their teachings.

7. Something in a spider's thread makes the bugs it catches _____adhere_____ to the web.

8. Vivian was about to buy a red dress when she noticed a small _____defect_____—some threads were loose on the collar.

9. My boss has a _____dogmatic_____ way of running things—he wants workers to do exactly what he tells them, without questions.

10. Dee thought Harry was _____absurd_____ to do a rain dance on their dry front lawn—until she saw the sky blacken and lightning flash immediately afterward.

Now check your answers to these questions by turning to page 164. Going over the answers carefully will help you prepare for the next two checks, for which answers are not given.

➤ Sentence Check 2

Complete each sentence below with two words from the following list. Use each word once.

absurd	adhere	affluent	alienate	assess
compile	contempt	defect	doctrine	dogmatic

1-2. To _____ *assess* _____ the value of their losses from the robbery, the Browns first had to _____ *compile* _____ a list of everything that was stolen.

3-4. I have _____ *contempt* _____ for any _____ *doctrine* _____ that teaches hatred of groups with other principles and beliefs.

5-6. _____ *Dogmatic* _____ parents who deny their children freedom to make some of their own decisions may eventually _____ *alienate* _____ those children.

7-8. It seems _____ *absurd* _____ that anyone should go hungry in a country as _____ *affluent* _____ as ours.

9-10. My little girl thought the roll of tape that is sticky on both sides had a _____ *defect* _____, but the tape is actually meant to _____ *adhere* _____ on both sides.

➤ Final Check: Unacceptable Boyfriends

Here is a final opportunity for you to strengthen your knowledge of the ten words. First read the following passage carefully. Then fill in each blank with a word from the box at the top of this page. (Context clues will help you figure out which word goes in which blank.) Use each word once.

My father has never liked any of my boyfriends. He always seems determined to find some (1)_____ *defect* _____ in them. His complaint against Victor was that "he wears rhinestone earrings." Could Victor help it if he wasn't (2)_____ *affluent* _____ enough for diamond earrings? My father (3)_____ *assess* _____(e)d Lance just as negatively. He claimed that Lance was brainwashed by a member of a cult. This was a(n) (4)_____ *absurd* _____ accusation. The truth is that Lance strictly follows the rules of a little-known religion. The religion preaches, among other things, that one should not allow one's T-shirts to (5)_____ *adhere* _____ to a sweaty body, which is why Lance changes so often in summer. When I tried to explain this to my father, he showed nothing but (6)_____ *contempt* _____ for Lance's beliefs. For that matter, my father doesn't tolerate any beliefs that differ greatly from his own. That's how (7)_____ *dogmatic* _____ he is when it comes to religious (8)_____ *doctrine* _____. Now my father is trying to (9)_____ *alienate* _____ me from my friend Joe Bob—he has started to (10)_____ *compile* _____ a long list of Joe Bob's "faults." For example, my father actually listed the fact that Joe Bob has a collection of poisonous snakes. I don't think it's fair to hold Joe Bob's love of nature against him.

SCORES:	Sentence Check 2 _____ %	Final Check _____ %

Enter your scores above and in the vocabulary performance chart on the inside back cover of the book.

Previewing the Word Parts

Common word parts—also known as *prefixes, suffixes, and roots*—are used in forming many words in English. This page will introduce you to ten common word parts.

Try to match each word part on the left with its definition on the right. Use the words in parentheses as hints to help you guess the meanings. If you can't decide on an answer, leave the space blank. Your purpose here is just to get a sense of the ten word parts and what you may know about them. (You'll have another chance to try this exercise after considering the word parts in context.)

Word Parts	Definitions
_c_ 1. **anti-** (antidote, antisocial)	a. after
_f_ 2. **bi-** (bifocal, binoculars)	b. something written or drawn
_d_ 3. **en-, em-** (enclose, encircle)	c. against, acting against
_b_ 4. **-graph, -gram** (paragraph, diagram)	d. into, in
_g_ 5. **inter-** (international, interfere)	e. under, below
_i_ 6. **-less** (thoughtless, fearless)	f. two
_j_ 7. **phon** (telephone, phonograph)	g. between, among
_a_ 8. **post-** (postpone, postwar)	h. look, watch
_h_ 9. **spect** (inspect, spectacle)	i. without
_e_ 10. **sub-** (submarine, subtract)	j. sound, speech

Now go on to "Ten Word Parts in Context" on the next page. Working through this chapter will help you to strengthen your knowledge of the word parts you already know and to master the word parts you're only half sure of, or don't know at all.

Keep in mind that learning word parts can pay several dividends. Word parts can help with the spelling and pronunciation of many words. They can also help you to unlock the meanings of unfamiliar words.

Ten Word Parts in Context

Figure out the meanings of the following ten word parts by looking *closely and carefully* at the context in which they appear. Doing so will prepare you for the matching test and the practices on the two pages that follow.

1 **anti-**
   a. **Antifreeze** prevents the water in a car radiator from freezing.
   b. During the Vietnam War, many students took part in **antiwar** marches.

2 **bi-**
   a. In addition to the expected pair of wheels, a **bicycle** built for two also has two seats.
   b. "You can have only one wife at a time," Judge Graves told the **bigamist,** "not both at once."

3 **en-, em-**
   a. A brief kiss, a quick **embrace,** and she was gone.
   b. On the boss's door were two signs: "**Enter**" and "Exit."

4 **-graph, -gram**
   a. My little sister practices her handwriting so that if she becomes a famous dancer, her **autograph** will look good.
   b. The **diagram** in my biology book shows that, strange as it may seem, the earthworm has two hearts.

5 **inter-**
   a. When my brother tries to speak while chewing gum, it's impossible to understand him without an **interpreter.**
   b. **International** law refers to the rules that apply to the relations between nations.

6 **-less**
   a. The mayor spoke sadly about the **homeless,** but he did nothing to build low-income housing.
   b. The Smiths' marriage was **loveless.** They stayed together for their children, but their constant fighting may have hurt the children more than a divorce would have.

7 **phon**
   a. Whenever Wayne played the **saxophone,** dogs howled, cats screamed, and lovebirds got divorced.
   b. Alexander Graham Bell invented not only the **telephone** but also a man-carrying kite.

8 **post-**
   a. Why are baseball games **postponed** because of a slight rain, but football games not called off if it rains rattlesnakes?
   b. My sister includes at least one **postscript** after each of her letters, even if it's only: "P.S. I don't have anything else to say."

9 **spect**
   a. Detective Blake amazed them all by **inspecting** the tuna casserole the thief was baking and then fishing the jewels out with a fork.
   b. There were several **spectators** at the robbery, but not one tried to help the old woman.

10 **sub-**
   a. Some people won't ride a **subway** because they fear being trapped underground.
   b. On the **submarine** ride at Disneyland, passengers can see models of such underwater life as seahorses and sharks.

Matching Word Parts and Definitions

Check your understanding of the ten word parts by matching each with its definition. See also the suggestions on page 4.

_c_ 1. **anti-**	a. after
_f_ 2. **bi-**	b. something written or drawn
_d_ 3. **en-, em-**	c. against, acting against
_b_ 4. **-graph, -gram**	d. into, in
_g_ 5. **inter-**	e. under, below
_i_ 6. **-less**	f. two
_j_ 7. **phon**	g. between, among
_a_ 8. **post-**	h. look, watch
_h_ 9. **spect**	i. without
_e_ 10. **.sub-**	j. sound, speech

CAUTION: Do not go any further until you are sure the above answers are correct. If you have studied the "Ten Word Parts in Context," you will know how to match each word part. Then you can use the matches to help you in the following practices. Your goal is to reach a point where you don't need to check definitions at all.

➤ Sentence Check 1

Complete each partial word in the following sentences with a word part from the box. Use each word part only once. You may want to check off each word part as you use it.

anti-	bi-	en-	-graph	inter-
-less	phon	post-	spect	sub-

1. Out on the ocean, sunsets can be (. . . *acular*) ___*spectacular*___ —color displays really worth seeing.

2. The French have trouble with English (. . . *etics*) ___*phonetics*___, especially the sound of "er," as in *murder* and *later*.

3. "We (. . . *rupt*) ___*interrupt*___ this program to bring you a special news bulletin."

4. You can keep brown sugar moist by (. . . *closing*) ___*enclosing*___ it in a container with a piece or two of apple.

5. In her (*autobio. . .y*) ___*autobiography*___, *The Story of My Life*, Helen Keller tells how she was able to learn despite her blindness and deafness.

6. Clark was (. . . *social*) ___*antisocial*___ in high school, but he became very outgoing in college.

7. Bird and animal watchers prefer rubber-coated (. . . *noculars*) ___*binoculars*___ because they don't click and bang against trees or equipment.

8. A (*cord. . .*) ___*cordless*___ phone allows a parent to talk to a caller while following a wandering child around the house.

9. Prenatal care for birds means sitting on the eggs. (. . . *natal*) ___*postnatal*___ care involves almost constant feeding during the day.

10. When we saw the floating log (. . . *merge*) ___*submerge*___, sliding under the water toward our canoe, we knew two things: one, it was no log; two, it meant to eat us.

Now check your answers to these questions by turning to page 164. Going over the answers carefully will help you prepare for the next two checks, for which answers are not given.

➤ Sentence Check 2

Complete each word in the sentences below with a word part from the following list. Use each word part once.

anti-	bi-	en-, em-	-graph, -gram	inter-
-less	phon	post-	spect	sub-

1-2. Because I'm allergic to all kinds of perfumes, my (. . . *perspirant*) __*antiperspirant*__ must be (*odor. . .*) ___*odorless*___ .

3-4. Long-playing records for (. . . *ographs*) __*phonographs*__ were thought up by a CBS (. . . *ployee*) ___*employee*___ who received no royalties for the invention.

5-6. In Nazi Germany, every (*tele. . .*) ___*telegram*___ sent was (*in. . .ed*) ___*inspected*___ by Hitler's secret police, making it hard to keep secrets.

7-8. No one (. . . *fered*) ___*interfered*___ with the mad scientist's plans because he worked in a hidden lab in a (. . . *basement*) __*subbasement*__ , under the laundry room in his basement.

9-10. I'm accustomed to being paid every two weeks, but for some reason, my expected (. . . *weekly*) ___*biweekly*___ check hasn't arrived yet, forcing me to (. . . *date*) ___*postdate*___ a check to my landlord.

➤ Final Check: Coping with Snow

Here is a final opportunity for you to strengthen your knowledge of the ten word parts. First read the following passage carefully. Then complete each partial word in the parentheses below with a word from the box at the top of this page. (Context clues will help you figure out which word part goes in which blank.) Use each word part once.

There are plenty of (. . *joyabl*e) (1)___*enjoyable*___ ways to keep your driveway free of snow. For example, you might (. . .*vene*) (2)___*intervene*___ between the snow and the driveway by simply extending the roof of your house until it covers the entire drive. Or you could paint the drive with (. . . *freeze*) (3)___*antifreeze*___ , so that snowflakes will melt as soon as they land. Or, with just one quick (*tele. . .e*) (4)___*telephone*___ call, you could order your kids to come shovel you out. Attaching a plow to the front of your (. . . *cycle*) (5)___*bicycle*___ and pedaling is another possibility. This method will provide you with plenty of leg exercise. At the same time, you will make a (. . .*acle*) (6)___*spectacle*___ of yourself in front of the neighborhood children, who can (*photo. . .*) (7)___*photograph*___ you and keep the pictures for possible later use in blackmail. Finally, since snow sticks only in (. . . *freezing*) (8)___*subfreezing*___ temperatures, you can always (. . . *pone*) (9)___*postpone*___ your actions until a later time—say, May or June. See? There's no reason to feel (*help. . .*) (10)___*helpless*___ just because a blizzard piles a foot of snow on your driveway.

SCORES: Sentence Check 2 _____%	Final Check _____%

Enter your scores above and in the vocabulary performance chart on the inside back cover of the book.

UNIT TWO: Test 1

PART A
Choose the word that best completes each sentence and write it in the space provided.

1. **phobia**
   doctrine
   diversity
   transition

   My sister's _____*phobia*_____ about snakes is so strong she actually faints if she sees one.

2. **pretense**
   remorse
   phobia
   defect

   A tiny _____*defect*_____ in the space shuttle led to its explosion.

3. **dogmatic**
   absurd
   chronic
   acute

   After you watch *Sesame Street* for a while, you forget how _____*absurd*_____ the enormous goggle-eyed Big Bird really is.

4. **dogmatic**
   ample
   moderate
   anonymous

   The editor refuses to print _____*anonymous*_____ letters. She believes people should know whose opinion they are reading.

5. **affluent**
   prudent
   moderate
   chronic

   Fred is a(n) _____*chronic*_____ complainer—as soon as one problem is solved, he'll come up with another.

6. **assessed**
   bestowed
   surpassed
   sustained

   I knew Jackie would do well in the pole-vault event, but her wonderful performance _____*surpassed*_____ even my expectations.

7. **prolong**
   verify
   alienate
   compile

   You have to admire Mayor Moss for not being afraid to _____*alienate*_____ some voters in order to do what he believes is right.

8. **prolong**
   deter
   verify
   assess

   We made the difficult decision to let our mother's life end rather than _____*prolong*_____ her suffering with artificial life-support systems.

9. **adhered**
   derived
   disclosed
   denounced

   We usually don't think about the fact that our books, newspapers, and wooden furniture are all _____*derived*_____ from trees.

10. **altered**
    deterred
    bestowed
    prolonged

    The new drug was pulled off the market when it was learned that researchers had _____*altered*_____ test results to show it was safe.

11. **alter**
    verify
    prolong
    bestow

    Since kids sometimes call in prank orders to pizza parlors, some pizza clerks

    now call back to _____*verify*_____ that each order is sincere.

12. **recipient**
    doctrine
    transition
    supplement

    At Gene's ten-year high school reunion, he was struck by how many of his classmates

    seemed to have already made the _____*transition*_____ to a middle-aged lifestyle.

13. **bestow**
    inhibit
    prolong
    disclose

    I can't imagine how actors play love scenes in front of the camera. Being watched by a

    film crew would certainly _____*inhibit*_____ my romantic feelings.

PART B
Circle **C** if the italicized word is used **correctly**. Circle **I** if the word is used **incorrectly**.

C Ⓘ 14.   The choir director assembled the children in *chronological* order, from shortest to tallest.

Ⓒ I 15.   After being the *recipient* of seven speeding tickets in one month, Marylee lost her license.

C Ⓘ 16.   Owen bragged that when he hit it rich he was going to buy his mom the most *moderate* diamond necklace in town.

C Ⓘ 17.   The twins are not only identical in appearance; they are *contrary* in their tastes and opinions as well.

Ⓒ I 18.   It's easy to find Dwight's house because of the *prominent* display of pink flamingos on the lawn.

C Ⓘ 19.   Goldie will never admit that she's been wrong about anything; she'll *concede* she was right to the bitter end.

Ⓒ I 20.   The soprano was famous for her ability to *sustain* even the highest notes for so long it thrilled her audiences.

Ⓒ I 21.   Once he laid his eyes on the mint-condition Corvette, nothing could *deter* Paolo from his goal of owning the car.

Ⓒ I 22.   Dad got Jen to the house for her surprise party on the *pretense* that Jen had left a jacket there.

C Ⓘ 23.   It's amazing how Davis turns even a bad situation to his own advantage. Somehow, he always ends up being admired as the *scapegoat*.

C Ⓘ 24.   I'm a little angry at our neighbor Henry. I told him to take just a few tomatoes from our garden, not to *bestow* all the ripe ones.

Ⓒ I 25.   Knowing that the thieves would be back again, Luisa *conceived* the plan of leaving a package of gift-wrapped garbage on the seat of her unlocked car.

> *SCORE:* (Number correct) _____ x 4 = _____ %

Enter your scores above and in the vocabulary performance chart on the inside back cover of the book.

UNIT TWO: Test 2

PART A
Complete each sentence with a word from the box. Use each word once.

adhered	compensate	disclosed	remorse
affluent	conservative	diversity	supplement
arrogant	denounce	prudent	tentative
blunt			

1. I can't stand that _____arrogant_____ movie critic; he always speaks as if his reviews come directly from God.

2. Our family isn't _____affluent_____ by American standards, but we're rich compared to people from many other countries.

3. Tom wouldn't take the hint, so Rebecca finally had to be _____blunt_____ and say she just didn't want to go out with him.

4. So many posters _____adhered_____ to the girls' bedroom walls that the color of the paint couldn't be seen.

5. Prisoners of war may be tortured until they are willing to publicly _____denounce_____ their own governments.

6. I hung my dress outside the cleaners when the owner refused to_____compensate_____ me for ruining it by running the colors together.

7. After I'd known Patty for years, she _____disclosed_____ to me that the girl known as her little sister was actually her daughter.

8. After running out of gas on the way to the hospital for an emergency, I decided it was_____prudent_____ to keep the tank full at all times.

9. The Monahans are famous in town for their _____conservative_____ ways. They have gone to the same church, eaten in the same restaurants and read the same newspaper for three generations.

10 The victim of the mugger made a _____tentative_____ identification of her attacker from a photo. But she said she would have to see him in person to be sure.

11. The young mother was still giving her toddler only milk. The doctor explained that it was time for

    her to _____supplement_____ the child's diet with solid food.

12. I like our women's group because of its _____diversity_____. Among the members are grandmothers, young mothers, and young single women as well as black, Hispanic and white women.

13. My brother expressed _____remorse_____ for having stolen my slice of chocolate pie, but I think he was just trying to avoid getting in trouble with Dad.

PART B
Circle **C** if the italicized word is used **correctly**. Circle **I** if the word is used **incorrectly**.

C (I) 14.   When my income was *ample*, I had to watch my expenses very carefully.

(C) I 15.   Mother warned us children to *refrain* from calling Uncle Milton "Mr. Pink Nose" to his face.

(C) I 16.   Working in a jewelry store, Gail learned how to *assess* the value of a diamond.

C (I) 17.   The high school seniors are *donors* of college scholarships, which they received from a generous local business owner.

(C) I 18.   When my sister doubled over with sudden, *acute* pain, we suspected her appendix had become infected.

C (I) 19.   A good *doctrine* for protecting tomato plants is to place a paper collar around them in the ground.

C (I) 20.   The first-grade teacher expressed her *contempt* for the responsible way her students behaved at the circus.

(C) I 21.   The defense attorneys *compiled* a great deal of evidence that showed their client was innocent.

C (I) 22.   Lucy was *apprehensive* about going to an Indian restaurant with Lloyd; she loved spicy Indian food more than anything.

(C) I 23.   Janie is such an *optimist* that I like to be on her volleyball team—she always makes me feel I can win.

C (I) 24.   The Chinese students were surprised by the American teachers' *dogmatic* style, which allowed for free discussion and debate with their students.

C (I) 25.   Professor Wise gained his *superficial* knowledge on the mating and parenting habits of bedbugs through years of research.

> *SCORE:* (Number correct) _____ x 4 = _____ %

Enter your scores above and in the vocabulary performance chart on the inside back cover of the book.

UNIT TWO: Test 3

PART A
Complete each sentence in a way that clearly shows you understand the meaning of the boldfaced word. Take a minute to plan your answer before you write.

    Example: I **altered** my appearance for the party by _____ *putting on a blonde wig.* _____

1. When Peter gained ten pounds, his **blunt** friend Buddy remarked _____ *(Answers will vary.)* _____

    _____

2. People who write letters to advice columns like to be **anonymous** because _____

    _____

3. Harold was filled with **contempt** when he saw the big, strong man _____

    _____

4. Fran decided to **supplement** her income by _____

    _____

5. Mrs. Carson was the most **dogmatic** teacher in school. For example, she used to tell students _____

    _____

    _____

6. If I suddenly discovered I had become **affluent,** the first thing I would do is _____

    _____

7. Pauline is so **arrogant** that when Greg told her she look pretty, she replied_____

    _____

8. While waiting for my turn for a haircut, I felt **apprehensive** because _____

    _____

9. My friend Ted was very **prudent** about his money. For instance, _____

    _____

10. When I served roast goose and a delicious peanut-butter pie for Thanksgiving dinner, my **conservative**

    brother said, " _____

    _____

PART B
After each boldfaced word are a *synonym* (a word that means the same as the boldfaced word), an *antonym* (a word that means the opposite of the boldfaced word), and a word that is neither. Mark the antonym with an *A*.

    Example: **endorse**   ___A___ disapprove   _____ support   _____ compel

11. **absurd**   _____ lively   _____ ridiculous   ___A___ sensible

12. **disclose**   _____ reveal   _____ shut   ___A___ hide

13. **arrogant**   _____ conceited   _____ skillful   ___A___ humble

14. **inhibit**   _____ analyze   ___A___ encourage   _____ prevent

15. **chronic**   _____ temporary   ___A___ continuing   _____ extreme

PART C
Use five of the following ten words in sentences. Make it clear that you know the meaning of the word you use. Feel free to use the past tense or plural form of a word.

adhere	assess	bestow	denounce	derive
diversity	phobia	pretense	remorse	surpass

16. _____ *(Answers will vary.)* _____

_____

17. _____

_____

18. _____

_____

19. _____

_____

20. _____

SCORE: (Number correct) _____ x 5 = _____ %

Enter your scores above and in the vocabulary performance chart on the inside back cover of the book.

UNIT TWO: Test 4 (Word Parts)

PART A

Listed in the left-hand column below are ten common word parts, along with words in which the parts are used. In each blank, write in the letter of the correct definition on the right.

Word Parts

a 1. **anti-**   antiwar, antidepressant

h 2. **bi**   bicycle, biweekly

j 3. **en-, em-**   enroll, embrace

d 4. **-graph, -gram**   autograph, monogram

i 5. **inter-**   interfere, interrupt

b 6. **-less**   hopeless, worthless

f 7. **phon**   phonograph, microphone

g 8. **post-**   postpone, postgraduate

c 9. **spect**   inspect, spectator

e 10. **sub-**   subway, substandard

Definitions

a. against, acting against

b. without

c. look

d. something written

e. under, below

f. sound, speech

g. after

h. two

i. between, among

j. into, in

PART B

Find the word part that correctly completes each word. Then write the full word in the blank space. Not every word part will be used.

anti-	bi-	en-	-graph	inter-
-less	phon	post-	spect	sub

11. "P.S." at the end of a note or letter stands for (. . . *script*) ___*postscript*___ .

12. Our fifth-grade teacher, who tried to teach us good grooming, (*in . . . ed*) ___*inspected*___ our fingernails every Monday morning.

13. In Moscow, taking a (. . . *way*) ___*subway*___ is a pleasant experience. The underground stations have marble floors, stained glass, and statues.

14. The flying squirrel is actually (*wing . . .*) ___*wingless*___ . It "flies" by spreading folds of skin as it glides short distances.

15. Zulu tribesmen are not allowed to (. . . *act*) ___*interact*___ directly with their mothers-in-law but may communicate with them only through another person.

PART C
Use your knowledge of word parts to determine the meaning of the boldfaced words. Circle the letter of each meaning.

16. Drugs **enslave** people.

    a. make against slavery   (b) put into slavery   c. put between slavery

17. My sister is learning **phonics** in her reading class.

    (a.) the study of sounds   b. the study of letters   c. the study of grammar

18. While Dean was in Europe, he sent me **aerograms**.

    a. tape-recorded messages   b. air-mail gifts   (c.) air-mail letters

19. The army experimented with several **antitank** weapons.

    a. with tanks   (b.) against tanks   c. in place of tanks

20. Twenty dollars seems a lot of money for a subscription to a magazine that is published **bimonthly**.

    a. every month   (b.) every two months   c. every three months

---

SCORE: (Number correct) _____ x 5 = _____ %

Enter your scores above and in the vocabulary performance chart on the inside back cover of the book.

Previewing the Words

Find out how many of the ten words in this chapter you already know. Try to complete each sentence with the most suitable word from the list below. Use each word once.

Leave a sentence blank rather than guessing at an answer. Your purpose here is just to get a sense of the ten words and what you may know about them.

accessible	awe	cite	compatible	exempt
prevail	propel	rational	retort	retrieve

1. Will's reason for running away wasn't _____*rational*_____ —it made no sense at all.

2. Ramps make buildings more _____*accessible*_____ to people in wheelchairs.

3. Tammy and her roommate are always quarreling; they certainly aren't _____*compatible*_____.

4. When I go bowling with Joan, she usually wins, but I always _____*prevail*_____ in Scrabble.

5. Before Mitch could _____*retrieve*_____ the papers he had dropped, the wind scattered them all over the street.

6. Darlene stood in line to get the autograph of her rock-star idol, but when her turn arrived she was too filled with _____*awe*_____ to speak.

7. No one with a steady job is _____*exempt*_____ from paying income taxes, although many wish they were.

8. Lisa was sent to the principal's office because of her sarcastic _____*retort*_____ to the teacher's question.

9. In her speech calling for better protection of children, the mayor will _____*cite*_____ examples of child abuse.

10. The wind at my back was so strong that it seemed to _____*propel*_____ me down the sidewalk.

Now check your answers by turning to page 164. Fix any mistakes and fill in any blank spaces by writing in the correct answers. By doing so, you will complete this introduction to the ten words.

You're now ready to strengthen your knowledge of the words you already know and to master the words you're only half sure of, or don't know at all. Turn to the next page.

Ten Words in Context

Figure out the meanings of the following ten words by looking *closely and carefully* at the context in which the words appear. Doing so will prepare you for the matching test and the practices on the two pages that follow.

1 **accessible**
(ak-ses'-ə-bəl)
-adjective

   a. The department store was not **accessible** from her side of the road, so Kristin looked ahead for a U-turn.

   b. We always hung the candy canes on the Christmas tree's highest branches, where they weren't **accessible** to the younger children.

2 **awe**
(ô)
-noun

   a. Sid is in **awe** of his gymnastics coach, whom he considers the greatest man he knows.

   b. Donna and Frank have different types of idols. While Donna admires Barbara Bush, Frank feels great **awe** for Bruce Springsteen.

3 **cite**
(sīt)
-verb

   a. Jeff was embarrassed but pleased when the teacher **cited** his essay as an example of good writing.

   b. Tired of picking up after her sister, Janet **cited** examples of her sloppiness: "stacks of papers, piles of dirty clothes, and unwashed dishes."

4 **compatible**
(kəm-pat'-ə-bəl)
-adjective

   a. My girlfriend and I weren't very **compatible;** whenever she wasn't angry with me, I was angry with her.

   b. Even though the sky and grass look beautiful together, people once thought blue and green were not **compatible** colors.

5 **exempt**
(ig-zempt')
-adjective

   a. Since he had never been spanked, my brother thought he was **exempt** from punishment — until he wrote on the walls in ink.

   b. Students with A averages were **exempt** from final exams, so the top three students went to the shore while the rest of us sweated it out on exam day.

6 **prevail**
(pri-vāl')
-verb

   a. Most Hollywood movies have a happy ending: good **prevails** over evil.

   b. Although Kennedy **prevailed** over Nixon in 1960, eight years later Nixon won the presidency.

7 **propel**
(prə-pel')
-verb

   a. In the sack race, participants stood in sacks and **propelled** themselves forward with big jumps.

   b. When the wind failed to **propel** the boat, we lowered the sails and turned on the motor.

8 **rational**
(rash'-ə-nəl)
-adjective

   a. Mr. Tibbs isn't **rational**; in addition to believing he came from another planet, he does crazy things like shoveling snow in his pajamas.

   b. The belief that breaking a mirror brings seven years of bad luck isn't **rational**. The only bad luck it could really bring is that of stepping on a sharp piece of broken mirror.

9 **retort**
(ri-tort')
-noun

   a. Sue, who is slender, boasted, "Thin is in." So Pat, who is heavy, gave this **retort**: "Well, fat is where it's at."

   b. When Shelley's balding boyfriend made fun of her new perm, her **retort** was "Jealous?"

10 **retrieve**
(ri-trēv')
-verb

   a. My dog Floyd refuses to **retrieve** a thrown Frisbee. Instead of running to bring it back, he only tilts his head and gives me a questioning look.

   b. I can't **retrieve** my sweater from the library until tomorrow, since the library was closed by the time I realized the sweater was missing.

Matching Words and Definitions

Check your understanding of the ten words by matching each word with its definition. Look back at the sentences in "Ten Words in Context" as needed to decide on the meaning of each word.

_e_	1. **accessible**	a.	reasonable; logical
_i_	2. **awe**	b.	to mention in support of a point
_b_	3. **cite**	c.	a sharp or clever reply
_g_	4. **compatible**	d.	to provide the force that moves something
_j_	5. **exempt**	e.	easily reached or entered
_h_	6. **prevail**	f.	to get (something) back
_d_	7. **propel**	g.	able to get along well together; combine well
_a_	8. **rational**	h.	to win out; triumph
_c_	9. **retort**	i.	a great respect with a touch of fear
_f_	10. **retrieve**	j.	free from some unpleasant duty or situation

CAUTION: Do not go any further until you are sure the above answers are correct. If you have studied the "Ten Words in Context," you will know how to match each word. Then you can use the matches to help you in the following practices. Your goal is to reach a point where you don't need to check definitions at all.

➤ Sentence Check 1

Complete each sentence below with the most suitable word from the box. Use each word once.

accessible	awe	cite	compatible	exempt
prevail	propel	rational	retort	retrieve

1. At the beginning of World War II, Hitler expected his military forces to _____*prevail*_____ over all others.

2. Jet engines _____*propel*_____ a plane forward.

3. I ran back to the ladies' room to _____*retrieve*_____ my purse, but someone had already taken it.

4. My brother was _____*exempt*_____ from the draft because his vision is so poor.

5. The general's uniform and medals filled Scott with _____*awe*_____, but Marla felt the general didn't deserve such respect.

6. The cabinet above the refrigerator was _____*accessible*_____ to Janet but not to her roommate Mieko, who was much shorter.

7. My husband thinks everything combines well with peanut butter. He even thinks peanut butter and onions are _____*compatible*_____ in a sandwich.

8. When Bridget writes up her experiment, she will _____*cite*_____ similar studies by other researchers, to show that her results match theirs.

9. Some people don't think in a(n) _____*rational*_____ way. Their thoughts are governed by emotion, not reason.

10. There are at least two versions of the joke in which a customer complains a fly is in his soup. The waiter's _____*retort*_____ is either "That's okay—there's no extra charge" or "Don't worry—he won't drink much."

Now check your answers to these questions by turning to page 164. Going over the answers carefully will help you prepare for the next two checks, for which answers are not given.

➤ *Sentence Check 2*

Complete each sentence below with two words from the following list. Use each word once.

accessible	awe	cite	compatible	exempt
prevail	propel	rational	retort	retrieve

1-2. Tony was in _____*awe*_____ of his athletic friend Ben, who seemed to _____*prevail*_____ in any contest of strength or speed.

3-4. The speaker told his high school audience, "I can _____*cite*_____ dozens of adults who thought they were _____*exempt*_____ from the harm of cocaine and eventually lost their jobs and their families."

5-6. Keith and Sara's matchmaking friends were so sure they'd be _____*compatible*_____ that they tried everything to _____*propel*_____ the two into each other's arms.

7-8. The _____*rational*_____ thing to do is to ask Michael to return your sweater before you sneak into his room to _____*retrieve*_____ it behind his back.

9-10. When I complained to the landlord that the kitchen shelves were so high they were _____*accessible*_____ only by ladder, his _____*retort*_____ was, "So get a ladder!"

➤ *Final Check:* My Headstrong Baby

Here is a final opportunity for you to strengthen your knowledge of the ten words. First read the following passage carefully. Then fill in each blank with a word from the box at the top of this page. (Context clues will help you figure out which word goes in which blank.) Use each word once.

Before my child was born, I truly believed I would be (1)_____*exempt*_____ from many of the restrictions of my friends who were parents. I was sure a baby and a nicely decorated home could be (2)_____*compatible*_____. I thought I could just explain to the baby in a calm, (3)_____*rational*_____ manner that there were certain objects in the house not to be touched. But now I am a mother, and I am in (4)_____*awe*_____ of a tiny infant's amazing abilities. I've learned that when an adult and a baby disagree, the baby will almost always (5)_____*prevail*_____. I've learned, too, that a child who can't even crawl can somehow (6)_____*propel*_____ its little body over to an object that attracts it. It took me a while to admit defeat—I could (7)_____*cite*_____ examples of vases broken and books chewed into pulp—but I finally gave up. I look at my formerly attractive house now and see that every surface (8)_____*accessible*_____ to the baby has been cleared of everything but toys. So now, when my childless friends laugh at me as I (9)_____*retrieve*_____ my belongings from the uppermost shelves of the house, this is my (10)_____*retort*_____: "I'll listen to you when you have a kid of your own."

SCORES: Sentence Check 2 _____ %   Final Check _____ %

Enter your scores above and in the vocabulary performance chart on the inside back cover of the book.

Previewing the Words

Find out how many of the ten words in this chapter you already know. Try to complete each sentence with the most suitable word from the list below. Use each word once.

Leave a sentence blank rather than guessing at an answer. Your purpose here is just to get a sense of the ten words and what you may know about them.

dubious	ecstatic	encounter	evolve	fallacy
fictitious	gullible	liable	miserly	pessimist

1. To avoid embarrassment, some authors of X-rated books use _____*fictitious*_____ names.

2. A _____*pessimist*_____ will greet a sunny day by thinking, "This sun is going to give me skin cancer."

3. Even after a long tutoring session, Adam was _____*dubious*_____ about his chances of passing the geometry exam.

4. If I'm nervous, I'm _____*liable*_____ to laugh. Once I giggled when a girl in my gym class fainted.

5. Our boss is so _____*miserly*_____ that in the winter he has us wear jackets in the stockroom so that he can keep the heat there low.

6. When Sue learned she had been given the lead in the school play, she became _____*ecstatic*_____ and danced down the hall.

7. My aunt was very _____*gullible*_____—she'd believe strangers' hard-luck stories, lend them money, and think they would really pay her back.

8. While camping, Don and Brenda _____*encounter*_____ (e)d a bear. Luckily, the bear was more interested in their food than in them.

9. Some people believed the moon was made of green cheese until astronauts landed there and proved that idea is a _____*fallacy*_____.

10. Working together on dances and service projects helped the class _____*evolve*_____ into a proud and friendly group.

Now check your answers by turning to page 164. Fix any mistakes and fill in any blank spaces by writing in the correct answers. By doing so, you will complete this introduction to the ten words.

You're now ready to strengthen your knowledge of the words you already know and to master the words you're only half sure of, or don't know at all. Turn to the next page.

Ten Words in Context

Figure out the meanings of the following ten words by looking *closely and carefully* at the context in which the words appear. Doing so will prepare you for the matching test and the practices on the two pages that follow.

1 **dubious**
(doo'-bē-əs)
-adjective

a. Her mother looked **dubious**. "I think it would be hard for you to live away from home for a whole summer, Janet."

b. Matt was **dubious** that graduate school would be useful for a career in clothing design. He felt work experience would be better.

2 **ecstatic**
(ik-stat'-ik)
-adjective

a. I wouldn't be just glad if I won the lottery; I'd be **ecstatic**.

b. The smallest thing, like an ice pop on a hot day or a train ride, or a ladybug in the grass, can make a child **ecstatic**.

3 **encounter**
(en-koun'-tər)
-verb

a. Strangely enough, I **encountered** my old boyfriend on my honeymoon.

b. I never expected to **encounter** anyone I knew at the crowded concert, but my friend Jeff sat just two rows in front of me.

4 **evolve**
(i-volv')
-verb

a. The women's club began as an informal group and then **evolved** into an educational and support group.

b. How did the plan for a block party **evolve** into a city-wide celebration?

5 **fallacy**
(fal'-ə-sē)
-noun

a. It is a **fallacy** for people to think that they can drink and drive safely.

b. To opponents of nuclear energy, the idea that nuclear power plants are safe for humans is a **fallacy**.

6 **fictitious**
(fik-tish'-əs)
-adjective

a. Many children have **fictitious** friends—people or animals who exist only in their imaginations.

b. Violence in TV movies may frighten very young children, who have not learned the difference between true and **fictitious** events.

7 **gullible**
(gul'-ə-bəl)
-adjective

a. Candace is so **gullible** that she believed me when I told her the White House is really yellow.

b. You might think I'm **gullible** enough to fall for that old line, but you can't put one over on me that easily.

8 **liable**
(lī'-ə-bəl)
-adjective

a. If you lie to me once, I will think you're **liable** to lie to me again.

b. I'm **liable** to start smoking again if I take even one puff of a cigarette, so I'm careful not to give in even for a moment.

9 **miserly**
(mī'-zər-lē)
-adjective

a. In *A Christmas Carol*, Scrooge at first hated to spend money, but he later regretted his **miserly** ways.

b. My rich uncle was so **miserly** that he never gave money to charity.

10 **pessimist**
(pes'-ə-mist)
-noun

a. A **pessimist** can see a bad side to even the best situation.

b. My family is very balanced: My father sees the best in everything, while my mother is usually a **pessimist**.

Matching Words and Definitions

Check your understanding of the ten words by matching each word with its definition. Look back at the sentences in "Ten Words in Context" as needed to decide on the meaning of each word.

_g_ 1. **dubious**   a. imaginary; made up

_d_ 2. **ecstatic**   b. to change gradually

_c_ 3. **encounter**   c. to meet, especially unexpectedly

_b_ 4. **evolve**   d. in a state of great joy

_i_ 5. **fallacy**   e. likely

_a_ 6. **fictitious**   f. a person who takes the most hopeless view of a situation

_j_ 7. **gullible**   g. doubtful

_e_ 8. **liable**   h. stingy and greedy

_h_ 9. **miserly**   i. a false idea

_f_ 10. **pessimist**   j. easily fooled

CAUTION: Do not go any further until you are sure the above answers are correct. If you have studied the "Ten Words in Context," you will know how to match each word. Then you can use the matches to help you in the following practices. Your goal is to reach a point where you don't need to check definitions at all.

➤ Sentence Check 1

Complete each sentence below with the most suitable word from the box. Use each word once.

dubious	ecstatic	encounter	evolve	fallacy
fictitious	gullible	liable	miserly	pessimist

1. My aunt is so _____*miserly*_____ that all she ever gives us for Christmas is a card.

2. When Lucas is drunk, he's _____*liable*_____ to become violent.

3. The characters in novels are usually totally _____*fictitious*_____, but some are based on real people.

4. I am _____*dubious*_____ about Andrew's ability to do the job alone, but I am willing to give him a try.

5. As I stepped into the garage, I _____*encounter*_____(e)d a surprise visitor — a raccoon.

6. "I'm _____*ecstatic*_____," said Christine on the day of her divorce. "I wasn't even this happy on my wedding day."

7. Don't be such a _____*pessimist*_____. Just because you did poorly on the midterm doesn't mean you won't pass the course.

8. It is a _____*fallacy*_____ that reading without good light ruins your sight. Actually, that does not harm your vision at all.

9. Surprising Allen on his birthday was easy. He's so _____*gullible*_____ that we knew he'd believe whatever story we told him.

10. Interest in the environment has _____*evolve*_____(e)d from a simple love of nature into a troubled awareness that we can destroy our world.

Now check your answers to these questions by turning to page 164. Going over the answers carefully will help you prepare for the next two checks, for which answers are not given.

➤Sentence Check 2

Complete each sentence below with two words from the following list. Use each word once.

dubious	ecstatic	encounter	evolve	fallacy
fictitious	gullible	liable	miserly	pessimist

1-2. When my brother visited California, he _____*encounter*_____(e)d Sally Field in a department store. He got her autograph and has been _____*ecstatic*_____ ever since.

3-4. A _____*miserly*_____ person is _____*liable*_____ to end up with lots of money and few friends.

5-6. Angel is so _____*gullible*_____ that her friends often tell her totally _____*fictitious*_____ stories and then tease her about believing them.

7-8. A _____*pessimist*_____ believes that bad luck can't be escaped and that good luck is a _____*fallacy*_____.

9-10. At first I was _____*dubious*_____ about our school's basketball team winning even one game. But as the season passed, the team _____*evolve*_____(e)d into an excellent group.

➤Final Check: Mr. Perfect?

Here is a final opportunity for you to strengthen your knowledge of the ten words. First read the following passage carefully. Then fill in each blank with a word from the box at the top of this page. (Context clues will help you figure out which word goes in which blank.) Use each word once.

Kathy was (1)_____*ecstatic*_____ as she told me that she had (2)_____*encounter*_____(e)d the "perfect man," as she called him. I was (3)_____*dubious*_____ right from the start. I think "perfection" is a (4)_____*fallacy*_____. Nobody I ever met was perfect—especially guys I've met in bars. I must admit that because of some of my experiences in bars over the years, I am (5)_____*liable*_____ to be more of a (6)_____*pessimist*_____ than most on this subject. One guy was so (7)_____*miserly*_____ that he never left a tip at a restaurant. Another was addicted to sausages. He ate sausages for breakfast, lunch and dinner. Our relationship quickly (8)_____*evolve*_____(e)d from bad to "wurst." Then there were all of those fellows who sort of forgot to mention that they were sort of married until we'd been seeing each other for months. As it turned out, they told me so many (9)_____*fictitious*_____ details that they should have been novelists. So I worry about Kathy, who is so (10)_____*gullible*_____ that she believes anything anyone says. I can't wait to meet Mr. Perfect. He's probably either an ax murderer or a married man. And I'm not sure which is worse.

SCORES:	Sentence Check 2 _____%	Final Check _____%

Enter your scores above and in the vocabulary performance chart on the inside back cover of the book.

Previewing the Words

Find out how many of the ten words in this chapter you already know. Try to complete each sentence with the most suitable word from the list below. Use each word once.

Leave a sentence blank rather than guessing at an answer. Your purpose here is just to get a sense of the ten words and what you may know about them.

elapse	evasive	fluent	futile	harass
infer	lethal	obsession	ordeal	persistent

1. His girl friend became such an ____obsession____ for my son that he could think of little else.

2. While Maria can hardly speak Spanish, her mother is ____fluent____ in it.

3. It is always a great ____ordeal____ for most people to give a speech in front of a crowd of strangers.

4. I realized that running for the bus would be ____futile____ — it was already a block away.

5. Just because a book is long is no reason to ____infer____ it is boring.

6. "If you ____harass____ me any more about going to the movies," said the children's mother, "we won't go for sure."

7. Several hours would ____elapse____ before the emergency-room doctor was able to tell me my father would live.

8. When the police questioned Mr. Shaw, he was ____evasive____, giving no specific details that the police could follow up on.

9. Abby was ____persistent____ in her efforts to change the Little League's boys-only rule. After seven months of trying, she was finally allowed to join the team.

10. The bite of a black widow spider can be ____lethal____, but if treatment is prompt, death can be prevented.

Now check your answers by turning to page 165. Fix any mistakes and fill in any blank spaces by writing in the correct answers. By doing so, you will complete this introduction to the ten words.

You're now ready to strengthen your knowledge of the words you already know and to master the words you're only half sure of, or don't know at all. Turn to the next page.

Ten Words in Context

Figure out the meanings of the following ten words by looking *closely and carefully* at the context in which the words appear. Doing so will prepare you for the matching test and the practices on the two pages that follow.

1 **elapse**
(i-laps')
-*verb*

   a. When I'm busy with work I enjoy, the hours seem to **elapse** quickly.

   b. Although four years had **elapsed** since I last saw Marian, we talked as if we'd never parted.

2 **evasive**
(i-vā'-siv)
-*adjective*

   a. The Roberts worried about their son when he became **evasive** about where he had been and what he'd been doing.

   b. We didn't want anyone at school to know our father was in jail, so we were **evasive** about him, saying only, "He has to be away for a while."

3 **fluent**
(floo'-ənt)
-*adjective*

   a. To work in a foreign country, it helps to be **fluent** in its language.

   b. Jenna wanted to hear what was wrong with her car in simple, everyday words. She was not **fluent** in the language of auto mechanics.

4 **futile**
(fyoot'-l)
-*adjective*

   a. My mother is so stubborn that once she has made a decision, it is **futile** to try to change her mind.

   b. Washing machines eat socks, so it is **futile** to try and find matching pairs in a clean load of laundry.

5 **harass**
(hə-ras')
-*verb*

   a. A few students in the cafeteria like to **harass** everyone else by frequently clinking their silverware and stamping their feet.

   b. Sometimes it doesn't help to **harass** people about quitting smoking. Bothering them all the time may make them stubborn about quitting.

6 **infer**
(in-fûr')
-*verb*

   a. The fact that the old man left his fortune to strangers led us to **infer** he was not fond of his children.

   b. Since you went hiking on Super Bowl Sunday, I **inferred** you were not a football fan.

7 **lethal**
(lē'-thəl)
-*adjective*

   a. My father is not alive today because of the **lethal** combination of driving and drinking.

   b. Jake is so good at karate that his hands are **lethal** weapons. Because he realizes he could kill somebody, he wouldn't use karate lightly.

8 **obsession**
(əb-sesh'-ən)
-*noun*

   a. Psychologists help people troubled by **obsessions** to gain control over their thinking, so they are not bothered by the same thoughts over and over.

   b. Going to the racetrack was at first just a hobby. But the track has become such an **obsession** that I can't seem to stop going there.

9 **ordeal**
(ôr-dēl')
-*noun*

   a. Even if you are in good physical condition, running cross-country is an **ordeal**.

   b. Hannah came out of the difficult three-hour test, sighed, and said, "What an **ordeal**. I'm worn out."

10 **persistent**
(pər-sis'-tənt)
-*adjective*

   a. At first Tony wouldn't go out with Lola, but she was **persistent** in asking him. Now they're engaged.

   b. I am a very **persistent** salesman. I work with customers for as long as it takes for them to buy something.

Matching Words and Definitions

Check your understanding of the ten words by matching each word with its definition. Look back at the sentences in "Ten Words in Context" as needed to decide on the meaning of each word.

<u>_h_</u> 1. **elapse**   a. to draw a conclusion from evidence

<u>_d_</u> 2. **evasive**   b. an idea or feeling which someone is overly concerned about

<u>_i_</u> 3. **fluent**   c. a very difficult or painful experience

<u>_e_</u> 4. **futile**   d. deliberately unclear

<u>_j_</u> 5. **harass**   e. useless; lacking an effective result

<u>_a_</u> 6. **infer**   f. able to cause death; deadly

<u>_f_</u> 7. **lethal**   g. refusing to quit; stubbornly continuing

<u>_b_</u> 8. **obsession**   h. to pass or slip by (usually said of time)

<u>_c_</u> 9. **ordeal**   i. able to speak a language with skill and ease

<u>_g_</u> 10. **persistent**   j. to constantly irritate or disturb; bother

CAUTION: Do not go any further until you are sure the above answers are correct. If you have studied the "Ten Words in Context," you will know how to match each word. Then you can use the matches to help you in the following practices. Your goal is to reach a point where you don't need to check definitions at all.

➤ Sentence Check 1

Complete each sentence below with the most suitable word from the box. Use each word once.

elapse	evasive	fluent	futile	harass
infer	lethal	obsession	ordeal	persistent

1. Roger knew a few Chinese phrases, but he was not _____*fluent*_____ enough in Chinese to carry on a conversation.

2. Photographers _____*harass*_____(e)d the movie star, photographing her even on a private beach.

3. When I'm on a diet, eating pizza becomes an _____*obsession*_____ for me.

4. Reporters tried to pin the President down on his plans to rescue the hostages, but he always gave a(n) _____*evasive*_____ answer.

5. After ten seconds _____*elapse*_____, a bell rings, and the game-show host reads the next question.

6. Selling drugs can be a _____*lethal*_____ occupation—there is almost one drug-related murder a day in Philadelphia alone.

7. Going to the veterinarian is a real _____*ordeal*_____ for our dog, who begins to shiver in fear at the sight of the vet's office.

8. It is _____*futile*_____ to try to have a conversation with Manny when a football game is on television— his eyes are glued to the set.

9. Carlos had to work full-time to support his family, but he still earned his college degree by being _____*persistent*_____ in his studies even when he was busy or tired.

10. It was easy for Professor Anderson to _____*infer*_____ that one of the girls had copied the other's paper — both had the same wording in several paragraphs.

   Now check your answers to these questions by turning to page 165. Going over the answers carefully will help you prepare for the next two checks, for which answers are not given.

➤ Sentence Check 2

Complete each sentence below with two words from the following list. Use each word once.

elapse	evasive	fluent	futile	harass
infer	lethal	obsession	ordeal	persistent

1-2. Wild mushrooms were an _____obsession_____ of my aunt, who picked and ate them whenever possible. Unfortunately, her abnormal interest proved _____lethal_____, for she died after a meal of poisonous creamed mushrooms on toast.

3-4. "From your _____evasive_____ answer," said the teacher, "I _____infer_____ you haven't studied the chapter."

5-6. Five days _____elapse_____(e)d before the forest fire was put out. It was an especially difficult _____ordeal_____ for the firefighters, who had to get by on very little sleep.

7-8. You must be _____persistent_____ in learning a language if you wish to become _____fluent_____ in it.

9-10. Cats on my street have learned they can safely _____harass_____ the dog chained in my neighbor's yard. The poor dog, however, hasn't seemed to learn that it is _____futile_____ to threaten the cats.

➤ Final Check: A Narrow Escape

Here is a final opportunity for you to strengthen your knowledge of the ten words. First read the following passage carefully. Then fill in each blank with a word from the box at the top of this page. (Context clues will help you figure out which word goes in which blank.) Use each word once.

"They're going to kill us or rape us. They're going to kill us or rape us." The thought had become an (1)_____obsession_____—I could think of nothing else. When Sharon and I hopped into the truck to hitch a ride toward Frankfurt, Germany, we were delighted these two Italian truck drivers were so friendly. Neither of us was (2)_____fluent_____ in Italian, but we knew a few Italian words, and they knew a little English. So we could (3)_____infer_____ from their words and motions that they would take us to Frankfurt after they delivered a package. But then they drove around for a long time and couldn't seem to make their delivery. Hours (4)_____elapse_____(e)d, and I became annoyed. But it still didn't occur to me to be afraid. We asked to be let out so we could get another ride. The men apologized for the delay and were (5)_____persistent_____ in repeating their promise to get us to Frankfurt. But they became more and more (6)_____evasive_____ about exactly when this ride would occur. We finally decided to stay wherever we were for the night, so we asked to be dropped off. Instead, they drove to an empty warehouse outside of town. The driver took out a long knife and said, "You sleep here." I cried, "Oh, no, thank you, we'll get out NOW!" and jumped for the door handle. But my effort was (7)_____futile_____—the men blocked our exit. They began to (8)_____harass_____ us about staying with them. That's when I knew they would kill or rape us. The knife was a (9)_____lethal_____ weapon, but even without it they could easily kill us. I just sat there shaking and Sharon sobbed and moaned and cried. Suddenly, one of the men threw up his hands and yelled, "OUT." He didn't have to ask twice. We flew out of that truck and back to town. We could hardly believe our (10)_____ordeal_____ was over and that we were around to tell the tale.

SCORES: Sentence Check 2 _____ %   Final Check _____ %

Enter your scores above and in the vocabulary performance chart on the inside back cover of the book.

Previewing the Words

Find out how many of the ten words in this chapter you already know. Try to complete each sentence with the most suitable word from the list below. Use each word once.

Leave a sentence blank rather than guessing at an answer. Your purpose here is just to get a sense of the ten words and what you may know about them.

convey	delusion	devise	savor	stimulate
subtle	unique	universal	versatile	vivid

1. "It's a ____*delusion*____ that she loves you," Lawrence warned. "She doesn't even care."

2. The actress was so ____*versatile*____ that she could play any kind of role, from a young villain to an elderly saint.

3. My aunt's remarks are often far from ____*subtle*____. Instead of giving a gentle hint, she will blurt out, "Don't be such a fool!"

4. I ____*savor*____ the smell of coffee almost more than I enjoy its taste.

5. Some of my dreams are in dull shades of grey. Others are in ____*vivid*____ colors.

6. When Edward saw the Grand Canyon, he made no attempt to describe it on a postcard. He felt the grandness of this natural wonder was too amazing to ____*convey*____ in words.

7. Even if Mr. Pierce sang his lecture while dancing on his desk, he couldn't ____*stimulate*____ my interest in geology—to me, the most boring of subjects.

8. Although countries differ in many of their customs, strict rules against murder seem to be nearly ____*universal*____.

9. The clever biology student was able to ____*devise*____ a number of experiments to test the effects of different amounts of light on plant growth.

10. This Egyptian bracelet is ____*unique*____—no other bracelet in the world is made with the same combination of gems and precious metals.

Now check your answers by turning to page 165. Fix any mistakes and fill in any blank spaces by writing in the correct answers. By doing so, you will complete this introduction to the ten words.

You're now ready to strengthen your knowledge of the words you already know and to master the words you're only half sure of, or don't know at all. Turn to the next page.

Ten Words in Context

Figure out the meanings of the following ten words by looking *closely and carefully* at the context in which the words appear. Doing so will prepare you for the matching test and the practices on the two pages that follow.

1 **convey**
(kən-vā')
-verb

   a. Using sign language, chimpanzees can **convey** such ideas as "Candy sweet" and "Gimme hug."

   b. On my parents' twenty-fifth wedding anniversary, I sent a telegram to **convey** my congratulations and love.

2 **delusion**
(di-lōō'-zhən)
-noun

   a. When drunk, Alec experienced the **delusion** of being in total control. Actually, he lacked both judgment and muscle control.

   b. The man suffered from the **delusion** that he had met aliens and traveled with them in their spaceship.

3 **devise**
(di-vīz')
-verb

   a. In the 1880's an American woman **devised** a machine that sprayed dinnerware with hot, soapy water—the first automatic dishwasher.

   b. The police had **devised** a plan to catch the thief, but he escaped through the freight elevator.

4 **savor**
(sā'-vər)
-verb

   a. Katie **savored** the candy bar, eating it bit by bit so that the pleasure would last as long as possible.

   b. Given a rare chance to enjoy the beach, I **savored** every moment under the warm sun.

5 **stimulate**
(stim'-yə-lāt')
-verb

   a. The teacher hoped to **stimulate** her students' interest in reading by choosing books that related to their own lives.

   b. When my father grew tomatoes as big as grapefruits, other neighborhood gardeners wanted to know which fertilizer **stimulated** such amazing growth.

6 **subtle**
(sut'-l)
-adjective

   a. Animal actors are trained to respond to human signals too **subtle** to be noticed by the audience.

   b. Although Virginia was born in Alabama, she has lived up North for many years. As a result, her Southern accent is so **subtle** that some of her friends don't even notice it.

7 **unique**
(yōō-nēk')
-adjective

   a. Any musical performance is **unique**—the music will never again be played in exactly the same way.

   b. My talents are **unique** in my family. For example, I'm the only one who can whistle through my nose.

8 **universal**
(yōō'-nə-vûr'-səl)
-adjective

   a. The United Nations was founded to advance **universal** freedom and peace.

   b. The film had **universal** success—it was a hit in all parts of the United States and in other countries as well.

9 **versatile**
(vûr'-sə-təl)
-adjective

   a. My new computer is **versatile**. It can balance my checkbook, do word processing, keep tax records, and play against me in chess.

   b. Edie is the most **versatile** person I know: she paints, sings, does gymnastics, and is a math whiz.

10 **vivid**
(viv'-id)
-adjective

   a. To make the living room bright and dramatic, we decorated it in **vivid** red.

   b. At funerals, most people wear black or dark grey clothing with no touch of **vivid** color.

Matching Words and Definitions

Check your understanding of the ten words by matching each word with its definition. Look back at the sentences in "Ten Words in Context" as needed to decide on the meaning of each word.

_e_	1. **convey**	a.	unlike any other
_i_	2. **delusion**	b.	to invent; think up; create
_b_	3. **devise**	c.	bright in color; striking
_h_	4. **savor**	d.	hardly noticeable; not obvious
_f_	5. **stimulate**	e.	to communicate; make known
_d_	6. **subtle**	f.	to cause to become active or grow; arouse
_a_	7. **unique**	g.	including everyone; covering all members of a group
_g_	8. **universal**	h.	to taste or smell with pleasure; enjoy with appreciation
_j_	9. **versatile**	i.	a false belief that clearly contradicts the evidence
_c_	10. **vivid**	j.	able to do many things well

CAUTION: Do not go any further until you are sure the above answers are correct. If you have studied the "Ten Words in Context," you will know how to match each word. Then you can use the matches to help you in the following practices. Your goal is to reach a point where you don't need to check definitions at all.

➤ Sentence Check 1

Complete each sentence below with the most suitable word from the box. Use each word once.

convey	delusion	devise	savor	stimulate
subtle	**unique**	**universal**	**versatile**	**vivid**

1. The chimp _____devise_____(e)d a way of reaching the banana that hung from the ceiling. She piled one box on top of another and climbed up.

2. The "terrible twos" is a _____universal_____ stage among babies. In every culture, they start demar.ding independence around the age of two..

3. Breathing deeply, I _____savor_____(e)d my favorite summer smell—freshly-cut grass.

4. Pam's eyes blinked a _____subtle_____ message that only her husband saw: "I think we should get ready to leave before it gets any later."

5. The painting—with its bright stripes of shocking pink, green, and yellow—was so _____vivid_____that it glowed even in dim light.

6. I tried to _____stimulate_____ my rabbit's appetite by offering him choice bits of carrots and celery.

7. Dina's body is so expressive that when she dances she seems able to _____convey_____ almost any mood with a single movement.

8. My uncle's wartime experience in the jungles of Vietnam left him with a _____delusion_____that people are trying to kill him.

9. The homemade quilt was prized by its owners for its seemingly _____unique_____ pattern, unlike any other they had ever seen.

10. From a child's point of view, a simple brown box is very _____versatile_____—it can be a dollhouse, a bucket, a desk, or even a funny hat.

Now check your answers to these questions by turning to page 165. Going over the answers carefully will help you prepare for the next two checks, for which answers are not given.

➤ Sentence Check 2

Complete each sentence below with two words from the following list. Use each word once.

convey	delusion	devise	savor	stimulate
subtle	unique	universal	versatile	vivid

1-2. When Jill applies for a job, it will be to her advantage to _____*convey*_____ to interviewers just how _____*versatile*_____ she is. Employers will welcome her many different skills.

3-4. I _____*savor*_____ the time I have alone with my brother, who is unlike anyone else. He has a _____*unique*_____ way of looking at things.

5-6. I wish someone would _____*devise*_____ a way to _____*stimulate*_____ my children's appetites so they will feel hungry for something besides pizza and peanut butter.

7-8. Rosa enjoys wearing _____*vivid*_____ colors, like red and purple, while I prefer more _____*subtle*_____ shades, such as pink and baby blue.

9-10. The crazed man thought it was a _____*universal*_____ belief that he was king of the world, but, of course, he was the only one to have this _____*delusion*_____.

➤ Final Check: The Power of Advertising

Here is a final opportunity for you to strengthen your knowledge of the ten words. First read the following passage carefully. Then fill in each blank with a word from the box at the top of this page. (Context clues will help you figure out which word goes in which blank.) Use each word once.

I am convinced that good advertising agencies could sell people last week's garbage. They make everything sound good. For example, newspaper ads never sell "brightly colored towels." Instead they sell "petal-soft bath sheets in a variety of (1)_____*vivid*_____ rainbow colors." Perfumes in ads don't make you "smell good"; they "invite you to please that special man in your life with this (2)_____*subtle*_____ yet unmistakable odor of tea roses." Food ads (3)_____*stimulate*_____ your appetite by offering "a sauce carefully blended to produce an unforgettable taste that you and your guests will (4)_____*savor*_____." Clothing ads (5)_____*convey*_____ the idea that if you wear a particular suit or dress, you will be classier than the next person. Other ads, such as those for computers, tell you how (6)_____*versatile*_____ their products will make you, suggesting that they will give you more skills than others have. Advertisements must have (7)_____*universal*_____ appeal to attract millions of people. Yet they must also convince all those people to accept the (8)_____*delusion*_____ that they will be (9)_____*unique*_____ if they buy a particular product. I bet if an advertising agency wanted to sell last week's garbage, it would simply (10)_____*devise*_____ an ad saying, "Nowhere else can you find a gift with so powerful an aroma that it overflows with bittersweet memories of yesterday, yet hints that it will grow stronger with each passing day."

SCORES: Sentence Check 2 _____% Final Check _____%

Enter your scores above and in the vocabulary performance chart on the inside back cover of the book.

Previewing the Words

Find out how many of the ten words in this chapter you already know. Try to complete each sentence with the most suitable word from the list below. Use each word once.

Leave a sentence blank rather than guessing at an answer. Your purpose here is just to get a sense of the ten words and what you may know about them.

defer	endeavor	equate	impose	indignant
inevitable	malicious	option	passive	patron

1. Don't _____ *equate* _____ years of schooling with intelligence; they aren't the same thing.

2. While Doreen is sometimes cruel on purpose, her twin sister is never _____ *malicious* _____.

3. My roommate failed half of his courses because he didn't even _____ *endeavor* _____ to learn the material.

4. "Hank is our best _____ *patron* _____," said the owner of the donut shop, pointing to a heavy customer eating from a plateful of donuts.

5. Graduating students have the _____ *option* _____ of either attending graduation or receiving their degrees in the mail.

6. Guy would not _____ *defer* _____ to his mother's request to have his long hair cut, but when his girlfriend asked, he headed straight to the barber.

7. My sister and brother-in-law had dated for so long it seemed _____ *inevitable* _____ they would get married.

8. Eddie allowed me to _____ *impose* _____ on him by agreeing to type up my ten-page research paper.

9. When his wife accused him of never helping around the house, Mac was _____ *indignant* _____. Hadn't he just built a deck off the kitchen?

10. I enjoy listening to the stereo, but I'm not just a _____ *passive* _____ music lover. I also like to sing and play piano.

Now check your answers by turning to page 165. Fix any mistakes and fill in any blank spaces by writing in the correct answers. By doing so, you will complete this introduction to the ten words.

You're now ready to strengthen your knowledge of the words you already know and to master the words you're only half sure of, or don't know at all. Turn to the next page.

Ten Words in Context

Figure out the meanings of the following ten words by looking *closely and carefully* at the context in which the words appear. Doing so will prepare you for the matching test and the practices on the two pages that follow.

1 **defer**
(di-fer')
-verb

   a. The children showed great respect for their grandmother and **deferred** to her every wish.

   b. When it comes to fixing cars, I **defer** to my son's judgment. He knows much more about auto mechanics than I do.

2 **endeavor**
(en-dev'-ər)
-verb

   a. Becky **endeavored** to raise money for Christmas presents by selling candy and cookies door to door.

   b. You are not likely to achieve a goal you will not even **endeavor** to reach.

3 **equate**
(i-kwāt')
-verb

   a. It would be a mistake to **equate** the two teams just because they both have perfect records. One team has played much stronger opponents.

   b. Don't **equate** all homework with busywork. Homework can increase one's understanding of a subject.

4 **impose**
(im-pōz')
-verb

   a. I'd rather rent a car for the trip than **impose** on my girlfriend by borrowing her car.

   b. Roy is always asking favors, yet no one ever seems to notice how much he **imposes** on them.

5 **indignant**
(in-dig'-nənt)
-adjective

   a. My mother becomes **indignant** when she sees parents treat their children with disrespect.

   b. When she was falsely accused of stealing the gold chain, the student became very **indignant.**

6 **inevitable**
(in-ev'-i-tə-bəl)
-adjective

   a. I am such a chocoholic that if you put a brownie in front of me, it is **inevitable** I will eat it.

   b. We try so many ways of looking and staying young, but aging is **inevitable.**

7 **malicious**
(ma-lish'-əs)
-adjective

   a. Bullies are **malicious**—they take pleasure in hurting others.

   b. Rachel loves **malicious** gossip. The more spiteful it is, the more she likes it, and the more she is likely to repeat it.

8 **option**
(op'-shən)
-noun

   a. When the mugger said to me, "Give me your wallet or I'll kill you," I didn't like either **option.**

   b. Harry thinks a multiple-choice test allows him to choose more than one **option.**

9 **passive**
(pas'-iv)
-adjective

   a. Taylor is very **passive.** He waits for things to happen instead of making them happen.

   b. Students learn more when they take part in class discussions, instead of being **passive** listeners.

10 **patron**
(pā'-trən)
-noun

   a. The punk-rock star was one of the beauty shop's best **patrons.** She came in at least once a week to change her hair color.

   b. Many of the diner's **patrons** were stagehands who worked at the theater across the street.

Matching Words and Definitions

Check your understanding of the ten words by matching each word with its definition. Look back at the sentences in "Ten Words in Context" as needed to decide on the meaning of each word.

_j_	1. **defer**	a.	a choice
_f_	2. **endeavor**	b.	to take advantage of
_e_	3. **equate**	c.	not active but acted upon
_b_	4. **impose**	d.	sure to happen; unavoidable
_g_	5. **indignant**	e.	to consider as equal, the same, or closely related
_d_	6. **inevitable**	f.	to try; attempt
_i_	7. **malicious**	g.	angry over some insult or injustice
_a_	8. **option**	h.	a steady customer
_c_	9. **passive**	i.	spiteful; harmful on purpose
_h_	10. **patron**	j.	to give in to someone else's wishes or judgment; yield out of respect

CAUTION: Do not go any further until you are sure the above answers are correct. If you have studied the "Ten Words in Context," you will know how to match each word. Then you can use the matches to help you in the following practices. Your goal is to reach a point where you don't need to check definitions at all.

➤ Sentence Check 1

Complete each sentence below with the most suitable word from the box. Use each word once.

defer	endeavor	equate	impose	indignant
inevitable	malicious	option	passive	patron

1. When rats are crowded, it's _____*inevitable*_____ they will fight with each other.

2. I have only two _____*option*_____s on my job: I can do what my boss asks, or I can be fired.

3. In our society, we too often _____*equate*_____ happiness with money.

4. Mort isn't a _____*passive*_____ football fan. He actively participates by jumping out of his seat and yelling until he's hoarse.

5. I was the store's most loyal _____*patron*_____ until new management raised the prices, and then I started shopping elsewhere.

6. Heidi is so _____*malicious*_____ that she makes up lies to ruin other people's reputations.

7. "I don't want to _____*impose*_____ on you," Scott said, "but if you're going to the post office, would you get me some stamps?"

8. Thomas was understandably _____*indignant*_____ when they fired him without a good reason.

9. Our boss doesn't expect us to _____*defer*_____ to his opinions just because he's the boss; he wants us to think for ourselves.

10. Mindy _____*endeavor*_____(e)d to stop her hiccups by putting a paper bag over her head.

Now check your answers to these questions by turning to page 165. Going over the answers carefully will help you prepare for the next two checks, for which answers are not given.

➤ Sentence Check 2

Complete each sentence below with two words from the following list. Use each word once.

defer	endeavor	equate	impose	indignant
inevitable	malicious	option	passive	patron

1-2.   _Indignant_   that the boys had thrown rocks at the monkeys and yelled at them, the zookeeper said,

"Don't _____equate_____ being an animal with having no feelings."

3-4. Rita, a _____patron_____ of Angelo's restaurant for several years, has _____endeavor_____(e)d without
success to copy Angelo's delicious spaghetti sauce.

5-6. "If you remain so _____passive_____ that you don't object when Jean takes advantage of you, she'll just
_____impose_____ on you more and more," my friend warned.

7-8. Since Sam's family is so poor, it seems _____inevitable____ he'll work full-time as soon as he finishes high
school. He won't have the _____option_____ of going to college.

9-10. Why do so many citizens _____defer_____ to the judgment of even the most _____malicious_____ leaders,
such as Stalin and Hitler?

➤ Final Check: Waiter

Here is a final opportunity for you to strengthen your knowledge of the ten words. First read the following passage carefully. Then fill in each blank with a word from the box at the top of this page. (Context clues will help you figure out which word goes in which blank.) Use each word once.

The loud voice of the young man at the next table startled me. He was (1)_indignant_____ about an
undeserved scolding the waiter had received. "Why did you just stand there and take all that abuse from
that old lady? You were like a(n) (2)____passive_____ little child."

"I beg your pardon, Sir," the waiter answered. "That woman is a(n) (3)_____patron_____ of this
restaurant. I (4)____endeavor_____ to treat our customers with respect."

"Even those who (5)____impose_____ on you by being so demanding? Even those who think they're
better than you because you're waiting on them?"

"You seem to (6)____equate_____ my polite manner with weakness," the waiter answered. "I don't
like rude customers, but they're part of the territory of a waiter. Standing up publicly to the woman may
seem like a smart move to you, but it would have made two things (7)____inevitable____: an ugly scene
and the loss of my job."

"But you have no (8)____option____," the customer insisted. "You can't let people step on you,
ever—especially when they're being (9)___malicious___, giving you a hard time for no good reason."

"You're giving me just as hard a time as that woman did," the waiter finally stated. "Why should I
(10) _____defer_____ to your opinion and not hers?"

SCORES:	Sentence Check 2 _____%	Final Check _____%

Enter your scores above and in the vocabulary performance chart on the inside back cover of the book.

Previewing the Words

Common word parts—also known as *prefixes, suffixes, and roots*—are used in forming many words in English. This page will introduce you to ten common word parts.

Try to match each word part on the left with its definition on the right. Use the words in parentheses as hints to help you guess the meanings. If you can't decide on an answer, leave the space blank. Your purpose here is just to get a sense of the ten word parts and what you may know about them. (You'll have another chance to try this exercise after considering the word parts in context.)

Word Parts	Definitions
_c_ 1. **con-** (conference, conform)	a. quality; ability, skill
_e_ 2. **dict** (dictate, diction)	b. three
_g_ 3. **dis-** (disorganized, displease)	c. with, together
_i_ 4. **micro-** (microscope, microwave)	d. far
_j_ 5. **ped** (pedal, pedestrian)	e. speak
_h_ 6. **script, scrib** (transcript, inscribe)	f. across, beyond, over
_a_ 7. **-ship** (friendship, penmanship)	g. do the opposite of; take away
_d_ 8. **tele-** (telescope, telegram)	h. write
_f_ 9. **trans-** (transmit, transfer)	i. small
_b_ 10. **tri-** (triple, triangle)	j. foot

Now go on to "Ten Word Parts in Context" on the next page. Working through this chapter will help you to strengthen your knowledge of the word parts you already know and to master the word parts you're only half sure of, or don't know at all.

Keep in mind that learning word parts can pay several dividends. Word parts can help with the spelling and pronunciation of many words. They can also help you to unlock the meanings of unfamiliar words.

Ten Word Parts in Context

Figure out the meanings of the following ten word parts by looking *closely and carefully* at the context in which the words appear. Doing so will prepare you for the matching test and the practices on the two pages that follow.

1 con-
    a. Members of the **congregation** screamed when the minister fell down in the middle of his sermon.
    b. "You know," Mr. Warner told his band, "the trombones are supposed to play WITH the **conductor,** not against him."

2 dict
    a. "The job of a **dictator** is to speak," said a Nazi officer. "He does not have to listen."
    b. "Why don't you see what the **dictionary** says about that word?"

3 dis-
    a. The icy mountain path would **discourage** all but the most daring hiker.
    b. Before they **disappeared** from the Earth, dinosaurs were around for 140 million years.

4 micro-
    a. In World War II, spies took **microphotographs** and made them even smaller, to the size of a printed period.
    b. **Microbiology** is the study of tiny life forms.

5 ped
    a. Humans and apes aren't the only **bipeds.** Birds also walk on two feet.
    b. I like to give myself a **pedicure** in the summer so my toes look neat and polished in open-toed shoes.

6 script, scrib
    a. The author of the play didn't like it when actors spoke words that were not in his **script.**
    b. In my grandfather's room I found an old locket **inscribed** with the words, "The two of us, always."

7 -ship
    a. Does good **citizenship** require following all the rules all the time?
    b. It took skilled **craftsmanship** to make that beautiful oak wall unit.

8 tele-
    a. Through the **telephoto** lens, the distant eagle came clearly into view.
    b. Before the **telephone** was invented, people could not speak to far-away loved ones.

9 trans-
    a. I had to **transfer** a large package from my right hand to my left in order to reach for my keys and open the door.
    b. It's hard to **translate** Zulu sounds into written English because Zulu uses clicks, ticks, and pops.

10 tri-
    a. Stan bought three rattles, three little blankets, and three knitted caps. He's the proud grandfather of **triplets.**
    b. Carol, Tod, and I have formed a guitar **trio.** Now we just need to get three guitars.

Matching Word Parts and Definitions

Check your understanding of the ten word parts by matching each with its definition. See also the suggestions on page 4.

_c_	1. **con-**	a.	quality; ability, skill
_e_	2. **dict**	b.	three
_g_	3. **dis-**	c.	with, together
_i_	4. **micro-**	d.	far
_j_	5. **ped**	e.	speak
_h_	6. **script, scrib**	f.	across, beyond, over
_a_	7. **-ship**	g.	do the opposite of; take away
_d_	8. **tele-**	h.	write
_f_	9. **trans-**	i.	small
_b_	10. **tri-**	j.	foot

CAUTION: Do not go any further until you are sure the above answers are correct. If you have studied the "Ten Word Parts in Context," you will know how to match each word part. Then you can use the matches to help you in the following practices. Your goal is to reach a point where you don't need to check definitions at all.

➤ Sentence Check 1

Complete each partial word in the following sentences with a word part from the box. Use each word part only once. You may want to check off each word part as you use it.

con-	dict-	dis-	micro-	ped
script, scrib	-ship	tele-	trans-	tri-

1. The company president wrote letters to his mother by (. . . *ating*) ____*dictating*____ them to his secretary.

2. Only one foot is required to operate the piano (. . . *als*) ____*pedals*____ .

3. To hold her camera still, the photographer put it on a (. . .*pod*) ____*tripod*____ , a three-legged support.

4. The organ (. . . *plant*) ____*transplant*____ involved replacing the child's damaged liver with liver tissue from his father.

5. My fifth-grade teacher cared more about how students wrote than what we wrote. She often said, "Good (*penman.* . .) _*penmanship*_ is a mark of education."

6. "Yes, teenagers don't like to be different. They want to (. . .*form*) ____*conform*____," said Mr. Gilbert, "but with their friends, who look like Martians, not with their parents."

7. On April 22, 1775, a British general ordered his troops to (. . . *arm*) ____*disarm*____ all the citizens of Boston.

8. You can study tiny things with a telescope by turning it into a (. . . *scope*) ____*microscope*____—simply look through the other end.

9. My grandfather is not very religious, but he reads the (. . . *ures*) ____*Scriptures*____ every morning.

10. Because the presentation of Academy Awards is (. . . *vised*) ____*televised*____ live, even people thousands of miles away can see it as it happens.

Now check your answers to these questions by turning to page 165. Going over the answers carefully will help you prepare for the next two checks, for which answers are not given.

➤ Sentence Check 2

Complete each word in the sentences below with a word part from the following list. Use each word part once.

con-	dict-	dis-	micro-	ped
script, scrib	-ship	tele-	trans-	tri-

1-2. We (. . . *approve*) ___*disapprove*___ of our children watching more than a couple of hours of (. . . *vision*) ___*television*___ each day.

3-4. (. . . *portation*) ___*Transportation*___ by subway is spoiled by all the graffiti (. . .*bled*) ___*scribbled*___ in the stations and on the trains.

5-6. No matter how hard my little nephew (. . .*als*) ___*pedals*___ his (. . . *cycle*) ___*tricycle*___, he can't keep up with his brother on a two-wheeler.

7-8. The word (*male. . .ion*) "___*malediction*___" means "curse." It (. . .*nects*) ___*connects*___ the two word parts meaning "badly" and "speak."

9-10. "The secret to (*scholar. . .*) ___*scholarship*___ in biology," Professor Kant told Don, "is to spend your time staring at cells through a (. . . *scope*) ___*microscope*___, not staring at all the females in the class!"

➤ Final Check: Black Widow Spiders

Here is a final opportunity for you to strengthen your knowledge of the ten word parts. First read the following passage carefully. Then complete each partial word in the parentheses below with a word from the box at the top of this page. (Context clues will help you figure out which word part goes in which blank.) Use each word part once.

If you stopped the average (. . .*estrian*) (1)___*pedestrian*___ walking down the street and asked, "What creature do you fear most?" you might get this answer: "The black widow spider." No matter that bees kill 120 times as many Americans as black widows do. People can tolerate bees, but they can't (. . . *cend*) (2)___*transcend*___ their fear of black widows. Perhaps that fear is fed by the knowledge of how the spiders got their name: the female, an hourglass-shaped red mark on her belly, sometimes eats the male.

My nephew in California has repeatedly told me over the (. . . *phone*) (3)___*telephone*___ of his war with black widows. And nearly every letter he sends (. . . *tains*) (4)___*contains*___ the (*post . . .*) (5)___*postscript*___ "P.S. House still has black widows." When he finds the black spider with the double red (. . . *angles*) (6)___*triangles*___ on her belly, the (*ver. . .*) (7)___*verdict*___ is always "Guilty." With a can of insect spray, he blasts the almost (. . . *scopic*) (8)___*microscopic*___ little lady in her web. And when he has finished (. . . *honoring*) (9)___*dishonoring*___ the spider in this way, he throws away any chance of gaining her (*friend. . .*) (10)___*friendship*___ by pounding her to death with a rolled-up magazine.

"Fine," I told him. "Fine. But how would you feel if spiders gave us honey?"

SCORES: Sentence Check 2 _____ % Final Check _____ %

Enter your scores above and in the vocabulary performance chart on the inside back cover of the book.

UNIT THREE: Test 1

PART A
Choose the word that best completes each sentence and write it in the space provided.

1. **propelled**
   devised
   inferred
   imposed

   The air escaping from the balloon ____*propelled*____ it across the table and into the punchbowl.

2. **savor**
   retrieve
   infer
   stimulate

   I used a fishing pole to ____*retrieve*____ my hat from the duck pond.

3. **ecstatic**
   passive
   unique
   futile

   When the usually peppy dog became ____*passive*____ and wouldn't play, Mickey knew he must be ill.

4. **subtle**
   indignant
   accessible
   vivid

   Lisa, who is unusually short, had her kitchen built with cabinets low enough to be ____*accessible*____ to her.

5. **versatile**
   fluent
   subtle
   lethal

   Separately, the seasonings I put in my pizza sauce are ____*subtle*____.
   Combined, however, they have a strong flavor.

6. **ordeal**
   pessimist
   retort
   patron

   Rita turned her ____*ordeal*____ of being lost in the desert into good fortune by selling the story to a movie studio.

7. **evolve**
   prevail
   devise
   elapse

   After denting the fender of my parents' car, I let several months____*elapse*____ before I asked to borrow the car again.

8. **harass**
   savor
   cite
   convey

   Using only motions, Tina managed to ____*convey*____ the message to Jerry that she would meet him at the Student Center at two o'clock.

9. **dubious**
   persistent
   malicious
   fluent

   I didn't tell my brother about the surprise party because I'm ____*dubious*____ about his ability to keep a secret.

10. **evasive**
    fictitious
    compatible
    inevitable

    Hal was foolish to believe he could go steady with two women at once. It was____*inevitable*____ they would find out about each other.

11. **vivid**
    versatile
    futile
    universal

    The Broadway dancer dyed her hair a _____*vivid*_____ red so she would stand out among all the blondes and brunettes in the chorus line.

12. **exempt**
    miserly
    liable
    rational

    My uncle is so _____*miserly*_____ that he refuses to give money to charity, claiming charity begins and ends at home.

13. **gullible**
    unique
    dubious
    lethal

    Marjorie wanted her prom dress to be _____*unique*_____, and it was—no one else wore a yellow-and-black gown that looked like a spotted banana.

PART B

Circle **C** if the italicized word is used **correctly**. Circle **I** if the word is used **incorrectly**.

Ⓒ   I   14.   Pearl and I went to the same party, but it was so big that we never *encountered* each other.

C   Ⓘ   15.   I think of myself as a *pessimist* because I can find something good in even the worst situation.

Ⓒ   I   16.   Although the movie seemed true to life, the writer swore it was entirely *fictitious*.

Ⓒ   I   17.   Gina and Steve are *patrons* of the local Japanese restaurant. They eat there every Friday night.

C   Ⓘ   18.   Efforts to teach chimpanzees to learn words have been *futile*. Some chimps know as many as 200 words.

Ⓒ   I   19.   During my history teacher's lecture, I was soon able to *infer* her opinion about the U.S. involvement in Vietnam.*

C   Ⓘ   20.   Tony was disappointed when he *prevailed* in the student council election. Maybe he'll do better next year.

C   Ⓘ   21.   I get tired of Pat's guitar playing. He's so *versatile* that he just plays the same three chords over and over.

Ⓒ   I   22.   After searching for months for a treasured bracelet, I was *ecstatic* to find it in the sleeve of an old sweater.

Ⓒ   I   23.   Marie always thinks handsome men are nice. She seems to *equate* good looks with good character.

Ⓒ   I   24.   It's dangerous to invite my brother to help himself in your kitchen. He's *liable* to eat a week's worth of groceries.

C   Ⓘ   25.   After Judy's wonderful performance in the play, friends rushed backstage to *harass* her with flowers and praise.

*The first printing of the text mistakenly contained another sentence here.

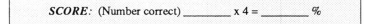
SCORE: (Number correct) _____ x 4 = _____ %

Enter your scores above and in the vocabulary performance chart on the inside back cover of the book.

UNIT THREE: Test 2

PART A

Complete each sentence with a word from the box. Use each word once.

awe	gullible	lethal	retort
cited	imposes	options	savor
delusion	indignant	rational	universal
evolved			

1. Having recently lent Trisha money, I was ___*indignant*___ when I learned she had been buying herself expensive jewelry.

2. It's thrilling to watch Michael Jordan play basketball. His athletic ability fills me with___ *awe* ___.

3. We considered several _____*options*_____for dinner: cooking, going out, or having a pizza delivered.

4. While in bed with a high fever, Joanne had the ___*delusion*___ that she was floating above the house.

5. Dad was embarrassed to admit he'd been ___*gullible*___ enough to buy a "genuine diamond wristwatch" from a stranger on the street.

6. As Gwen got to know Peter better, her feelings for him _____*evolved*_____ from interest to affection to love.

7. It's dangerous to mix chlorine bleach and other household cleaners. The combination can produce _____*lethal*_____ fumes.

8. My sister _____*imposes*_____ on her husband's good nature by having him run errands for her all the time.

9. Knowing the ice cream would be his last before beginning his diet, Jon took time to ___*savor*___ every rich spoonful.

10. The German and American children didn't mind that they couldn't talk together. They all knew the _____*universal*_____ language of play.

11. Rosa is very _____*rational*_____ about her love life. She lists a guy's good and bad qualities before deciding if she'll date him again.

12. When Paul complained, "Women and computers are both impossible to understand," his wife gave this _____*retort*_____: "No, you just don't know how to turn either one on."

13. To make my point that college can be as stressful as a full-time job, I _____*cited*_____ the pressures of being a student.

PART B
Circle **C** if the italicized word is used **correctly**. Circle **I** if the word is used **incorrectly**.

C (I) 14.   If a friend suffers a *fallacy*, it is proper to send a note of sympathy.

(C) I 15.   Although our teacher is *fluent* in French and Italian, her Russian is shaky.

(C) I 16.   At some health clinics, people with little income are *exempt* from all fees.

C (I) 17.   Bob *endeavored* to save the diseased tree, saying, "Let's just chop it down for firewood."

(C) I 18.   I felt like having pizza, but since it was my girlfriend's birthday, I *deferred* to her desire for Chinese food.

C (I) 19.   The couple next door often yell and throw things at each other. Clearly, they're *compatible*.

C (I) 20.   After my sister turned down Gabe's first request for a date, he was so *persistent* that he gave up.

(C) I 21.   Lynn has repeatedly asked Brian what exactly he does for a living, but she always gets an *evasive* answer like "I'm in sales."

(C) I 22.   The interracial couple were the victims of *malicious* acts. Their windows were smashed, and a cross was burned on their lawn.

C (I) 23.   Phil has such an *obsession* with his looks that he sometimes wears socks that don't match or forgets to comb his hair.

C (I) 24.   My overactive young nephew takes medicine to *stimulate* his tendency to race around the house and throw things.

(C) I 25.   Someone has *devised* sunglasses that serve as "eyes in the back of your head." Put them on and you see what's behind you.

SCORE: (Number correct) _____ x 4 = _____ %

Enter your scores above and in the vocabulary performance chart on the inside back cover of the book.

UNIT THREE: Test 3

PART A
Complete each sentence in a way that clearly shows you understand the meaning of the boldfaced word. Take a minute to plan your answer before you write.

Example: Two ways a boat can be **propelled** are by _____ *motor and wind.* _____

1. A **unique** color combination for a car would be _____ *(Answers will vary.)* _____

2. My sister is so **versatile** that _____

3. Lonnie needs to get from New York to Florida. One of his **options** is to _____

4. Because of her **obsession** with clothes, Sheila _____

5. Here's an **evasive** answer to "What did you do over vacation?": " _____

6. Glen is so **miserly** that _____

7. A man who believes he and his date are **compatible** might say at the end of an evening, _____

8. Wild teenagers on the street **harassed** passing cars by _____

9. An animal-lover would become **indignant** if _____

10. An obviously **fictitious** detail about my past is that I _____

PART B

After each boldfaced word are a *synonym* (a word that means the same as the boldfaced word), an *antonym* (a word that means the opposite of the boldfaced word), and a word that is neither. Mark the antonym with an *A*.

	Example:	**malicious**	____ eager	*A* kindly	____ spiteful
11.	**prevail**		*A* lose	____ triumph	____ disguise
12.	**dubious**		*A* certain	____ foolish	____ doubtful
13.	**vivid**		____ bright	____ angry	*A* colorless
14.	**futile**		____ evil	____ useless	*A* effective
15.	**awe**		____ wisdom	*A* contempt	____ respect

PART C

Use five of the following ten words in sentences. Make it clear that you know the meaning of the word you use. Feel free to use the past tense or plural form of a word.

accessible	delusion	elapse	encounter	impose
inevitable	liable	ordeal	retrieve	savor

16. _____ *(Answers will vary.)* _____

_____

17. _____

_____

18. _____

_____

19. _____

_____

20. _____

SCORE: (Number correct) _____ x 5 = _____ %

Enter your scores above and in the vocabulary performance chart on the inside back cover of the book.

UNIT THREE: Test 4 (Word Parts)

PART A
Listed in the left-hand column below are ten common word parts, along with words in which the parts are used. In each blank, write in the letter of the correct definition on the right.

Word Parts

			Definitions
_j_ 1. **con-**	consent, convention		a. quality; ability, skill
_c_ 2. **dict**	dictator, dictation		b. write
_i_ 3. **dis-**	dishonor, disarm		c. speak
_g_ 4. **micro-**	microscope, microfilm		d. foot
_d_ 5. **ped**	pedal, pedestrian		e. three
_b_ 6. **script, scrib**	scribble, scriptwriter		f. far
_a_ 7. **-ship**	hardship, leadership		g. small
_f_ 8. **tele-**	telephone, telecast		h. across, beyond, over
_h_ 9. **trans-**	transfer, translate		i. the opposite of; take away
_e_ 10. **tri-**	triplets, trio		j. with; together

PART B
Find the word part that correctly completes each word. Then write the full word in the blank space. Not every word part will be used.

con-	dict	dis-	micro-	ped
script	-ship	tele-	trans-	tri-

11. The easiest way to catch a cold is through skin (. . . *tact*) _____*contact*_____.

12. Other kids fall from bicycles, but I was so clumsy as a child that I even lost my balance on a

    (. . . *cycle*) _____*tricycle*_____.

13. (*Horseman*. . .) _*Horsemanship*_ was a much more common skill before automobiles became popular.

14. Is there anything more amazing than the (. . . *formation*) _*transformation*_ of a creepy caterpillar into a butterfly?

15. Allergy medicine bought with a doctor's (*pre*. . . *ion*) _*prescription*_ is likely to cost much more than the same medicine on the drugstore shelf.

PART C

Use your knowledge of word parts to determine the meaning of the boldfaced words. Circle the letter of each meaning.

16. I'd like to own a **microcomputer.**

    a. large computer   b. computer with a sound system   (c.) small computer

17. The horror movie's plot centered on a **malediction.**

    (a.) curse   b. serious illness   c. child

18. A lion's head was carved into the **pedestal** of the statue.

    a. top   b. middle   (c.) foot

19. While trying to fix Martha's car, Phil **disabled** it.

    (a.) made unable   b. made able   c. wrote about its abilities

20. In 1608, the **telescope** was invented by accident when the inventor happened to look through two lenses at once.

    An instrument which makes it easier to see:

    (a.) distant things   b. very small things   c. writings

SCORE: (Number correct) _____ x 5 = _____ %

Enter your scores above and in the vocabulary performance chart on the inside back cover of the book.

Unit Four

Previewing the Words

Find out how many of the ten words in this chapter you already know. Try to complete each sentence with the most suitable word from the list below. Use each word once.

Leave a sentence blank rather than guessing at an answer. Your purpose here is just to get a sense of the ten words and what you may know about them.

adapt	dismay	exile	gesture	recede
reciprocate	refute	retain	revert	ritual

1. Plastic storage containers often ____*retain*____ the odors of foods. I have one that still smells like spaghetti sauce after ten washings.

2. Since Arnie drove me to softball practice last week, I'll ____*reciprocate*____ and drive him to this week's practice.

3. Although Lena was ____*dismay*____(e)d to learn the application was due in only three days, she decided to try to get it in on time.

4. The flood was over, and the waters began to ____*recede*____. Soon land was visible again.

5. The tribe performed an ancient dance, a(n) ____*ritual*____ meant to please the gods and bring rain.

6. In a ____*gesture*____ of cooperation, the manager and the head of the union shook hands.

7. I ____*refuted*____(e)d the bill by showing that the cashier had overcharged me for one item.

8. Many Jews were forced to flee Nazi Germany and live in ____*exile*____, never to return to their native land.

9. When Greg moved from a small Southern town to Boston, he had to ____*adapt*____ to new weather conditions, accents, and customs.

10. Sylvia works to control her temper, but sometimes she ____*revert*____s to her childhood habit of screaming and stamping her feet.

Now check your answers by turning to page 165. Fix any mistakes and fill in any blank spaces by writing in the correct answers. By doing so, you will complete this introduction to the ten words.

You're now ready to strengthen your knowledge of the words you already know and to master the words you're only half sure of, or don't know at all. Turn to the next page.

Ten Words in Context

Figure out the meanings of the following ten words by looking *closely and carefully* at the context in which the words appear. Doing so will prepare you for the matching test and the practices on the two pages that follow.

1 **adapt**
(ə-dapt')
-*verb*

   a. After many years of being only a student, I found it hard to **adapt** to the schedule of a full-time job.

   b. Surprisingly, Gina **adapted** well to California. She thought she would have trouble adjusting to living so far from her family and friends.

2 **dismay**
(dis-mā')
-*verb*

   a. Carmen was **dismayed** when he realized that he wouldn't have enough money to buy a special birthday present for his girlfriend.

   b. The doctor knew it would **dismay** Karl to learn his injured leg would never regain its previous strength.

3 **exile**
(eg'-zīl')
-*noun*

   a. The political rebel decided to end his five-year **exile** and return to his native land to oppose the government.

   b In the movie *The Sound of Music*, the Von Trapp family is forced into **exile** when the Nazis take control of their homeland.

4 **gesture**
(jes'-chər)
-*noun*

   a. As a **gesture** of sympathy, the neighborhood association sent flowers to Milly when her husband died.

   b. The other workers' **gestures** of friendship made Vic feel at home on the first day of his new job.

5 **recede**
(ri-sēd')
-*verb*

   a. The heavy blanket of clouds finally began to **recede,** allowing the sun to warm the crowd at the football game.

   b. Walter had to wait until the flood water **receded** before he could get to his house to see the damage.

6 **reciprocate**
(ri-sip'-rə-kāt')
-*verb*

   a. I've done many favors for Anne, but she never **reciprocates** by doing a favor in return.

   b. Alonso treated me to dinner, so I'm going to **reciprocate** by taking him to my favorite restaurant.

7 **refute**
(ri-fyoot')
-*verb*

   a. The lawyer was able to **refute** the defendant's claim that she was home the night of the murder. He had found a witness who saw her in a town bar that night.

   b. Some science-fiction fans were disappointed when photos of Mars **refuted** the idea that intelligent life exists there.

8 **retain**
(ri-tān')
-*verb*

   a. The chairman of the board **retained** control of the firm by firing the president, who opposed him.

   b. "I can usually **retain** my sense of humor," Janice said. "But I lose it totally when I'm laid off and break up with my boyfriend in the same week."

9 **revert**
(ri-vûrt')
-*verb*

   a. After his release from jail, Sam **reverted** to his old habit of stealing.

   b. Helene gave up smoking while she was pregnant, but she **reverted** to a pack a day after her daughter was born.

10 **ritual**
(rich'-oo-əl)
-*noun*

   a. **Rituals**—set practices that are repeated regularly—are important in most religious traditions.

   b. Each time Mary Ann must fly, she writes a check to a charity, carries it on the plane, and mails it at her destination. She believes this **ritual** guarantees a safe flight.

Matching Words and Definitions

Check your understanding of the ten words by matching each word with its definition. Look back at the sentences in "Ten Words in Context" as needed to decide on the meaning of each word.

_g_   1. **adapt**

_j_   2. **dismay**

_d_   3. **exile**

_h_   4. **recede**

_c_   5. **reciprocate**

_f_   6. **refute**

_b_   7. **gesture**

_i_   8. **retain**

_a_   9. **revert**

_e_   10. **ritual**

a. to return to a previous habit, opinion, or condition

b. anything said or done to show one's attitude or intentions

c. to do in return; pay back

d. separation from one's native country through force or choice

e. a ceremony; any actions done regularly in a set manner

f. to prove wrong or false

g. to adjust to a situation

h. to move back; draw back

i. to keep

j. to discourage; make fearful or uneasy

CAUTION: Do not go any further until you are sure the above answers are correct. If you have studied the "Ten Words in Context," you will know how to match each word. Then you can use the matches to help you in the following practices. Your goal is to reach a point where you don't need to check definitions at all.

➤ Sentence Check 1

Complete each sentence below with the most suitable word from the box. Use each word once.

adapt	dismay	exile	gesture	recede
reciprocate	refute	retain	revert	ritual

1. Getting a D on the first math test of the semester _____*dismay*_____(e)d Sean.

2. If the shoreline continues to _____*recede*_____, there soon won't be any sandy beach there at all.

3. Antonio tried to _____*refute*_____ my argument, but I was able to prove I was right.

4. As a _____*gesture*_____ of support and encouragement, Jeri's friends cheered when it was her turn to bowl in the tournament.

5. To _____*retain*_____ her strength and energy, Mrs. Green does push-ups, sit-ups, and leg-lifts three times a week.

6. My brother vowed to eat only one Oreo a day, but I'm afraid he'll _____*revert*_____ to his old habit of eating the entire bag of cookies at at sitting.

7. As the Ice Age ended, some animals were able to _____*adapt*_____ to the new climate. Those who could not adjust failed to survive.

8. The country's new dictator feared having certain political enemies in the country, so he sent them into _____*exile*_____.

9. I always send Gordon a birthday card, but he doesn't bother to _____*reciprocate*_____ with a card or phone call on my birthday.

10. Homer always repeats the same baseball _____*ritual*_____ before he bats: he twirls his bat three times, stretches his arms, and says, "Okay, okay, this one will be good."

Now check your answers to these questions by turning to page 165. Going over the answers carefully will help you prepare for the next two checks, for which answers are not given.

➤ *Sentence Check 2*

Complete each sentence below with two words from the following list. Use each word once.

adapt	dismay	exile	gesture	recede
reciprocate	refute	retain	revert	ritual

1-2. "I don't want to _____*dismay*_____ you," Jack's lawyer told him, "but it's going to be difficult to _____*refute*_____ the charges against you."

3-4. The Reillys have been so kind to me that I want to _____*reciprocate*_____ in some way. I don't have much money, so I hope they'll understand that a small gift is meant as a _____*gesture*_____ of great appreciation.

5-6. My husband is afraid his hairline will _____*recede*_____, causing him to _____*revert*_____ to the bald head he was born with.

7-8. Any customary _____*ritual*_____, such as the Roman Catholic Mass, helps a church to _____*retain*_____ a sense of tradition.

9-10. The Howards had _____*adapt*_____(e)d well to other cultures, but they were still pleased to retire from the Foreign Service and return to America after their long _____*exile*_____ in Europe and Asia.

➤ *Final Check:* Adjusting to a New Culture

Here is a final opportunity for you to strengthen your knowledge of the ten words. First read the following passage carefully. Then fill in each blank with a word from the box at the top of this page. (Context clues will help you figure out which word goes in which blank.) Use each word once.

When En-Mei first came to the United States from China, any little problem was enough to (1)____*dismay*____ her. As a lonely student, she felt as if she were in forced (2)_____*exile*_____ from her native country. She didn't like American food and tried to limit her diet to Chinese dishes. Otherwise, however, she worked hard to (3)_____*adapt*_____ to an unfamiliar country. Soon she overcame her shyness and learned to (4)____*reciprocate*____ other students' (5)_____*gesture*_____s of friendship. When she was with her new friends, homesickness would (6)_____*recede*_____ into the background. But En-Mei didn't try to become "all-American"; she wanted to (7)_____*retain*_____ her Chinese identity. She taught her new friends about modern China and tried to (8)_____*refute*_____ mistaken ideas they had about her country. She even found a group of friends willing to learn tai chi, an ancient Chinese exercise (9)_____*ritual*_____ that benefits body and spirit. Living in America wasn't always easy. Sometimes En-Mei would miss her family so badly that she would (10)_____*revert*_____ to her former unhappiness. But such times were increasingly rare. By the end of her first year here, En-Mei even found she had become a devoted fan of pizza and apple pie.

SCORES:	Sentence Check 2 _____%	Final Check _____%	

Enter your scores above and in the vocabulary performance chart on the inside back cover of the book.

Previewing the Words

Find out how many of the ten words in this chapter you already know. Try to complete each sentence with the most suitable word from the list below. Use each word once.

Leave a sentence blank rather than guessing at an answer. Your purpose here is just to get a sense of the ten words and what you may know about them.

elaborate	emerge	exotic	frugal	impulsive
indifferent	indulgent	liberal	mediocre	notable

1. Since I'm not earning much money, I try to be ___*frugal*___.

2. The bride planned the wedding in ___*elaborate*___ detail, not forgetting the least thing; the groom, however, forgot to come.

3. Usually a C grade indicates neither the best nor the worst job, but work that is average, or ___*mediocre*___.

4. Looking out over the water, we saw a tiny submarine ___*emerge*___ from below the surface.

5. I'm tired of Robin's self-___*indulgent*___ temper tantrums; she expects others to satisfy her every desire.

6. Tamara is such a talented actress that we all expect her to become a ___*notable*___ film or TV star.

7. The advice "Look before you leap" encourages people to think carefully before they act, rather than to be ___*impulsive*___.

8. The kiwi fruit, grown in New Zealand, is one of several ___*exotic*___ fruits now commonly sold in supermarkets.

9. I care greatly whether a Democrat or Republican wins the election. But my brother, who has no real interest in politics, is ___*indifferent*___ about the election.

10. The ice-cream parlor was known for its ___*liberal*___ servings—huge scoops dripping with syrup.

Now check your answers by turning to page 165. Fix any mistakes and fill in any blank spaces by writing in the correct answers. By doing so, you will complete this introduction to the ten words.

You're now ready to strengthen your knowledge of the words you already know and to master the words you're only half sure of, or don't know at all. Turn to the next page.

Ten Words in Context

Figure out the meanings of the following ten words by looking *closely and carefully* at the context in which the words appear. Doing so will prepare you for the matching test and the practices on the two pages that follow.

1 **elaborate**
(i-lab'-ər-it)
-adjective

   a. The dinner required **elaborate** preparation. Each course included a complicated favorite dish of one of the guests.

   b. Irma's quilt was very **elaborate**. She used tiny stitches to sew on the very detailed pattern.

2 **emerge**
(i-mûrj')
-verb

   a. Anna **emerged** from the dressing room, looking beautiful in a blue prom gown.

   b. When the chick **emerged** from its egg, it was tired and wet, but a day later it was a fluffy yellow ball of energy.

3 **exotic**
(ig-zot'-ik)
-adjective

   a. Orchids are grown in the U.S., not just in foreign countries. So Americans really should not consider the flower **exotic**.

   b. Ross has an **exotic** accent of some kind, but I can't put my finger on just what country he comes from.

4 **frugal**
(froo'-gəl)
-adjective

   a. You can stretch your dollars by being **frugal**. For example, using store coupons and waiting for expensive items to be on sale can save a lot of money.

   b. Diane buys designer jeans, but because I need to be more **frugal**, I buy store-brand jeans.

5 **impulsive**
(im-pul'-siv)
-adjective

   a. Ved is too **impulsive** to make plans. He always prefers to act on the spur of the moment.

   b. Kids are usually more **impulsive** than adults. Children will follow such sudden urges as the desire to climb a tree while in their best clothes, regardless of the results.

6 **indifferent**
(in-dif'-ər-ənt)
-adjective

   a. Does our society have no interest in homeless children? Are we **indifferent** to the many families who can no longer afford to pay rent?

   b. Because her husband was **indifferent** to how the apartment would be decorated, Kathy felt free to do the job any way she wanted.

7 **indulgent**
(in-dul'-jənt)
-adjective

   a. Monica's grandparents are too **indulgent** with her. They don't scold her even when she splatters the walls with baby food.

   b. My self-**indulgent** brother spends hours playing video games and never helps out around the house.

8 **liberal**
(lib'-ər-əl)
-adjective

   a. Martin Lopez has no children, so he gives **liberal** Christmas and birthday gifts to his nephews and nieces.

   b. Norma left the waiter a **liberal** tip because he had been especially friendly and helpful.

9 **mediocre**
(mē-dē-ō'-kər)
-adjective

   a. The mystery movie was neither terrible nor great; it was **mediocre**.

   b. Although Hank can be quite funny, his jokes are only **mediocre** compared to those of the best comedians.

10 **notable**
(nō'-tə-bəl)
-adjective

   a. Winning the Nobel Prize can make a little-known scientist into a **notable** world figure.

   b. Abraham Lincoln's "Gettysburg Address" is surely his most **notable** speech, especially among those many Americans who memorized it in school.

Matching Words and Definitions

Check your understanding of the ten words by matching each word with its definition. Look back at the sentences in "Ten Words in Context" as needed to decide on the meaning of each word.

_e_	1. **elaborate**	a.	to rise up or come forth
_a_	2. **emerge**	b.	famous; widely known
_h_	3. **exotic**	c.	having no real interest; unconcerned
_i_	4. **frugal**	d.	generous
_g_	5. **impulsive**	e.	done with great attention to details; complex
_c_	6. **indifferent**	f.	average; ordinary; neither very bad nor very good
_j_	7. **indulgent**	g.	tending to act on sudden urges; not in the habit of planning ahead
_d_	8. **liberal**	h.	foreign; from a different part of the world; strange or different in an appealing way
_f_	9. **mediocre**	i.	thrifty; avoiding unnecessary expenses
_b_	10. **notable**	j.	giving in to someone's desires, often too much so

CAUTION: Do not go any further until you are sure the above answers are correct. If you have studied the "Ten Words in Context," you will know how to match each word. Then you can use the matches to help you in the following practices. Your goal is to reach a point where you don't need to check definitions at all.

➤ Sentence Check 1

Complete each sentence below with the most suitable word from the box. Use each word once.

elaborate	emerge	exotic	frugal	impulsive
indifferent	indulgent	liberal	mediocre	notable

1. While my father didn't do badly in school, he wasn't a great student. So he's proof it's possible to have a successful career despite _____*mediocre*_____ grades.

2. It was Gwen's birthday, so her parents were especially _____*indulgent*_____, letting her stay up much later than her usual bedtime.

3. The puppy _____*emerge*_____(e)d from her bath much cleaner than when she entered it, but we doubted she'd stay clean for long.

4. Paul Newman is _____*notable*_____ not only for his acting ability, but also for his charity work.

5. My boss gave each of us such a(n) _____*liberal*_____ bonus that I was able to buy a new sofa with the money.

6. Ella embroidered a(n) _____*elaborate*_____ design on the back of her sweatshirt. She used four colors in a complicated pattern of swirls and flowers.

7. "Gowns are so expensive," Mimi said, "that I've decided to be _____*frugal*_____ and rent a wedding dress instead of buying one."

8. People walked past the bleeding, moaning man without even pausing; they were _____*indifferent*_____ to his need for help.

9. Bruce, as _____*impulsive*_____ as ever, suddenly changed his mind about going to a restaurant and announced, "Let's have a picnic."

10. An Indian rain dance may seem _____*exotic*_____ to many Americans, but it is actually more native to this country than square-dancing.

Now check your answers to these questions by turning to page 165. Going over the answers carefully will help you prepare for the next two checks, for which answers are not given.

➤ Sentence Check 2

Complete each sentence below with two words from the following list. Use each word once.

elaborate	emerge	exotic	frugal	impulsive
indifferent	indulgent	liberal	mediocre	notable

1-2. The actress, _____ *notable* _____ for great acting, deserved her Academy Award. Compared to her performance, all of the others appeared _____ *mediocre* _____.

3-4. Every time Sylvia shops, she manages to _____ *emerge* _____ from the store without a single foolish purchase. I wish I could be such a(n) _____ *frugal* _____ shopper.

5-6. The _____ *exotic* _____ meal, full of strange but delicious foods, involved _____ *elaborate* _____ preparation that took up most of the afternoon.

7-8. Americans find it difficult to be _____ *indifferent* _____ to the suffering of disaster victims, so they send _____ *liberal* _____ donations to the Red Cross when disasters strike.

9-10. Rafael is so _____ *impulsive* _____ that he often decides he wants to go out for dinner or to a movie at the last minute. Overly _____ *indulgent* _____, his wife agrees every time—even when he wants to eat out after she's already cooked dinner.

➤ Final Check: A Dream About Wealth

Here is a final opportunity for you to strengthen your knowledge of the ten words. First read the following passage carefully. Then fill in each blank with a word from the box at the top of this page. (Context clues will help you figure out which word goes in which blank.) Use each word once.

When I was a very poor student, I sometimes daydreamed about being rich. I imagined being such a (1)_____ *notable* _____ member of society that my name would turn up in the newspaper columns every time I remarried. I pictured myself traveling to (2)_____ *exotic* _____ places in faraway lands. I would forget no detail when planning (3)_____ *elaborate* _____ parties for five hundred of my closest friends. There would be nothing (4)_____ *mediocre* _____ in my life, not even an ordinary, average toaster. No, I would have the finest toasters, the biggest houses, the most glamorous wardrobe—the best. Of course, I would be quite (5)_____ *impulsive* _____: whenever I had the urge, I would buy diamond rings or go swimming nude in my Olympic-size pool. But I wouldn't only be self- (6)_____ *indulgent* _____. I'd also be very (7)_____ *liberal* _____ in spending my money to help the poor and underprivileged. I would not be (8)_____ *indifferent* _____ to their needs. After graduating, I began saving money, and I stopped daydreaming about being rich. Having some earnings to spend, I had finally (9)_____ *emerge* _____(e)d from a life of endless budgeting, a life in which I was forced to be extremely (10)_____ *frugal* _____. Of course, I am still thrifty because I don't want to waste my hard-earned money. But now that I have enough money to be comfortable, I no longer daydream about being super-rich.

SCORES: Sentence Check 2 _____ %	Final Check _____ %

Enter your scores above and in the vocabulary performance chart on the inside back cover of the book.

Previewing the Words

Find out how many of the ten words in this chapter you already know. Try to complete each sentence with the most suitable word from the list below. Use each word once.

Leave a sentence blank rather than guessing at an answer. Your purpose here is just to get a sense of the ten words and what you may know about them.

affirm	alleged	allude	coerce	elite
essence	immunity	impair	query	sadistic

1. Not only was the _____ *alleged* _____ car thief out of town on the day of the theft; he cannot drive.

2. We are all free to the extent that no one can _____ *coerce* _____ us into holding certain beliefs.

3. Augusto will _____ *query* _____ the banker about the proper way to apply for a car loan.

4. Staring at the sun during an eclipse can _____ *impair* _____ vision and even cause blindness.

5. Trust is the _____ *essence* _____ of a good relationship; without it, the relationship won't last.

6. New U.S. Presidents _____ *affirm* _____ under oath that they will uphold the Constitution.

7. As a child, Lee was so _____ *sadistic* _____ that he would smile as he pulled legs off live grasshoppers.

8. In joining the Olympic team, Kelly became a member of an _____ *elite* _____ group of athletes.

9. Although the mayor won't name her opponent, she plans to _____ *allude* _____ to him by mentioning the scandal in which he's involved.

10. Leon's mother was the high school principal, but that didn't give Leon _____ *immunity* _____ from following the rules. In fact, she was very strict with him.

Now check your answers by turning to page 165. Fix any mistakes and fill in any blank spaces by writing in the correct answers. By doing so, you will complete this introduction to the ten words.

You're now ready to strengthen your knowledge of the words you already know and to master the words you're only half sure of, or don't know at all. Turn to the next page.

Ten Words in Context

Figure out the meanings of the following ten words by looking *closely and carefully* at the context in which the words appear. Doing so will prepare you for the matching test and the practices on the two pages that follow.

1 **affirm**
(ə-fûrm')
-verb

    a. The witness **affirmed** in court that he had seen the defendant commit the robbery.

    b. Lana did **affirm** during the wedding ceremony that she would love and honor Joseph, but she did not state that she would obey him.

2 **alleged**
(ə-ledjd')
-adjective

    a. The **alleged** killer was never proven guilty in court, but most people believe he committed the murder.

    b. The senator lost the election because of his **alleged** drinking problem, which has yet to be proved.

3 **allude**
(ə-lo͞od')
-verb

    a. In his speeches, Martin Luther King often **alluded** to the Bible's familiar stories by referring to Biblical personalities.

    b. Regina **alluded** to Sal's weight gain by calling him "Santa," instead of referring to it directly.

4 **coerce**
(kō-ûrs')
-verb

    a. The rebels tried to **coerce** the general into giving up by kidnapping his daughter.

    b. The Puritan colonists **coerced** Indians into slavery by capturing and selling them to buyers in the West Indies.

5 **elite**
(i-lēt')
-adjective

    a. The 57th was the **elite** military unit. Its members were the toughest and the smartest and had trained the longest.

    b. The **elite** neighborhood in town is surrounded by a high fence and has a guard at its gates.

6 **essence**
(es'-əns)
-noun

    a. New life is the **essence** of spring.

    b. The **essence** of the hour-long lecture was the idea that much important work gets done in America by volunteers.

7 **immunity**
(i-myo͞o'-ni-tē)
-noun

    a. Because the foreign ambassador has **immunity** from parking fines, she is never ticketed when she parks in a no-parking zone.

    b. When the actor punched a police officer, even his wealth and fame didn't get him **immunity** from jail.

8 **impair**
(im-pâr')
-verb

    a. Listening to loud music **impairs** hearing by damaging the inner ear.

    b. The rifle shot didn't kill the deer, but it **impaired** her running ability, leaving her with a limp.

9 **query**
(kwēr'-ē)
-verb

    a. Since no printed schedule was available, I had to **query** the man at the information booth to learn when the train would leave.

    b. Reporters repeatedly **queried** the President about taxes, but his only reply was "No comment."

10 **sadistic**
(sə-dis'-tik)
-adjective

    a. Instead of killing his victims quickly, the **sadistic** murderer first made them suffer.

    b. Our **sadistic** science teacher had a strange way of teaching about electrical currents: First, he had us hold hands in a circle. Then he put one student's hand on a wire with a slight electrical charge.

Matching Words and Definitions

Check your understanding of the ten words by matching each word with its definition. Look back at the sentences in "Ten Words in Context" as needed to decide on the meaning of each word.

_f_ 1. **affirm**	a. to damage; weaken
_i_ 2. **alleged**	b. to refer indirectly to
_b_ 3. **allude to**	c. tending to take pleasure in cruelty
_h_ 4. **coerce**	d. a fundamental characteristic or the most important quality of something; the heart of a matter
_g_ 5. **elite**	e. the freedom from something unpleasant or something required of others
_d_ 6. **essence**	f. to indicate to be true
_e_ 7. **immunity**	g. being or for the best, most powerful, or most privileged; superior
_a_ 8. **impair**	h. to force
_j_ 9. **query**	i. supposed to be true but not proved or not decided in a court
_c_ 10. **sadistic**	j. to question; ask

CAUTION: Do not go any further until you are sure the above answers are correct. If you have studied the "Ten Words in Context," you will know how to match each word. Then you can use the matches to help you in the following practices. Your goal is to reach a point where you don't need to check definitions at all.

➤ Sentence Check 1

Complete each sentence below with the most suitable word from the box. Use each word once.

affirm	alleged	allude	coerce	elite
essence	immunity	impair	query	sadistic

1. Our gym teacher used to _____coerce_____ us into doing fifty sit-ups by refusing to let anyone leave before we all had finished.

2. The _____sadistic_____ Nazi laughed while his victim was tortured.

3. Drugs and alcohol _____impair_____ a person's ability to drive.

4. The _____essence_____ of a paragraph is stated in its topic sentence.

5. As a child, I didn't enjoy total _____immunity_____ from punishment, but my parents rarely hit me.

6. During the spelling bee, the judge would _____affirm_____ that a spelling was correct by nodding silently.

7. Nan, who believed Luther was innocent of the car theft, reminded her friends that his guilt was only _____alleged_____.

8. A(n) _____elite_____ group of doctors, including the country's top brain surgeons, met to discuss two new operations.

9. When two people are arrested for the same crime, the police _____query_____ them separately, to see if they give the same answers.

10. My brother and I used secret names to _____allude_____ to certain relatives. For example, if we wished to speak about Aunt Dotty, we instead spoke about "an old Chevy."

Now check your answers to these questions by turning to page 165. Going over the answers carefully will help you prepare for the next two checks, for which answers are not given.

➤ *Sentence Check 2*

Complete each sentence below with two words from the following list. Use each word once.

affirm	alleged	allude	coerce	elite
essence	immunity	impair	query	sadistic

1-2. The senator would neither deny nor _____*affirm*_____ that the _____*elite*_____, expensive country club he belonged to allowed no minority members.

3-4. I need to _____*query*_____ my professor more closely about the chemistry theory. Although I've grasped the _____*essence*_____, I don't understand all the details yet.

5-6. When my roommate wants to _____*coerce*_____ me into doing her some favor, all she has to do is _____*allude*_____ to certain dark secrets of mine. The hint that she might tell them is enough to make me help her out.

7-8. One terrible beating by her _____*sadistic*_____ husband was enough to _____*impair*_____ the woman's sight for life.

9-10. The _____*alleged*_____ crime was never investigated because the chief suspect was given _____*immunity*_____ from arrest by a powerful political figure.

➤ *Final Check:* Children and Drugs

Here is a final opportunity for you to strengthen your knowledge of the ten words. First read the following passage carefully. Then fill in each blank with a word from the box at the top of this page. (Context clues will help you figure out which word goes in which blank.) Use each word once.

One of the disturbing things about drug selling is the involvement of children. Police regularly pick up pre-teens who are used as lookouts and delivery boys for drug dealers. When the police (1)____*query*____ them, the children often say the drug dealers (2)____*coerce*____ them into doing these jobs. At least sometimes, this (3)____*alleged*____ forcing isn't necessary; some poor kids are naturally attracted by the money the dealers offer. When the children speak of the dealers, they (4)____*allude*____ to them with admiration. With their fancy cars and wads of money, the dealers seem like members of a(n) (5)____*elite*____ club.

Dealers like using kids because their age gives them (6)____*immunity*____ from serious criminal charges. The police (7)____*affirm*____ that arresting the children doesn't (8)____*impair*____ the dealers' business much.

To some of the children, serving as lookouts and drug runners is almost a game. They don't realize what harm could come to them if they got involved with a really (9)____*sadistic*____ dealer, someone who enjoys violence. The use of these children shows that the (10)____*essence*____ of drug dealing is abuse of people.

SCORES: Sentence Check 2 _____%   Final Check _____%

Enter your scores above and in the vocabulary performance chart on the inside back cover of the book.

Previewing the Words

Find out how many of the ten words in this chapter you already know. Try to complete each sentence with the most suitable word from the list below. Use each word once.

Leave a sentence blank rather than guessing at an answer. Your purpose here is just to get a sense of the ten words and what you may know about them.

plausible	provoke	recur	reprimand	revoke
ridicule	shrewd	skeptical	stereotype	tactic

1. The judge usually _____*revoke*_____s a person's license for driving while drunk.

2. The county board decided that the annual fair would _____*recur*_____ each year during the last week in July.

3. One _____*tactic*_____ for getting a raise is to show your boss a list of your accomplishments.

4. Sandra was _____*skeptical*_____ that the fortune teller could really tell her future.

5. Steven understood how to make his sister angry. For example, he knew it would _____*provoke*_____ her if he used a toy of hers without asking.

6. "When a worker breaks a rule, I give him a _____*reprimand*_____," said the strict boss. "If he breaks it again, he's fired."

7. Evan is not a _____*shrewd*_____ flea-market shopper. Instead of bargaining, he pays the full asking price, no matter how high.

8. My excuse for missing the English final did not sound _____*plausible*_____ to my teacher. Nevertheless, my grandmother really had died, and I was attending her funeral.

9. Bev still accepts the _____*stereotype*_____ of all athletes as dumb, even though the school's star quarterback is her math tutor.

10. Eugene knew his friends would _____*ridicule*_____ him for wearing a shirt and shorts with two different plaids, but he had no other clean clothes to wear.

Now check your answers by turning to page 165. Fix any mistakes and fill in any blank spaces by writing in the correct answers. By doing so, you will complete this introduction to the ten words.

You're now ready to strengthen your knowledge of the words you already know and to master the words you're only half sure of, or don't know at all. Turn to the next page.

Ten Words in Context

Figure out the meanings of the following ten words by looking *closely and carefully* at the context in which the words appear. Doing so will prepare you for the matching test and the practices on the two pages that follow.

1 **plausible**
(plô'-zə-bəl)
-adjective

   a. Was Buck's excuse for being late **plausible**? Or did he tell you some unbelieveable story?

   b. "Some TV shows are just not **plausible**," said the producer. "Who ever heard of a talking horse or a flying nun?"

2 **provoke**
(prə-vōk')
-verb

   a. "Mr. Jackson **provoked** me by saying nasty things about my mother, so I hit him," Terry told the judge.

   b. My father is slow to anger, but this morning my sister's wisecracks began to **provoke** him.

3 **recur**
(ri-kûr')
-verb

   a. Jordan has headaches that **recur** as often as once a day.

   b. "The labor pains are **recurring** every minute," I told the nurse. "Do you think it's about time?"

4 **reprimand**
(rep'-rə-mand')
-noun

   a. If a boss wants to blame a worker, the union requires the **reprimand** to be written.

   b. My father gave me verbal **reprimands,** but my mother would not hesitate to give me a slap on the rear end.

5 **revoke**
(ri-vōk')
-verb

   a. Mrs. Byers said she would **revoke** Ken's computer-lab privileges if he ever again squirted glue between the computer keys.

   b. To avoid having his driver's license **revoked,** Art paid the $467 for all of his speeding tickets.

6 **ridicule**
(rid'-i-kyōol')
-verb

   a. People often **ridicule** my brother because he is so overweight.

   b. Fellow students used to **ridicule** Eric for being so poor, but no one has mocked him since he got a full scholarship to an Ivy League school.

7 **shrewd**
(shrōod)
-adjective

   a. Eddie is a fine musician, but he's no good with money. So he hired a friend with a **shrewd** business sense to handle his financial affairs.

   b. Sherry is a **shrewd** flirt. She ignores men wearing a Timex watch so she'll be available for one with a Rolex.

8 **skeptical**
(skep'-ti-kəl)
-adjective

   a. Jessica's family is so rich that she is **skeptical** about any man who asks her out. She wonders if he's interested in her or in her money.

   b. I am **skeptical** about the articles on movie stars and space aliens in supermarket newspapers. My brother, however, believes every word he reads in those papers.

9 **stereotype**
(ster'-ē-ə-tīp')
-noun

   a. The used car salesman did not fit our **stereotype.** He was quiet and informative, not loud and pushy.

   b. Because all members of a group are not alike, **stereotypes** lead to inaccurate judgments of people.

10 **tactic**
(tak'-tic)
-noun

   a. The teacher finally caught on to Greg's **tactic** for getting his homework done—having his sister do it.

   b. The best **tactic** for keeping young children from fighting is to separate them.

Matching Words and Definitions

Check your understanding of the ten words by matching each word with its definition. Look back at the sentences in "Ten Words in Context" as needed to decide on the meaning of each word.

_c_	1. **plausible**	a.	doubting; questioning
_d_	2. **provoke**	b.	clever; tricky
_i_	3. **recur**	c.	believeable; appearing truthful or reasonable
_g_	4. **reprimand**	d.	to stir up anger or resentment in someone
_e_	5. **revoke**	e.	to cancel or make ineffective by taking back, withdrawing, or reversing
_h_	6. **ridicule**	f.	a means to reach a goal; method
_b_	7. **shrewd**	g.	a harsh or formal criticism
_a_	8. **skeptical**	h.	to make fun of; mock
_j_	9. **stereotype**	i.	to occur again; occur over and over
_f_	10. **tactic**	j.	an oversimplified image of a person or group, with no individuality taken into account

CAUTION: Do not go any further until you are sure the above answers are correct. If you have studied the "Ten Words in Context," you will know how to match each word. Then you can use the matches to help you in the following practices. Your goal is to reach a point where you don't need to check definitions at all.

➤ Sentence Check 1

Complete each sentence below with the most suitable word from the box. Use each word once.

plausible	provoke	recur	reprimand	revoke
ridicule	shrewd	skeptical	stereotype	tactic

1. Lauri never got used to being ____*ridicule*____(e)d by the other children for speaking with an accent.

2. Italian-Americans are rightly bothered by the ____*stereotype*____ of all Italians as members of the Mafia.

3. Amber's excuse for missing the party did not seem ____*plausible*____. She said she was too sick, but I saw her shopping that afternoon.

4. It was ____*shrewd*____ of Connie to move to California last year. Now she can pay in-state fees when she begins college at San Bernadino University.

5. Five-year-old Arnie's nightmare of ghosts chasing him tended to ____*recur*____ at least once a week.

6. Some divorced parents who want to see more of their children use an illegal ____*tactic*____: kidnapping.

7. When the roofer gave us an estimate that was much lower than what others charged, we became ____*skeptical*____ about the quality of his work.

8. The principal wrote our gym teacher a note of ____*reprimand*____ for not having his class leave the gym right after the fire alarm rang.

9. Dustin usually doesn't let his older sister's teasing ____*provoke*____ him, but he gets angry whenever she calls him "baby."

10. Eleanor's parents said she could not attend the prom because of her bad grades, but later they ____*revoke*____(e)d the punishment and let her go anyway.

Now check your answers to these questions by turning to page 165. Going over the answers carefully will help you prepare for the next two checks, for which answers are not given.

➤ Sentence Check 2

Complete each sentence below with two words from the following list. Use each word once.

plausible	provoke	recur	reprimand	revoke
ridicule	shrewd	skeptical	stereotype	tactic

1-2. When it comes to preventing cheating, our science teacher is _____*shrewd*_____. His _____*tactics*_____s include checking our hands before a test and having us sit in alternate seats during a test.

3-4. _____*Stereotype*_____s may get their start when certain behavior patterns _____*recur*_____ among members of a particular group.

5-6. "Of course I'm _____*skeptical*_____ of your excuse," Mel's boss said. "You have to give me a more _____*plausible*_____ reason for not having the sales report ready than that you couldn't find a pen or pencil."

7-8. "This time you're just getting a _____*reprimand*_____," said the judge to the owner of the hot-dog stand. "Next time your license may be _____*revoke*_____(e)d."

9-10. When some boys pushed and _____*ridicule*_____(e)d a retarded student for being "dumb," the principal was greatly _____*provoke*_____(e)d. So she kept the boys after school to write "I am not as smart as I think" five hundred times.

➤ *Final Check:* Party House

Here is a final opportunity for you to strengthen your knowledge of the ten words. First read the following passage carefully. Then fill in each blank with a word from the box at the top of this page. (Context clues will help you figure out which word goes in which blank.) Use each word once.

The loud parties at the Phi Gamma fraternity house had (1)_____*provoke*_____(e)d its neighbors all year. The neighbors complained to the college, but the Phi Gammas were (2)_____*shrewd*_____ enough to come up with a (3)_____*plausible*_____ explanation each time. For example, they claimed that one of their members tended to have nightmares which would (4)_____*recur*_____ throughout finals week, making him cry out loudly throughout the night. This, they said, woke up all of the other members, who had gone to bed early that evening. Again and again, the Phi Gammas were let off by the college dean with only a (5)_____*reprimand*_____. But members of the other fraternities were (6)_____*skeptical*_____ of Phi Gamma's excuses. They also disliked the way the group contributed to a negative (7)_____*stereotype*_____ of fraternities. So they decided on a (8)_____*tactic*_____ to get back at Phi Gamma. They secretly tape-recorded one of the Phi Gamma meetings. During that meeting, members (9)_____*ridicule*_____(e)d the dean by mocking the way he always believed their excuses. They also made plans for more loud parties. When the dean heard the recording, he (10)_____*revoke*_____(e)d Phi Gamma's campus license.

SCORES:	Sentence Check 2 _____%	Final Check _____%

Enter your scores above and in the vocabulary performance chart on the inside back cover of the book.

Previewing the Words

Find out how many of the ten words in this chapter you already know. Try to complete each sentence with the most suitable word from the list below. Use each word once.

Leave a sentence blank rather than guessing at an answer. Your purpose here is just to get a sense of the ten words and what you may know about them.

consequence	destiny	detain	diminish	procrastinate
simultaneous	strategy	tedious	transaction	vital

1. Because Carrie left out a _____ *vital* _____ ingredient, the apple cake came out looking like a pancake.

2. Kyle and Tara's births were almost _*simultaneous*_ —they're twins.

3. Susanna forgot to buy milk. As a _____ *consequence* _____, she had to wash down dry cereal with her coffee the next morning.

4. When it comes to housework, it pays to _*procrastinate*_ for a week. Then the next week, you can do two weeks' worth of cleaning at once.

5. Some people's dating _____ *strategy* _____ is to "play cool"; others prefer to "come on strong."

6. "May I _____ *detain* _____ you one minute, for some directions?" asked a stranger as I hurried to work.

7. Using an automatic bank machine takes less time than a _*transaction*_ with a human bank teller.

8. Shakespeare wrote that Romeo and Juliet's _____ *destiny* _____ is written in the stars, but I don't believe in fate.

9. Beth hoped her headache would _____ *diminish* _____ after she took two aspirins, but it didn't lessen at all.

10. _____ *Tedious* _____ chores, like washing dishes, are less boring if you do them while you listen to the radio or talk with a friend.

Now check your answers by turning to page 166. Fix any mistakes and fill in any blank spaces by writing in the correct answers. By doing so, you will complete this introduction to the ten words.

You're now ready to strengthen your knowledge of the words you already know and to master the words you're only half sure of, or don't know at all. Turn to the next page.

Ten Words in Context

Figure out the meanings of the following ten words by looking *closely and carefully* at the context in which the words appear. Doing so will prepare you for the matching test and the practices on the two pages that follow.

1 **consequence**
(kon'-si-kwens)
-noun

   a. As a **consequence** of her heavy spending at the mall, Lily was short of cash until her next paycheck.

   b. When children reach for something hot or sharp, it's because they don't know the **consequences** of such actions.

2 **destiny**
(des'-tə-nē)
-noun

   a. Believing in fate, the soldier wondered if his **destiny** was to die in the coming battle.

   b. Marc believes much of his life is set by **destiny**. For example, he feels that he and Debbie were born for each other.

3 **detain**
(di-tān')
-verb

   a. Paul's history teacher **detained** him after class to speak privately about his surprisingly low test results.

   b. **Detained** at home by a friend in urgent need of advice, Gloria was late for work.

4 **diminish**
(di-min'-ish)
-verb

   a. After Mother yelled, "Turn that thing down!" the sound from the stereo **diminished** from a roar to a soft hum.

   b. As the cost of living rises, the value of a person's life savings **diminishes.**

5 **procrastinate**
(prə-kras'-tə-nāt')
-verb

   a. Morgan **procrastinated** so long that when she finally returned the dress to the store, it was too late for a refund.

   b. I can't **procrastinate** any longer. I must study tonight because the final exam is tomorrow morning.

6 **simultaneous**
(sī'-məl-tā'-nē-əs)
-adjective

   a. In a fair race, all starts must be **simultaneous**.

   b. Lightning and thunder don't seem **simultaneous**—we see the lightning before we hear the thunder.

7 **strategy**
(strat'-ə-jē)
-noun

   a. The best **strategy** for teaching your children manners is to use good manners yourself.

   b. The general's **strategy** was to trap the enemy troops by surrounding them in the course of the night.

8 **tedious**
(tē'-dē-əs)
-adjective

   a. Is anything more **tedious** than lugging a heavy sack of clothes to a laundromat and then waiting forever for the laundry to be done?

   b. John found the homework assignment very **tedious**; the questions were dull and repetitious.

9 **transaction**
(tran-sak'-shən)
-noun

   a. A police officer spotted the **transaction** between the drug dealer and an addict.

   b. Among some business people, a **transaction** is finalized with a handshake. These business deals are never put in writing.

10 **vital**
(vīt'-l)
-adjective

   a. Water is **vital** to the survival of all living things.

   b. For Teresa to pass her math course, it is **vital** that she pass the final exam.

Matching Words and Definitions

Check your understanding of the ten words by matching each word with its definition. Look back at the sentences in "Ten Words in Context" as needed to decide on the meaning of each word.

_d_	1. **consequence**	a.	occurring, existing, or done at the same time
_j_	2. **destiny**	b.	to lessen or become smaller
_h_	3. **detain**	c.	a method; plan
_b_	4. **diminish**	d.	a result
_i_	5. **procrastinate**	e.	a business deal or action; exchange of money, goods, or services
_a_	6. **simultaneous**	f.	necessary; important
_c_	7. **strategy**	g.	boring; uninteresting because of great length, slowness, or repetition
_g_	8. **tedious**	h.	delay; to keep from continuing
_e_	9. **transaction**	i.	to put off doing something until later
_f_	10. **vital**	j.	fate; an unavoidable occurrence

CAUTION: Do not go any further until you are sure the above answers are correct. If you have studied the "Ten Words in Context," you will know how to match each word. Then you can use the matches to help you in the following practices. Your goal is to reach a point where you don't need to check definitions at all.

➤ *Sentence Check 1*

Complete each sentence below with the most suitable word from the box. Use each word once.

consequence	destiny	detain	diminish	procrastinate
simultaneous	strategy	tedious	transaction	vital

1. The ___*transaction*___ at the checkout counter was delayed by an incorrect price label.

2. The afternoon sunshine caused the snowman's height to ___*diminish*___ from six feet to three.

3. To ___*procrastinate*___ is to follow the old saying, "Never do today what you can put off until tomorrow."

4. As a ___*consequence*___ of his staying out too late, Wilson wasn't allowed out for a week.

5. The dancers' movements were meant to be ___*simultaneous*___. But when the ballerina leaped, her partner failed to move in time to catch her.

6. Helen's chess ___*strategy*___ is to make her moves so quickly that her opponent believes she's an expert.

7. After his wife died in a fire, Ryan felt such tragedies are decided by ___*destiny*___. He refused to believe her death was meaningless.

8. The secret agent paid for information he thought was ___*vital*___ to our national safety, but he had been tricked into buying useless knowledge.

9. "If my science teacher didn't ___*detain*___ us past the bell every day, I wouldn't be late for my next class," explained George.

10. To make raking autumn leaves less ___*tedious*___, my sister and I took turns jumping into the newly created piles.

   Now check your answers to these questions by turning to page 166. Going over the answers carefully will help you prepare for the next two checks, for which answers are not given.

➤ Sentence Check 2

Complete each sentence below with two words from the following list. Use each word once.

consequence	destiny	detain	diminish	procrastinate
simultaneous	strategy	tedious	transaction	vital

1-2. Before the tug-of-war started, the blue team decided on a ___strategy___: each time the captain shouted "Go!" all team members would give a hard __simultaneous__ pull.

3-4. "I'm sorry to ___detain___ you," the salesman said, "but any ___transaction___ involving payment with a personal check takes longer than a cash purchase."

5-6. The __consequence__ of poor nutrition is illness. A balanced diet is ___vital___ for health.

7-8. Unfortunately, it doesn't help to __procrastinate__ in paying your bills—putting them off doesn't make them ___diminish___ or disappear.

9-10. "This job is so ___tedious___ I'm afraid I'll die of boredom," said the file clerk. "Is it my ___destiny___ to put things in alphabetical order for the rest of my life?"

➤ Final Check: Procrastinator

Here is a final opportunity for you to strengthen your knowledge of the ten words. First read the following passage carefully. Then fill in each blank with a word from the box at the top of this page. (Context clues will help you figure out which word goes in which blank.) Use each word once.

One of these days there is going to be a "new me": I will no longer (1) _procrastinate_ . I'm making this my New Year's resolution. Well, yes, I know it's March. I was going to make this resolution in January, but all that Christmas shopping and cookie-baking (2)___detain___(e)d me. In February I figured out a (3)___strategy___ to help me stop putting things off, and I'll get around to it soon because I know that it's (4)___vital___ for me to change my ways. My problem is that some jobs are so (5)___tedious___ that just thinking of them makes me want to yawn. But I know that the (6)_consequence_ of putting things off is that nothing actually gets done. And once I get started on my New Year's resolution, my tendency to delay things will surely gradually (7)___diminish___. I'll finish every household project and financial (8)___transaction___ that I start. Maybe I'll even make a list of (9)_simultaneous_ activities, such as sewing while watching TV, or cleaning my junk drawer while I talk to my mother on the phone. I'd make a list now if I could just find a pen. I was going to buy pens yesterday, but I figured I'd be at the mall on Friday, so why make a special trip? I'll make the list later. Oh well, maybe it's just my (10)___destiny___ to put things off.

> **SCORES:** Sentence Check 2 _____ %   Final Check _____ %

Enter your scores above and in the vocabulary performance chart on the inside back cover of the book.

Previewing the Word Parts

Common word parts—also known as *prefixes, suffixes, and roots*—are used in forming many words in English. This page will introduce you to ten common word parts.

Try to match each word part on the left with its definition on the right. Use the words in parentheses as hints to help you guess the meanings. If you can't decide on an answer, leave the space blank. Your purpose here is just to get a sense of the ten word parts and what you may know about them. (You'll have another chance to try this exercise after considering the word parts in context.)

Word Parts

_j_ 1. **-able** (comfortable, reliable)

_c_ 2. **cent-, centi-** (cents, century)

_a_ 3. **in-** (insane, invisible)

_b_ 4. **-logy, -ology** (biology, astrology)

_g_ 5. **mal-** (malpractice, malignant)

_e_ 6. **man** (manual, manuscript)

_i_ 7. **mem** (memory, memo)

_f_ 8. **mono-, mon-** (monotone, monopoly)

_h_ 9. **port** (portable, transportation)

_d_ 10. **therm-, thermo-** (thermometer, thermal)

Definitions

a. not

b. study, science, theory

c. hundred

d. heat

e. by hand

f. one

g. bad, badly

h. carry

i. remember

j. able to

Now go on to "Ten Word Parts in Context" on the next page. Working through this chapter will help you to strengthen your knowledge of the word parts you already know and to master the word parts you're only half sure of, or don't know at all.

Keep in mind that learning word parts can pay several dividends. Word parts can help with the spelling and pronunciation of many words. They can also help you to unlock the meanings of unfamiliar words.

Ten Word Parts in Context

Figure out the meanings of the following ten word parts by looking *closely and carefully* at the context in which they appear. Doing so will prepare you for the matching test and the practices on the two pages that follow.

1 -able
   a. The couch was too hard to make a **comfortable** bed.
   b. Come on, now. Can you really say a movie like *Slaughter in the Subway* is **enjoyable?**

2 cent-, centi-
   a. The 19th **century** didn't start in 1900 or 1800. It started in 1801 and ran through 1900.
   b. The **centipede** doesn't really have a hundred feet; it just has so many that it seems there are a hundred of them.

3 in-
   a. The glass on the door was so clean that it was **invisible,** which explains why I walked into the door instead of opening it.
   b. "Only an **inexperienced** burglar leaves fingerprints," said the detective.

4 -logy, -ology
   a. "I'd probably major in **biology,**" Cybil explained, "if I didn't have to kill those little frogs."
   b. In a famous **psychology** experiment, people were tested to see if they would follow instructions to give other people electrical shocks.

5 mal-
   a. What should we do about the many neglected and **maltreated** children?
   b. When the doctor gave his patient a medicine with harmful side effects, the patient sued for **malpractice.**

6 man
   a. Mark Twain may have been the first author ever to give a publisher an entire **manuscript** that was typed, rather than handwritten.
   b. The man's rough hands show he's done much **manual** labor.

7 mem
   a. I wrote a memo to help me **remember** what to do today, but I forgot where I put it.
   b. Against the smooth, black wall of the Vietnam War **memorial,** every flower left in memory of a loved one shows up brightly.

8 mono-, mon-
   a. When Pastor Brook preached in a **monotone,** he found his congregation snoring in stereo.
   b. Human "wolves" may play the field, but actual wolves are **monogamous,** having one mate throughout their lives.

9 port
   a. **Porters** on early African safaris earned a penny a day carrying sixty-pound bundles of equipment and food.
   b. "My daughter is overly tender toward others," said Reginald. "She feeds the hungry and **supports** both the weak and her husband."

10 therm-, thermo-
   a. In the fall, a **thermos** full of hot soup is a great addition to any hiking gear.
   b. An electronic **thermometer** beeps when the body heat has been fully measured.

Matching Word Parts and Definitions

Check your understanding of the ten word parts by matching each with its definition. See also the suggestions on page 4.

_j_	1. **-able**	a.	not
_c_	2. **cent-, centi-**	b.	study, science, theory
_a_	3. **in-**	c.	hundred
_b_	4. **-logy, -ology**	d.	heat
_g_	5. **mal-**	e.	by hand
_e_	6. **man**	f.	one
_i_	7. **mem**	g.	bad, badly
_f_	8. **mono-, mon-**	h.	carry
_h_	9. **port**	i.	remember
_d_	10. **therm-, thermo-**	j.	able to

CAUTION: Do not go any further until you are sure the above answers are correct. If you have studied the "Ten Word Parts in Context," you will know how to match each word part. Then you can use the matches to help you in the following practices. Your goal is to reach a point where you don't need to check definitions at all.

➤ Sentence Check 1

Complete each partial word in the following sentences with a word part from the box. Use each word part only once. You may want to check off each word part as you use it.

-able	centi-	in-	-ology	mal-
man	mem	mono-	port	thermo-

1. The dogs had been fed so poorly that they suffered from (. . . *nutrition*) __malnutrition__ .

2. Five (. . . *meters*) ___centimeters___ means 5/100 of a meter—the length of a long eyebrow.

3. (*Crimin*. . .) ___Criminology___ now includes the study of computer crime.

4. I always feel unsafe on a (. . . *rail*) ___monorail___. I think a train is more safe running on two rails than on one.

5. To (. . . *orize*) ___memorize___ the names of the five Great Lakes, remember "HOMES," which is made up of the lakes' initials: Huron, Ontario, Michigan, Erie, and Superior.

6. Automatic transmission makes driving easier, but repairs on (. . .*ual*) ___manual___ transmissions are cheaper.

7. Explorer Robert Scott and his party died in Antarctica because they brought (. . . *adequate*) ___inadequate___ supplies of food and fuel.

8. The union representative objected, saying, "Asking the workers to take a 20 percent pay cut would be (*laugh*. . .) ___laughable___ if it weren't so awful."

9. A (. . . *gram*) ___thermogram___, or heat picture, shows that a single cigarette can lower the temperature of the smoker's hands by six degrees, by reducing the blood flow.

10. On May 14, 1856, the U.S. Cavalry (*im*. . .*ed*) ___imported___ thirty-three camels from Egypt to use in chasing Indians across Texas.

Now check your answers to these questions by turning to page 166. Going over the answers carefully will help you prepare for the next two checks, for which answers are not given.

➤ *Sentence Check 2*

Complete each word in the sentences below with a word part from the following list. Use each word part once.

-able	cent-	in-	-ology	mal-
man	mem	mon, mono-	port	therm-

1-2. "There is room for only one (. . . *arch*) ___monarch___ in this country," announced the king. "Anyone who disagrees with me will get free sea (*trans . . . ation*) _transportation_ —without a boat."

3-4. In 1963, during the (. . . *ennial*) ___centennial___ of the Civil War (1861-1865), we visited a (. . . *orial*) ___memorial___ to some of the soldiers who had died.

5-6. While others study (*climat. . .*) ___climatology___, I ignore the weather and simply leave my (. . .*ostat*) ___thermostat___ set at a constant, comfortable 68 degrees.

7-8. I (. . . *icure*) ___manicure___ my nails the (. . . *expensive*) ___inexpensive___ way—by biting them.

9-10. It was (*debat. . .*) ___debatable___ whether the cake looked so weird because the oven (. . . *functioned*) _malfunctioned_ or because I forgot an ingredient.

➤ *Final Check:* King of Cats

Here is a final opportunity for you to strengthen your knowledge of the ten word parts. First read the following passage carefully. Then complete each partial word in the parentheses below with a word from the box at the top of this page. (Context clues will help you figure out which word part goes in which blank.) Use each word part once.

They called him King of Cats. He was young and so hot-headed that he had an (. . . *ability*) (1)___inability___ to keep his temper. He lived in an Italian city baked by (. . . *al*) (2)___thermal___ winds in the summer. Life in that hot city was never (. . . *tonous*) (3)___monotonous___ when his street gang met a rival gang. (*Re. . . s*) (4)___Reports___ of bloodshed often followed such meetings. He was raised to fight for his family, including his beautiful cousin. He was willing to do anything to keep her safe from insult or (. . . *treatment*) (5)_maltreatment_.

This girl fell in love with the leader of a rival gang. Perhaps today (*psych . . .*) (6)___psychology___ could explain why. At the time, it seemed she was simply (. . . *ipulated*) (7)___manipulated___ by fate to fall in love with someone (*unaccept . . .*) (8)___unacceptable___ to her relatives. One (. . . *orable*) (9)___memorable___ afternoon of that sad year in the 16th (. . . *ury*) (10)___century___, blades flashed. The King of Cats stabbed a member of that rival gang. In return, his cousin's lover cut him dead.

The King of Cats' name was Tybalt Capulet. His cousin was called Juliet; her lover was Romeo.

SCORES: Sentence Check 2 _____% Final Check _____%

Enter your scores above and in the vocabulary performance chart on the inside back cover of the book.

UNIT FOUR: Test 1

PART A
Choose the word that best completes each sentence and write it in the space provided.

1. frugal
   tedious
   elaborate
   plausible

   It may not seem ____*plausible*____, but it's true—some people need only fifteen minutes of sleep a day.

2. simultaneous
   liberal
   mediocre
   frugal

   In ____*simultaneous*____ translation, words are translated as they are spoken.

3. adapt
   retain
   provoke
   allude

   Usually, a bee will not sting unless you ____*provoke*____ it first by swatting at it.

4. strategies
   reprimands
   destinies
   rituals

   In kindergarten, an afternoon nap was required. Yet, in English class, my napping has earned me ____*reprimands*____.

5. tedious
   impulsive
   frugal
   sadistic

   Many ____*frugal*____ shoppers buy soy-based foods because they are inexpensive sources of protein.

6. notable
   mediocre
   vital
   elite

   The singer's voice is only ____*mediocre*____, but he's very popular because his personality is so appealing.

7. ritual
   immunity
   destiny
   ridicule

   For an Arab Moslem man, the entire divorce ____*ritual*____ consists of announcing to his wife before two witnesses, "I divorce you."

8. exotic
   indulgent
   alleged
   indifferent

   Although the police report mentioned an ____*alleged*____ break-in, the gold theft may actually have been an "inside" job.

9. exile
   stereotype
   strategy
   immunity

   Tokyo, Japan, has a simple ____*strategy*____ for fitting as many people as possible onto rush-hour trains: Men are paid to push people on.

10. detain
    recede
    query
    allude

    My teacher meant to ____*query*____, "Why did you miss the history lecture?"
    Instead he asked, "Why did you hiss the mystery lecture?"

125

11. **procrastinate** Why doesn't crabgrass ever _____ *diminish* _____? Because every time you yank some out,
    diminish
    revoke you spread its seeds, causing more crabgrass to grow.
    coerce

12. **stereotype** Although buying a pair of panty hose seems like a minor _____ *transaction* _____, the
    essence
    query customer gets about four miles of thread knitted into some three million loops.
    transaction

13. **refuted** Experts have _____ *refuted* _____ the idea that giant redwood trees are the oldest living
    coereced
    emerged things on Earth. Some pine trees, aged about 4,600 years, are now known to be older.
    provoked

PART B
Circle C if the italicized word is used **correctly**. Circle I if the word is used **incorrectly**.

C (I) 14. A tornado's winds can *recede* to speeds as high as 200 miles an hour.

C (I) 15. Arthur came down with the flu because he has a built-in *immunity* to it.

(C) I 16. *Elite* members of our society include movie stars and athletes.

C (I) 17. The *sadistic* herring gull gives a special call that invites other gulls to share its food.

(C) I 18. As a *gesture* of respect, my boyfriend makes a point of greeting my parents and grandmother whenever he comes to call for me.

(C) I 19. Although most *notable* as a scientist, Albert Einstein was also well known as a spokesman for world peace.

(C) I 20. The owl can hardly move its eyes. So the ability to turn its head nearly completely around is *vital* to its survival.

(C) I 21. Before eyeglasses were invented, some people whose vision was *impaired* looked through clear gemstones shaped like lenses.

C (I) 22. The Liberty Bell, so *exotic* to all Americans, was once offered for sale as scrap metal.

(C) I 23. If you're entering a movie theater with a crowd, it's *shrewd* to bear left. Since most people head right, you'll get a better choice of seats that way.

C (I) 24. The old belief that men prefer blonde women to brunettes was *affirmed* by a poll of college students: Most males liked brunettes better than blondes.

(C) I 25. My brother *ridiculed* me for talking on the phone so much. He would holler to the family, "Get a doctor! A phone is growing out of Stacy's head."

SCORE: (Number correct) _____ x 4 = _____ %

Enter your scores above and in the vocabulary performance chart on the inside back cover of the book.

UNIT FOUR: Test 2

PART A
Complete each sentence with a word from the box. Use each word once.

adapt	coerce	elaborate	essence
exile	indulgent	procrastinate	reciprocated
recur	retained	reverted	stereotype
tactic			

1. After my brother gave me the measles, I ___reciprocated___ by giving him the mumps.

2. The ___elaborate___ dollhouse included many realistic details, such as tiny lamps, clocks, and flowers in vases.

3. The ___essence___ of a thunderstorm is energy—energy sometimes equal to that of a dozen atomic bombs.

4. Although mono doesn't generally ___recur___ in the same individual, some people do get the disease more than once.

5. There's a club for people who like to ___procrastinate___. They haven't met yet because they keep postponing their first meeting.

6. The ___stereotype___ of the cowboy is of a rough and romantic fighter, but most cowboys spent their days working steadily at a series of routine chores.

7. A native author had to leave China to avoid being imprisoned. He was forced into___exile___ for attacking the Chinese government in his writings.

8. On New Year's Eve I decided to stop eating chocolate, but by January 4th I ___reverted___ to my old ways—stocking up on on Mars bars and M&M's.

9. Trained dogs help deaf people ___adapt___ to a silent world by alerting them to the sounds of such things as doorbells and smoke alarms.

10. Many students have used the ___tactic___ of blaming the computer for their missed deadlines. They say, for example, "It erased my whole paper."

11. In ancient Rome, some of the wealthiest and most self-___indulgent___ people powdered their hair with pure gold dust every day.

12. Built of white marble and decorated with gems, the famous Taj Mahal of India has___retained___ its beauty for more than three hundred years.

13. Because a thief might ___coerce___ you into handing over a wallet, carry an extra one with little money, an old ID card, and out-of-date credit cards.

PART B
Circle **C** if the italicized word is used **correctly.** Circle **I** if the word is used **incorrectly.**

C (I) 14. Judging by the smile of relief on his face, the X-ray *dismayed* Dr. Fry.

C (I) 15. Iris is so *impulsive* that she won't even take a step outside without first listening to a weather report.

(C) I 16. I was *skeptical* when the salesman said I could get a month's worth of frozen food for under fifty dollars a person.

(C) I 17. Because so many of the rain forests are being destroyed, the *destiny* of many animals and insects may be to die out.

C (I) 18. People who get around in wheelchairs are bound to be *indifferent* to a new wheelchair that follows spoken instructions.

C (I) 19. According to a study, most working couples spend a *liberal* amount of time talking with their children—on average, less than a minute a day.

(C) I 20. The poem *alludes* to so many 18th-century events that it is difficult for today's readers to get its full meaning.

(C) I 21. The construction company had its building license *revoked* when its materials were found to be dangerously weak.

C (I) 22. Early Latin American Indians had a *tedious* way of making the world's first sneakers. They simply dipped their feet into liquid rubber straight from the tree.

(C) I 23. A camel's hump stores fat that breaks down into water. As a *consequence,* a camel can survive for as long as two weeks without drinking.

(C) I 24. Today, those who walk or drive in the city are *detained* by stoplights and traffic. In the future, however, moving sidewalks may do away with the need for buses and cars in the city.

C (I) 25. Every day, the original Declaration of Independence is on display in a glass case. Every evening, however, it *emerges* into an underground container that resists extreme heat or cold, water, fire, and explosions.

SCORE: (Number correct) _____ x 4 = _____ %

Enter your scores above and in the vocabulary performance chart on the inside back cover of the book.

UNIT FOUR: Test 3

PART A
Complete each sentence in a way that clearly shows you understand the meaning of the boldfaced word. Take a minute to plan your answer before you write.

Example: A **mediocre** essay is likely to _____ *receive a grade of C.* _____

1. One especially **tedious** activity is _____ *(Answers will vary.)* _____

2. A cab driver might respond to a **liberal** tip by _____

3. When the heater broke, I **adapted** to the sudden drop in temperature by _____

4. A **tactic** for dieting is _____

5. When Gina invited Daniel out for coffee, he **reciprocated** by _____

6. One **impulsive** thing I once did was _____

7. An **indulgent** parent might react to a screaming child by _____

8. I often **procrastinate** when _____

9. To achieve my career goals, it is **vital** that I _____

10. A **skeptical** response to "I love you" is " _____

PART B

After each boldfaced word are a *synonym* (a word that means the same as the boldfaced word), an *antonym* (a word that means the opposite of the boldfaced word), and a word that is neither. Mark the antonym with an *A*.

Example: **plausible**	_____ believable	_A_ doubtful	_____ soft
11. **retain**	_A_ lose	_____ keep	_____ limit
12. **frugal**	_____ hasty	_A_ wasteful	_____ thrifty
13. **consequence**	_____ pattern	_____ result	_A_ cause
14. **impair**	_____ weaken	_____ call	_A_ strengthen
15. **ridicule**	_A_ praise	_____ mock	_____ disprove

PART C

Use five of the following ten words in sentences. Make it clear that you know the meaning of the word you use. Feel free to use the past tense or plural form of a word.

coerce	**diminish**	**emerge**	**gesture**	**indifferent**
recur	**ritual**	**sadistic**	**shrewd**	**strategy**

16. _____ *(Answers will vary.)* _____

_____

17. _____

_____

18. _____

_____

19. _____

_____

20. _____

SCORE: (Number correct) _____ x 5 = _____ %

Enter your scores above and in the vocabulary performance chart on the inside back cover of the book.

UNIT FOUR: Test 4 (Word Parts)

PART A

Listed in the left-hand column below are ten common word parts, along with words in which the parts are used. In each blank, write in the letter of the correct definition on the right.

Word Parts   **Definitions**

_c_ 1. **-able**   affordable, reliable   a. carry

_d_ 2. **cent-, centi-**   century, cent   b. by hand

_e_ 3. **in-**   invisible, inhuman   c. able to

_g_ 4. **-ology, -logy**   astrology, biology   d. hundred

_i_ 5. **mal-**   maltreat, malnourish   e. not

_b_ 6. **man**   manual, manuscript   f. heat

_j_ 7. **mem**   memo, memorial   g. study, science, theory

_h_ 8. **mono-, mon-**   monogamy, monotheism   h. one

_a_ 9. **port**   porter, export   i. bad, badly

_f_ 10. **therm-, thermo-** thermometer, thermostat   j. remember

PART B

Find the word part that correctly completes each word. Then write the full word in the blank space. Not every word part will be used.

-able	cent-	in-	-ology	mal-
man	mem	mono-	port	therm-

11. Someone who knows we all make mistakes invented an (*eras. . .*) ___erasable___ ink.

12. (*Soci. . .*) ___Sociology___ is the study of the origins, development, and institutions of human society.

13. One mental patient has such a damaged (*. . . ory*) ___memory___ that he can't remember what happened only a few minutes before.

14. After working so hard on my flower garden, I wish it were (*. . . able*) ___portable___. Then I could take it with me next month when I move to a new house.

15. People who can't resist yanking their hair out are not (*. . . sane*) ___insane___. They simply have an illness that can be cured with therapy.

PART C
Use your knowledge of word parts to determine the meaning of the boldfaced words. Circle the letter of each meaning.

16. My grandmother will be a **centenarian** next month, so we're having a huge party.

    a. bride   (b) 100-year-old   c. great-great-grandmother

17. The first clay pot I ever made was very **malformed.**

    a. formed too small   (b) poorly formed   c. without form

18. Tarzan's vocabulary included many **monosyllabic** words: "Me Tarzan. You Jane. Come. We find Boy."

    (a) one-syllable   b. few-syllable   c. short-syllable

19. The sheriff reached for **manacles** to put on the violently drunk driver.

    a. ropes   b. chains   (c) handcuffs

20. For silly fun, my family used to go on picnics in the winter. Mother would pack steaming thick soup in a **thermos** jug.

    a. a plastic jug   b. a jug that can be carried (c) a jug that keeps things warm

SCORE: (Number correct) _____ x 5 = _____ %

Enter your scores above and in the vocabulary performance chart on the inside back cover of the book.

Previewing the Words

Find out how many of the ten words in this chapter you already know. Try to complete each sentence with the most suitable word from the list below. Use each word once.

Leave a sentence blank rather than guessing at an answer. Your purpose here is just to get a sense of the ten words and what you may know about them.

discriminate	dismal	dispense	profound	severity
site	subside	summon	theoretical	vocation

1. Women now take on many ___*vocation*___s once thought to be mainly for men, including carpentry and firefighting.

2. The ___*severity*___ of the judge's sentence—death by hanging—shocked the family of the defendant.

3. Billy Joel stepped onto the stage, and the audience's cheering didn't ___*subside*___ for ten minutes.

4. I can use the geometry formulas, but I don't understand the ___*theoretical*___ basis for them.

5. The principal liked to ___*summon*___ students to his office by calling their names over the loudspeaker.

6. The ___*site*___ of the future library was only a block from the present library.

7. Martin Luther King's "I Have a Dream" speech had a ___*profound*___ effect on me. I still cry whenever I hear it.

8. Andy's favorite gift on his fifth birthday was a machine that would ___*dispense*___ a gumball when a penny was put in.

9. Jessica, tone deaf, can't ___*discriminate*___ between good music and bad. To her, a song by Stevie Wonder is barely more satisfying than one by a local band.

10. This room is too ___*dismal*___. It needs a party to brighten it up.

Now check your answers by turning to page 166. Fix any mistakes and fill in any blank spaces by writing in the correct answers. By doing so, you will complete this introduction to the ten words.

You're now ready to strengthen your knowledge of the words you already know and to master the words you're only half sure of, or don't know at all. Turn to the next page.

Ten Words in Context

Figure out the meanings of the following ten words by looking *closely and carefully* at the context in which the words appear. Doing so will prepare you for the matching test and the practices on the two pages that follow.

1 **discriminate**
(di-skrim'-ə-nāt')
-verb

   a. It's easy to **discriminate** between frozen and fresh vegetables—fresh taste much better.

   b. Tests show that women tend to **discriminate** better among colors than men. Cherry red, cranberry red, and purplish red are all simply dark red to many men.

2 **dismal**
(diz'-məl)
-adjective

   a. Most New York subway stations are **dismal** compared to the cheerful stations in Washington, D.C.

   b. "It is a **dismal,** rainy day," Mona told her disappointed children. "But we don't have to cancel the picnic—we can have it on the kitchen floor."

3 **dispense**
(di-spens')
-verb

   a. The broken soda machine **dispensed** either a cup or soda, but not both together.

   b. Restroom soap holders that are supposed to **dispense** liquid soap at each pull seem to be empty most of the time.

4 **profound**
(prə-found')
-adjective

   a. The death of a spouse can cause **profound** depression that, in some cases, can even lead to the death of the partner.

   b. Ever since her stepfather slapped her mother, Stacy has had a **profound** hatred of him.

5 **severity**
(sə-ver'-ə-tē)
-noun

   a. The **severity** of the fire could be seen in the burnt, smoking ruins of the once beautiful building.

   b. Mark believes the **severity** of his punishment was too great. A hundred hours of weekend trash cleanup seemed too harsh a penalty for throwing two Coke cans onto the highway.

6 **site**
(sīt)
-noun

   a. The oldest private home in the New England town was named an historical **site.**

   b. Wounded Knee, S.D., is the **site** of a 1971 conflict between the federal government and the Sioux Indians.

7 **subside**
(səb-sīd')
-verb

   a. When I'm really furious, a walk around the block helps the anger **subside.**

   b. Consuela sat in the car until the storm **subsided.** Then she dashed up the sidewalk and into school.

8 **summon**
(sum'-ən)
-verb

   a When the king couldn't sleep, he would **summon** the court clown to entertain him.

   b. When my father quietly **summoned** me to the den, I realized that he was angry about something.

9 **theoretical**
(thē'-ə-ret'-i-kəl)
-adjective

   a. Einstein's theory that time is relative is largely **theoretical**—it has yet to be fully proved.

   b. The teacher explained the **theoretical** basis for the chemistry formula before the class tried to prove it in an experiment.

10 **vocation**
(vō-kā'-shən)
-noun

   a. Raising German shepherds was just a hobby for Louise. Her **vocation** was library science.

   b. If you can't decide on a career, you might wish to take a test that reveals which **vocations** you're suited for.

Matching Words and Definitions

Check your understanding of the ten words by matching each word with its definition. Look back at the sentences in "Ten Words in Context" as needed to decide on the meaning of each word.

_b_	1. **discriminate**	a.	deeply felt or realized
_f_	2. **dismal**	b.	to see the difference(s); distinguish
_h_	3. **dispense**	c.	the spot where a place or event was, is, or will be located
_a_	4. **profound**	d.	a profession or occupation
_i_	5. **severity**	e.	about or based on theory (as opposed to practice or practical use); limited to theory
_c_	6. **site**	f.	gloomy; cheerless; depressing
_j_	7. **subside**	g.	to send for; order to come; call to come
_g_	8. **summon**	h.	to give out in portions or amounts
_e_	9. **theoretical**	i.	a harshness; intensity; seriousness; harmful extent
_d_	10. **vocation**	j.	to become less active; calm down; become less in amount or degree

CAUTION: Do not go any further until you are sure the above answers are correct. If you have studied the "Ten Words in Context," you will know how to match each word. Then you can use the matches to help you in the following practices. Your goal is to reach a point where you don't need to check definitions at all.

➤ Sentence Check 1

Complete each sentence below with the most suitable word from the box. Use each word once.

discriminate	dismal	dispense	profound	severity
site	subside	summon	theoretical	vocation

1. Most people cannot ____*discriminate*____ between an alligator and a crocodile.

2. Today there is a ____*profound*____ interest in the rights of animals.

3. The waves were enormous in the bay, but they began to ____*subside*____ as the boat moved out into open water.

4. I thought I was in trouble when my boss ____*summon*____(e)d me to her office—until she told me I was getting a raise.

5. Among the most dangerous ____*vocation*____s are deep-sea diving, mining, and construction.

6. Kyle was annoyed by the ____*dismal*____ news that mono would keep him out of college for a whole semester.

7. Do you think food machines at public schools should ____*dispense*____ only nutritious foods, such as fruit and juices?

8. Medication should match the ____*severity*____ of an illness. For example, a powerful medicine isn't needed for a cold.

9. Astronomers are often limited to ____*theoretical*____ explanations because their subject matter cannot be easily examined or tested.

10. Although the ____*site*____ where the hiker claimed a spaceship had landed was burned, no one believed him.

Now check your answers to these questions by turning to page 166. Going over the answers carefully will help you prepare for the next two checks, for which answers are not given.

➤ Sentence Check 2

Complete each sentence below with two words from the following list. Use each word once.

discriminate	dismal	dispense	profound	severity
site	subside	summon	theoretical	vocation

1-2. My visit to the school for retarded children had a _____*profound*_____ effect on me. I knew that day that my _____*vocation*_____ would be in special education.

3-4. It was not until I was ten miles away from the _____*site*_____ of the accident that my shaking began to _____*subside*_____.

5-6. The movie was meant to be a dark comedy, but I found it to be _____*dismal*_____. I often couldn't _____*discriminate*_____ between lines that were meant to be funny and lines that were just depressing.

7-8. If you have a question on the principles of this music, we will have to _____*summon*_____ Mr. Burns from his office. He has studied music for years. I can play the music, but I have no _____*theoretical*_____ knowledge.

9-10. Some hospitals now allow patients to judge the _____*severity*_____ of their own pain and to _____*dispense*_____ small amounts of medication to themselves as necessary.

➤ Final Check: Changes in View

Here is a final opportunity for you to strengthen your knowledge of the ten words. First read the following passage carefully. Then fill in each blank with a word from the box at the top of this page. (Context clues will help you figure out which word goes in which blank.) Use each word once.

What an education I got yesterday! I am studying to be a nurse. Part of my preparation for this (1)_____*vocation*_____ is (2)_____*theoretical*_____ and part is practical experience. Yesterday, after weeks of studying about mental illness in textbooks, I began my training in a mental hospital. I was scared. I imagined (3)_____*dismal*_____, dark rooms where people sat staring and drooling. I pictured screaming patients trying to hurt me so badly that I would have to (4)_____*summon*_____ the guards. But yesterday my views of mental hospitals went through a (5)_____*profound*_____ change. First of all, the (6)_____*site*_____ of the hospital is at the edge of a lovely small town, and its grounds are green and neat. When I arrived there, I was brought to a big, cheerful room where patients were talking, playing ping-pong or cards, or doing craft projects.

I spoke to one patient. She seemed like a nice, normal person who happened to have problems. She told me her illness had been of much greater (7)_____*severity*_____ when she first came to this hospital. At that time, she could not always (8)_____*discriminate*_____ between what was real and what she imagined. Like many patients, she was often upset and confused. But the doctors put her on medicine, which the nurses still (9)_____*dispense*_____ three times a day. The medicine, as well as talks with the doctors, nurses and other patients, have helped her illness (10)_____*subside*_____. Perhaps our conversation was helpful to her; I know it helped me. Now I'm thinking about working in the mental health field after I get my nursing degree.

> **SCORES:** Sentence Check 2 _____% Final Check _____%

Enter your scores above and in the vocabulary performance chart on the inside back cover of the book.

Previewing the Words

Find out how many of the ten words in this chapter you already know. Try to complete each sentence with the most suitable word from the list below. Use each word once.

Leave a sentence blank rather than guessing at an answer. Your purpose here is just to get a sense of the ten words and what you may know about them.

ascend	finite	infinite	inflict	ingenious
initiate	literally	lure	mania	nostalgia

1. A(n) _____ingenious_____ person did away with the need for can openers by creating the pop-top can.

2. There are so many stars in the sky that their number seems _____infinite_____.

3. By working hard, Lisa quickly _____ascend_____(e)d the ladder of success, from secretary to administrative assistant to office manager.

4. I'm so clumsy that I often _____inflict_____ pain on myself, like when I cut my finger instead of a bagel.

5. We decided to _____initiate_____ a campaign to improve the school's food by asking other students to sign a petition.

6. Bar managers sometimes _____lure_____ male customers by featuring waitresses in short, low-cut outfits.

7. Barbara's mother has such a _____mania_____ for Willie Nelson that she constantly plays his music.

8. When Carey said she'd given an arm and leg for tickets to a Rolling Stones concert, her little boy burst out crying—he took her _____literally_____.

9. Some say that the _____finite_____ years we live make life more meaningful, that unlimited years would make life less significant.

10. Now that I live far from home, I'm filled with _____nostalgia_____ for my early Christmases, when my family was all together.

Now check your answers by turning to page 166. Fix any mistakes and fill in any blank spaces by writing in the correct answers. By doing so, you will complete this introduction to the ten words.

You're now ready to strengthen your knowledge of the words you already know and to master the words you're only half sure of, or don't know at all. Turn to the next page.

Ten Words in Context

Figure out the meanings of the following ten words by looking *closely and carefully* at the context in which the words appear. Doing so will prepare you for the matching test and the practices on the two pages that follow.

1 **ascend**
(ə-send')
-*verb*

   a. The express elevator **ascends** directly from the lobby to the twentieth floor.

   b. Edgar is the boss's son, so he expects to **ascend** to the presidency of the company after his father retires.

2 **finite**
(fī'-nīt)
-*adjective*

   a. The earth's supply of natural resources is **finite,** not unlimited.

   b. Judging by their endless requests for money, my children don't seem to realize our income is **finite.**

3 **infinite**
(in'-fə-nit)
-*adjective*

   a. Scientists no longer believe the universe is **infinite;** they now actually think it has limits.

   b. Dealing with my baby brother, who cries a lot, requires almost an **infinite** amount of patience on the part of my parents.

4 **inflict**
(in-flikt')
-*verb*

   a. When Marge is angry, she tries to **inflict** pain with a cutting remark, a habit that does not make her popular with her classmates.

   b. Loud music can eventually **inflict** permanent damage on the ears.

5 **ingenious**
(in-gēn'-yəs)
-*adjective*

   a. Fran had an **ingenious** plan to sneak out of the house unseen, but it wasn't clever enough to fool her grandmother.

   b. Few people have been as **ingenious** as Thomas Edison, inventor of the electric light, the phonograph, and the movie camera.

6 **initiate**
(i-nish'-ē-āt')
-*verb*

   a. Eric **initiated** a change in his company's hiring policy by suggesting all job openings be advertised.

   b. True leaders **initiate** new practices, rather than simply following other people's programs.

7 **literally**
(lit'-ər-ə-lē)
-*adverb*

   a. As a child, Jan took the term "man in the moon" **literally.** She was sure she saw his eyes, nose and mouth up there.

   b. When I told my nephew to "go fly a kite," I was speaking **literally**—I gave him an eagle kite for his birthday.

8 **lure**
(loor)
-*verb*

   a. The bakery **lured** customers by displaying richly decorated cakes and cookies in its windows.

   b. The music and lights **lured** many teens to the carnival.

9 **mania**
(mā'-nē-ə)
-*noun*

   a. My sister has such a **mania** for bird watching that she once climbed a tree to get a better view of a woodpecker.

   b. Because he's so thin, you'd never guess Ken has a **mania** for chocolate.

10 **nostalgia**
(no-stal'-jə)
-*noun*

   a. Music from the 1940s fills my grandparents with **nostalgia** because it reminds them of their carefree youth.

   b. When he came across an old photo of his Little League team, Jerry felt **nostalgia.**

Matching Words and Definitions

Check your understanding of the ten words by matching each word with its definition. Look back at the sentences in "Ten Words in Context" as needed to decide on the meaning of each word.

_e_	1. **ascend**	a.	to begin something; start
_f_	2. **finite**	b.	without limits; endless
_b_	3. **infinite**	c.	with the exact meaning of the words
_d_	4. **inflict**	d.	to give or cause (something painful)
_g_	5. **ingenious**	e.	to go up; move upward; go from a lower to a higher level or degree
_a_	6. **initiate**	f.	having limits; limited
_c_	7. **literally**	g.	clever; inventive
_j_	8. **lure**	h.	a desire for something in the past
_i_	9. **mania**	i.	an extreme enthusiasm
_h_	10. **nostalgia**	j.	to attract with temptation; tempt

CAUTION: Do not go any further until you are sure the above answers are correct. If you have studied the "Ten Words in Context," you will know how to match each word. Then you can use the matches to help you in the following practices. Your goal is to reach a point where you don't need to check definitions at all.

➤ Sentence Check 1

Complete each sentence below with the most suitable word from the box. Use each word once.

ascend	finite	infinite	inflict	ingenious
initiate	literally	lure	mania	nostalgia

1. We often ___*initiate*___ conversations with routine questions or comments, such as "How are you today?" or "Hello there."

2. Although the English alphabet is ___*finite*___, the possible combinations of its letters are almost endless.

3. Many people think of the dentist as someone who actually likes to ___*inflict*___ pain.

4. Sue has feelings of ___*nostalgia*___ when she thinks about the happy days of her childhood on the farm.

5. The opportunity to be helpful ___*lure*___s people to certain fields, such as nursing and teaching.

6. Shoppers once showed such a ___*mania*___ for Cabbage Patch dolls that stores couldn't keep enough in stock.

7. In spite of the cold and wind, the group continued to ___*ascend*___ toward the snow-covered mountain top.

8. When you see the force of Niagara Falls, the power behind it seems limitless. The force of ocean waves also seems ___*infinite*___.

9. When temperatures are in the 90s, I'm grateful to the ___*ingenious*___ person who invented the air conditioner.

10. Fred kicked the bucket—___*literally*___. So he only stubbed his toe; he didn't die.

Now check your answers to these questions by turning to page 166. Going over the answers carefully will help you prepare for the next two checks, for which answers are not given.

➤ Sentence Check 2

Complete each sentence below with two words from the following list. Use each word once.

ascend	finite	infinite	inflict	ingenious
initiate	literally	lure	mania	nostalgia

1-2. Though the possibilities for life in the universe seem _____*infinite*_____, intelligent life might exist only on our own _____*finite*_____ earth.

3-4. The West continues to _____*lure*_____ my grandfather, who was raised there. Every summer, he feels enough _____*nostalgia*_____ for his youth to drive from Florida to Colorado.

5-6. Some cult followers develop a _____*mania*_____ for pleasing their leader. They will even _____*inflict*_____ injury on themselves to show their loyalty. For example, the teenage girlfriends of the murderer Charles Manson cut a symbol into their foreheads to prove their love.

7-8. A red-tailed hawk can _____*ascend*_____ hundreds of feet into the air by locking its wings open and riding an upward wind. But it merely folds its wings and aims at the ground to _____*initiate*_____ a dive.

9-10. One of the world's most _____*ingenious*_____ scientists, Albert Einstein, _____*literally*_____ gave his brain to science. His will directed that his brain be given to a laboratory in Wichita, Kansas for study.

➤ Final Check: Balloon Flight

Here is a final opportunity for you to strengthen your knowledge of the ten words. First read the following passage carefully. Then fill in each blank with a word from the box at the top of this page. (Context clues will help you figure out which word goes in which blank.) Use each word once.

Human flight was (1)_____*initiated*_____(e)d by a rooster, a duck, and a sheep. A(n) (2)_____*ingenious*_____ inventor got them to try out the first flying machine. For eight minutes, the animals left the (3)_____*finite*_____ world of the ground to fly into the endless sky. The year was 1783, the place was France, and the aircraft was a hot-air balloon. (Because hot air rises, heating the air in the balloon causes it to (4)_____*ascend*_____.)

Since the experience didn't (5)_____*inflict*_____ any serious injury on the animals, three months later the idea of flying (6)_____*lure*_____(e)d a man named de Rozier, who became the first human to look down on the rooftops of Paris from a hot-air balloon.

Jump ahead 125 years to the early 1900's and you find ballooning at its peak. One retail company said of ballooning in its 1910 catalogue: "The whole world is before us in the (7)_____*infinite*_____ loveliness of dawn!" (Daybreak, with its calm air, is the best as well as one of the most beautiful times to fly.)

Today, balloons are still available for rent in some places. For people with (8)_____*nostalgia*_____ for the olden days, before the (9)_____*mania*_____ for faster and faster travel, a balloon flight is a wonderful way to spend some delightful time (10)_____*literally*_____ floating on air.

SCORES: Sentence Check 2 _____%	Final Check _____%

Enter your scores above and in the vocabulary performance chart on the inside back cover of the book.

Previewing the Words

Find out how many of the ten words in this chapter you already know. Try to complete each sentence with the most suitable word from the list below. Use each word once.

Leave a sentence blank rather than guessing at an answer. Your purpose here is just to get a sense of the ten words and what you may know about them.

data	inept	innate	intervene	lament
morbid	obstinate	parallel	perceptive	sedate

1. My two-year-old son is so ___obstinate___ that he refuses to eat his dinner without his Mickey Mouse spoon.

2. Peter is such a(n) ___inept___ dancer that he nearly always slips on the dance floor.

3. At a funeral, mourners are able to ___lament___ a death while feeling the sympathy and support of friends and relatives.

4. My brother is so ___perceptive___ that he knows what I am thinking just by looking at me.

5. Before Phyllis can finish her research paper on acid rain, she needs to collect more ___data___ on its effects.

6. "All of this talk of sickness and death is too ___morbid___ for me," Blake said. "Let's talk about something more cheerful."

7. When two children get into a fight, it is sometimes best not to ___intervene___ but to let them work it out themselves.

8. At four, Sandra could already multiply. Since her talent for math showed up at such an early age, it must be ___innate___.

9. The railroad workers laid the track carefully, making sure the rails were ___parallel___, exactly the same distance apart at every point.

10. On the roller coaster, most of us screamed with excitement and fear. In contrast, Michael somehow was able to look ___sedate___.

Now check your answers by turning to page 166. Fix any mistakes and fill in any blank spaces by writing in the correct answers. By doing so, you will complete this introduction to the ten words.

You're now ready to strengthen your knowledge of the words you already know and to master the words you're only half sure of, or don't know at all. Turn to the next page.

Ten Words in Context

Figure out the meanings of the following ten words by looking *closely and carefully* at the context in which the words appear. Doing so will prepare you for the matching test and the practices on the two pages that follow.

1   **data**
(dā'-tə)
-*noun*

   a. Jodi considers the available **data** on a car—including its fuel economy, safety, and repair record—before deciding whether to buy it.

   b. Jane Goodall collected important **data** on chimpanzees by observing their behavior in the wild.

2   **inept**
(in-ept')
-*adjective*

   a. I am so **inept** at carpentry that a hammer in my hand is a dangerous weapon.

   b. Since the actress was **inept** at playing comic characters, she chose to try out only for dramatic roles.

3   **innate**
(i-nāt')
-*adjective*

   a. Rick's musical ability must be **innate** because even as an infant he could play the piano by ear and make up his own tunes.

   b. Psychologists try to learn how many of our abilities and interests are **innate** and how many of them we gain through experience.

4   **intervene**
(in'-tər-vēn')
-*verb*

   a. The two boxers would have killed each other if the referee hadn't finally decided to **intervene**.

   b. When my parents argue, I get out of the way rather than trying to **intervene**.

5   **lament**
(lə-ment')
-*verb*

   a. When her mother died, Evelyn **lamented** for weeks, crying every day.

   b. Blues songs **lament** loneliness, sadness, and hardship, rather than celebrating happy situations.

6   **morbid**
(môr'-bid)
-*adjective*

   a. Great comedians can make even as **morbid** a topic as murder or terrorism a source of laughter.

   b. The movie, about people dying of cancer, was so **morbid** I felt gloomy for hours after seeing it.

7   **obstinate**
(ob'-stə-nit)
-*adjective*

   a. No matter how I prodded, Andrew remained **obstinate**; he refused to move out of the city.

   b. My father has a reputation for being **obstinate**. But he never insists on having his own way with his sister, who is even more stubborn.

8   **parallel**
(par'-ə-lel')
-*adjective*

   a. On Jeff's first bookcase, the shelves weren't **parallel**—they were two inches closer on the left than on the right.

   b. **Parallel** lines run alongside each other but never meet.

9   **perceptive**
(pər-sep'-tiv)
-*adjective*

   a. Children are more **perceptive** than many people think. They can usually sense their parents' moods and know whether or not it is a good time to ask for something.

   b. Professor Banks is especially **perceptive** when it comes to her students. She always seems to know which ones are under special stress.

10 **sedate**
(si-dāt')
-*adjective*

   a. While the officer wrote out the ticket, Beverly remained **sedate** and even wished the officer a pleasant day. But after he left, she pounded the steering wheel and loudly cursed the police force.

   b. As an experienced surgeon, Dr. Greenbaum remains **sedate** even in an emergency, performing the most complicated operations with complete calm.

Matching Words and Definitions

Check your understanding of the ten words by matching each word with its definition. Look back at the sentences in "Ten Words in Context" as needed to find the meaning of each word.

_e_	1. **data**	a.	to come in or between for some purpose
_i_	2. **inept**	b.	calm; serious and unemotional
_f_	3. **innate**	c.	the same distance apart at every point along a length
_a_	4. **intervene**	d.	understanding and insightful; observant; aware
_g_	5. **lament**	e.	information gathered for a study or a decision
_h_	6. **morbid**	f.	possessed at birth; inborn
_j_	7. **obstinate**	g.	to feel or express sorrow; mourn
_c_	8. **parallel**	h.	causing horror or disgust
_d_	9. **perceptive**	i.	clumsy; unskillful
_b_	10. **sedate**	j.	stubborn

CAUTION: Do not go any further until you are sure the above answers are correct. If you have studied the "Ten Words in Context," you will know how to match each word. Then you can use the matches to help you in the following practices. Your goal is to reach a point where you don't need to check definitions at all.

➤Sentence Check 1

Complete each sentence below with the most suitable word from the box. Use each word once.

data	inept	innate	intervene	lament
morbid	obstinate	parallel	perceptive	sedate

1. For his psychology experiment, Rudy is gathering _____data_____ to show which memory aids work best for students.

2. I'm so _____inept_____ at bowling that I usually roll the ball straight into the gutter.

3. Since his father died, Fred's conversation is often _____morbid_____, overly concerned with such gloomy topics as funerals and death.

4. While my dog gets excited easily, my cat remains _____sedate_____ even when everyone around her is in a whirl of activity.

5. Kwan is so _____perceptive_____ that she often correctly judges a person's character after a brief conversation.

6. When you frame a picture, the picture's edges should be _____parallel_____ to those of the frame, not dipping down or slanting up.

7. The referee had to _____intervene_____ and separate the two hockey players, who had started hitting each other.

8. I tried to convince my son to join the family for dinner, but he was _____obstinate_____, refusing to leave his room no matter what I said.

9. People all over the United States _____lament_____(e)d the death of Martin Luther King, who is now honored with a national holiday on his birthday.

10. Richard's gift for fixing machines seems _____innate_____. Even as a child, he could take one look at a broken machine and know what was wrong with it.

Now check your answers to these questions by turning to page 166. Going over the answers carefully will help you prepare for the next two checks, for which answers are not given.

➤ Sentence Check 2

Complete each sentence below with two words from the following list. Use each word once.

data	inept	innate	intervene	lament
morbid	obstinate	parallel	perceptive	sedate

1-2. As a child, Calvin was _____*sedate*_____, rarely excited or upset. As a teenager, however, he is often angry and ___*obstinate*___—so stubborn that he hates to change his mind.

3-4. Angie's work is quite _____*morbid*_____. She collects _____*data*_____ on all the serious diseases and the top ten causes of death.

5-6. Jason's math ability must be _____*innate*_____—by age two he could add and subtract, and by age seven he could tell whether two lines were _____*parallel*_____ without even using a ruler.

7-8. "I _____*lament*_____ the passing of the days when I could depend on my employees to do the job right," the shop owner said. "These days, workers are not only _____*inept*_____; they do nothing to improve their skills."

9-10. A good marriage counselor, _____*perceptive*_____ enough to understand both the husband's and the wife's points of view, doesn't _____*intervene*_____ in the couple's arguments, but helps them decide how to solve their problems themselves.

► Final Check: Family Differences

Here is a final opportunity for you to strengthen your knowledge of the ten words. First read the following passage carefully. Then fill in each blank with a word from the box at the top of this page. (Context clues will help you figure out which word goes in which blank.) Use each word once.

I am always amazed at how different all of my brothers and sisters are. Sheila, who succeeds at everything she tries, has no patience with the rest of us. She thinks we are (1)_____*inept*_____ at everything and that it's up to her to (2)_____*intervene*_____ in what we do so that things will be done the right way—her way. Jack, on the other hand, is very (3)_____*sedate*_____. He doesn't let anything bother him, and so he rarely loses his temper. Chris is the one who never gives in. As a baby, he was already so (4)_____*obstinate*_____ that he would spit food he didn't like right at my mother. Stacey, the most social, likes people and seems to have an (5)_____*innate*_____ ability to make them feel good. She has always been very (6)_____*perceptive*_____, knowing just what mood others were in and what they might need. Frank has always seemed a little sad. While the rest of us kids would be riding bikes or jumping ropes, he would be doing something (7)_____*morbid*_____, like holding a funeral for a dead frog or bird. He got mad at us whenever we failed to (8)_____*lament*_____ a death as much as he did. Betty has the quickest mind of us all. When she was just four, she told my dad, "Those two shelves aren't (9)_____*parallel*_____—the books are farther apart on the left than on the right." By age six, she was collecting (10)_____*data*_____ for a book she was writing on insects. Yes, my brothers and sisters are all different. They may be strange at times, but they're never boring.

> **SCORES:**   Sentence Check 2 _____ %   Final Check _____ %

Enter your scores above and in the vocabulary performance chart on the inside back cover of the book.

28

Previewing the Words

Find out how many of the ten words in this chapter you already know. Try to complete each sentence with the most suitable word from the list below. Use each word once.

Leave a sentence blank rather than guessing at an answer. Your purpose here is just to get a sense of the ten words and what you may know about them.

controversy	deduction	dimensions	disperse	distort
dominant	sequence	sophisticated	treacherous	trivial

1. Don't believe everything you hear; people often _____*distort*_____ facts when they gossip.

2. The program lists the actors in the _____*sequence*_____ in which they appear in the play.

3. Molly's sprained ankle suddenly seemed _____*trivial*_____ when she heard about her friend's broken leg.

4. We'd better measure the _____*dimensions*_____ of the doorway to be sure we can carry the piano through it.

5. The _____*treacherous*_____ pirate promised a safe journey to his king and queen and then robbed them.

6. When the soccer game ended, police told the wild crowd to _____*disperse*_____ and go to their cars.

7. Having already worked for four years, twelve-year-old Eddie is more _____*sophisticated*_____ about the world of work than all of his friends.

8. The question of where to build a mental health center brought much _____*controversy*_____—everybody wanted it in someone else's neighborhood.

9. Fran was the _____*dominant*_____ partner in her business. Her partner, Pat, wasn't the type to take charge of things.

10. When the dog barked, I reasoned he had to go out again. But my _____*deduction*_____ was incorrect—he was barking at the raccoon in our trashcan.

Now check your answers by turning to page 166. Fix any mistakes and fill in any blank spaces by writing in the correct answers. By doing so, you will complete this introduction to the ten words.

You're now ready to strengthen your knowledge of the words you already know and to master the words you're only half sure of, or don't know at all. Turn to the next page.

Ten Words in Context

Figure out the meanings of the following ten words by looking *closely and carefully* at the context in which the words appear. Doing so will prepare you for the matching test and the practices on the two pages that follow.

1 **controversy**
(kon'-trə-vûr'-sē)
-noun

   a. There was no longer any **controversy**—everyone agreed the all-male dining club should now accept female members.

   b. The students debated the **controversy** over whether or not we should have the death penalty.

2 **deduction**
(di-duk'-shən)
-noun

   a. Since the lights were out and nobody came to the door when I rang, my **deduction** was that no one was home.

   b. The great fictional detective Sherlock Holmes was a master at making **deductions**, at reasoning out solutions to puzzling crimes.

3 **dimensions**
(di-men'-shənz)
-noun

   a. The pool's **dimensions** were odd—its length and width were huge, yet it wasn't very deep.

   b. Let's measure the **dimensions** of the kitchen walls so we can buy the right amount of wallpaper.

4 **disperse**
(di-spûrs')
-verb

   a. The basketball landed in the midst of some pigeons, causing them to **disperse** in all directions.

   b. The police made the large crowd **disperse** because people are easier to manage in small groups.

5 **distort**
(di-stôrt')
-verb

   a. To sell more papers, some newspapers **distort** the news.

   b. Even if people don't mean to **distort** facts, they may misrepresent the truth because their memories are inaccurate.

6 **dominant**
(dom'-ə-nənt)
-adjective

   a. The **dominant** members of the baboon troop are the biggest, most aggressive males. Fearful of these males, the others yield to them.

   b. Mr. Green may be quiet, but he's the **dominant** person in this office. No one questions his authority.

7 **sequence**
(sē'-kwəns)
-noun

   a. The code's **sequence** was essential: 342 would turn off the alarm, but 432 or 234 would not.

   b. The lawyer established the **sequence** of events: The robber first climbed the roof and then entered the house through the attic. Then he went to the bedroom and stole the jewelry.

8 **sophisticated**
(sə-fis'-ti-kā'-tid)
-adjective

   a. Good music doesn't have to be **sophisticated**. An uncomplicated folk tune, for example, can be very moving.

   b. Don't let the professor's simple clothes and manner fool you. When it comes to teaching and to science, he's very **sophisticated**.

9 **treacherous**
(trech'-ər-əs)
-adjective

   a. During the American Revolution, the **treacherous** American soldier Benedict Arnold tried to aid the British.

   b. I felt it was **treacherous** of my friend Jack to go out with my old girlfriend the day after we broke up.

10 **trivial**
(triv'-ē-əl)
-adjective

   a. The principal had a bad reputation for suspending students for **trivial** offenses, such as talking too loudly in the hallways.

   b. When I'm nervous, it helps me to concentrate on some **trivial** activity, such as washing dishes or watching a game show.

Matching Words and Definitions

Check your understanding of the ten words by matching each word with its definition. Look back at the sentences in "Ten Words in Context" as needed to decide on the meaning of each word.

_e_ 1. **controversy**   a. to break up and spread out

_c_ 2. **deduction**   b. disloyal; traitorous

_h_ 3. **dimensions**   c. a conclusion reached through reasoning

_a_ 4. **disperse**   d. unimportant; not significant

_i_ 5. **distort**   e. a debate; argument; a discussion of an important issue with opposing views

_f_ 6. **dominant**   f. having or using more control, influence or authority

_j_ 7. **sequence**   g. wise about the ways of the world; knowledgeable; not simple or childlike; complicated

_g_ 8. **sophisticated**   h. measurements in width, length and sometimes depth

_b_ 9. **treacherous**   i. to misrepresent; tell in an untrue or misleading way

_d_ 10. **trivial**   j. the order in which one thing follows another

CAUTION: Do not go any further until you are sure the above answers are correct. If you have studied the "Ten Words in Context," you will know how to match each word. Then you can use the matches to help you in the following practices. Your goal is to reach a point where you don't need to check definitions at all.

➤Sentence Check 1

Complete each sentence below with the most suitable word from the box. Use each word once.

controversy	deduction	dimensions	disperse	distort
dominant	sequence	sophisticated	treacherous	trivial

1. When I flipped on the kitchen light, roaches _____*disperse*_____(e)d wildly in all directions.

2. Scientists observe facts and then make _____*deduction*_____s based on those facts.

3. There's great _____*controversy*_____ in this country over abortion.

4. In nursery school, shy Alex was often bossed around by the more _____*dominant*_____ children.

5. With each retelling of the story, Wes _____*distort*_____(e)d the facts even more. Before long, the fish had become a giant tuna, and the battle had lasted for hours.

6. Children often argue about things that seem _____*trivial*_____ to adults, such as who gets to sit in the front seat of the car and whose turn it is to feed the cats.

7. In Tokyo, space is so limited that most apartments and homes are very small. The _____*dimensions*_____ of some bedrooms are barely larger than a closet's.

8. After my family moved and I joined the baseball team at a new school, I felt _____*treacherous*_____ when I had to pitch against the team from my old school.

9. If Artie were a more _____*sophisticated*_____ dresser, he might be promoted. But if he continues to wear tennis shoes and earrings to work, he'll be in the mail room forever.

10. The _____*sequence*_____ of moves for a basketball layup is simple: first leap toward the hoop, and then release the ball with one hand so that it gently hits the backboard and drops into the net.

Now check your answers to these questions by turning to page 166. Going over the answers carefully will help you prepare for the next two checks, for which answers are not given.

➤ *Sentence Check 2*

Complete each sentence below with two words from the following list. Use each word once.

controversy	deduction	dimensions	disperse	distort
dominant	sequence	sophisticated	treacherous	trivial

1-2. "Check the _____*dimensions*_____ of your bookcases very carefully," said the carpentry teacher. "Even a quarter of an inch off is not _____*trivial*_____, as it can make the whole thing crooked."

3-4. After learning that a _____*treacherous*_____ member of their unit had told the enemy their location, the sergeant ordered his men to _____*disperse*_____ throughout the forest.

5-6. My boss often _____*distort*_____s the truth by suggesting he's the _____*dominant*_____ person in the shoe store. In reality, the store owner makes all the important decisions.

7-8. Based on my experience, I have made this _____*deduction*_____: managers are often _____*sophisticated*_____ about finances but not so knowledgable when it comes to handling people.

9-10. The _____*controversy*_____ on the movie set was about the _____*sequence*_____ of scenes. Some actors thought the love scene should come before the chase scene, but the director wanted the opposite.

➤ *Final Check:* **Murder Mystery**

Here is a final opportunity for you to strengthen your knowledge of the ten words. First read the following passage carefully. Then fill in each blank with a word from the box at the top of this page. (Context clues will help you figure out which word goes in which blank.) Use each word once.

There was a great deal of (1)_____*controversy*_____ and disagreement among the London police over who could have killed the city's richest citizen. They finally agreed to call in the world-famous detective Ernest G. Mann. Mr. Mann was a (2)_____*sophisticated*_____ gentleman—he knew the world and understood people. And when it came to murder, he spoke with such authority that no one doubted who was the (3)_____*dominant*_____ person in the room.

Mr. Mann ordered the crowd of policemen to (4)_____*disperse*_____ throughout the house so he would have space to work where the murder occurred, in the dining room. One quick glance told him its (5)_____*dimensions*_____ down to the nearest inch. After studying the mess in the room, he also knew the (6)_____*sequence*_____ of events—the word, the angry toss, the punch, the shot. He circled the room, eyeing every single item in it. "Nothing can be considered (7)_____*trivial*_____ when murder is concerned," he said. "Everything is important. I must see everything! Everything!"

Next he read the police report and questioned the butler. "Ah, Mr. Butler, what you have just told me is different from what you told the police. Are you trying to (8)_____*distort*_____ the truth?"

At that, the red-faced butler jumped up and headed for the door. "Wait!" called Mr. Mann. "You are only making it worse. But no matter. The mystery is solved." Then he said to the police in the hallway, "That butler is a (9)_____*treacherous*_____ man. Anyone who would kill his employer over a comment about lumpy gravy is too traitorous to walk the streets. Arrest him, officers."

"But. . .but, how did you know?" cried the butler.

"It was a simple (10)_____*deduction*_____, sir. The facts were all here. They just needed a logical mind to put them together correctly." And with that, Ernest G. Mann spun around and left.

SCORES:	Sentence Check 2 _____ %	Final Check _____ %	

Enter your scores above and in the vocabulary performance chart on the inside back cover of the book.

Previewing the Words

Find out how many of the ten words in this chapter you already know. Try to complete each sentence with the most suitable word from the list below. Use each word once.

Leave a sentence blank rather than guessing at an answer. Your purpose here is just to get a sense of the ten words and what you may know about them.

confirm	deceptive	defy	restrain	seclusion
submit	susceptible	transmit	valid	vigorous

1. In a courtroom, gossip isn't considered _____*valid*_____ testimony—it's too unreliable.

2. Telephones _____*transmit*_____ voice signals through electrical wires.

3. Maya called the airline to _____*confirm*_____ her flight reservation before she drove to the airport.

4. Any prisoner who dared to _____*defy*_____ the guards was badly beaten.

5. Because Lenny refused to _____*submit*_____ to his grandfather's wishes, he was removed from the will.

6. Fran is so _____*susceptible*_____ to blushing that she turns away whenever she is embarrassed, so no one will see her turn red.

7. The little boy tried to _____*restrain*_____ his big dog from chasing a car, but he could not hold the dog back.

8. The _____*seclusion*_____ of the man's farm—many miles from other homes—made it difficult for him to get help in an emergency.

9. The seeming ease with which Nadia plays the piano is _____*deceptive*_____; she practices hours each day.

10. My 80-year-old grandmother is still _____*vigorous*_____ enough to walk four miles every day.

Now check your answers by turning to page 166. Fix any mistakes and fill in any blank spaces by writing in the correct answers. By doing so, you will complete this introduction to the ten words.

You're now ready to strengthen your knowledge of the words you already know and to master the words you're only half sure of, or don't know at all. Turn to the next page.

Ten Words in Context

Figure out the meanings of the following ten words by looking *closely and carefully* at the context in which the words appear. Doing so will prepare you for the matching test and the practices on the two pages that follow.

1 **confirm**
(kən-fûrm')
-*verb*

  a. Because his doctor's appointment had been made weeks before, Daniel phoned to **confirm** the date and time.

  b. "Yes, it's true," the union leader said, **confirming** the report that the teachers would refuse to do lunch duty from now on.

2 **deceptive**
(di-sep'-tiv)
-*adjective*

  a. Certain car mirrors are **deceptive**. They make other cars seem farther away than they really are.

  b. After stealing the radio, Meg remained silent while another student was wrongly accused. Her silence was as **deceptive** as an outright lie.

3 **defy**
(di-fī')
-*verb*

  a. The automotive plant workers voted to **defy** the company and go on strike.

  b. After being forbidden to go out three evenings in a row, Ted **defied** his parents by walking right out the front door.

4 **restrain**
(ri-strān')
-*verb*

  a. I **restrained** myself from laughing when my brother made a funny face while Uncle William told us—yet again—the story of his operation.

  b. Larry was so angry that we had to **restrain** him by force from punching Neal.

5 **seclusion**
(si-kloo'-zhən)
-*noun*

  a. The **seclusion** of the mountain cabin started to bother Veronica. She missed the city and being with other people.

  b. I work best in **seclusion**, where no one can interrupt the flow of my thoughts.

6 **submit**
(səb-mit')
-*verb*

  a. After bucking wildly for several minutes, the horse calmed down and **submitted** to the rider.

  b. For safety reasons, travelers must **submit** to being inspected at airports.

7 **susceptible**
(sə-sep'-tə-bəl)
-*adjective*

  a. Some people view falling in love as an illness to which romantic people are especially **susceptible**.

  b. People who smoke are more **susceptible** to colds than others.

8 **transmit**
(trans-mit')
-*verb*

  a. The emergency broadcast was **transmitted** over all the nation's radio stations.

  b. Before the microscope was invented, no one knew a person could **transmit** a disease to someone else through "invisible" germs.

9 **valid**
(val'-id)
-*adjective*

  a. The research study was not **valid** because the researcher had lied about the facts, which really did not support his conclusion.

  b. "Your accusation that I'm not responsible isn't **valid**," Mona told her father. "I've done all my homework already and even cleaned the living room."

10 **vigorous**
(vig'-ər-əs)
- *adjective*

  a. Joanie is so **vigorous** that she constantly needs to release energy. She often roller-skates for hours at a time.

  b. The best teachers have **vigorous** personalities. They are lively enough to make any lesson interesting.

Matching Words and Definitions

Check your understanding of the ten words by matching each word with its definition. Look back at the sentences in "Ten Words in Context" as needed to decide on the meaning of each word.

_e_	1. **confirm**	a. separation from others; being apart or far from others
_c_	2. **deceptive**	b. likely to be affected by; likely to be stricken with
_d_	3. **defy**	c. misleading; intended or intending to deceive
_j_	4. **restrain**	d. to boldly oppose; openly resist; stand up to
_a_	5. **seclusion**	e. to check or establish that something is true or correct; support the truth of something
_h_	6. **submit**	f. firmly based on facts or logic; logical; well grounded
_b_	7. **susceptible to**	g. lively; energetic
_i_	8. **transmit**	h. to give in to another's power or authority
_f_	9. **valid**	i. to send out as an electrical signal; pass or spread (an illness, etc.)
_g_	10. **vigorous**	j. to hold back from action

CAUTION: Do not go any further until you are sure the above answers are correct. If you have studied the "Ten Words in Context," you will know how to match each word. Then you can use the matches to help you in the following practices. Your goal is to reach a point where you don't need to check definitions at all.

➤ Sentence Check 1

Complete each sentence below with the most suitable word from the box. Use each word once.

confirm	deceptive	defy	restrain	seclusion
submit	susceptible	transmit	valid	vigorous

1. I gave the bottle such a _____vigorous_____ shake that it leaked Russian dressing all over my hands.

2. The dinosaur theory seemed _____valid_____ because all the available evidence supported it.

3. I don't go to the beach because I'm so _____susceptible_____ to sunburn.

4. At the party tonight, Nick will _____confirm_____ he is engaged by introducing his date as "my fiancee."

5. In prison, the criminal had to _____submit_____ to more rules than he had ever thought possible.

6. The widow stayed in _____seclusion_____ for a period of mourning, not seeing visitors or going to any social events.

7. Frankenstein's monster was so strong that even tying him down couldn't _____restrain_____ him; he could escape whenever he wished.

8. "Looks can be _____deceptive_____," Ray's big brother warned. "Wendy may have a cute, childish face, but she's far from sweet."

9. With a special attachment, you can _____transmit_____ a document directly from one computer to another over the phone line.

10. The daring thief liked to openly _____defy_____ the police by leaving this note at the scene of the crime: "Love and Kisses from 'The Uncatchable One.'"

Now check your answers to these questions by turning to page 166. Going over the answers carefully will help you prepare for the next two checks, for which answers are not given.

➤ Sentence Check 2

Complete each sentence below with two words from the following list. Use each word once.

confirm	deceptive	defy	restrain	seclusion
submit	susceptible	transmit	valid	vigorous

1-2. It took a _____*vigorous*_____ effort on the part of the police to _____*restrain*_____ the angry mob from pushing through the gates.

3-4. Children who must _____*submit*_____ to overly strict rules often openly _____*defy*_____ their parents when they get older.

5-6. Buddy is so _____*susceptible*_____ to ear infections that he is never surprised to hear the doctor_____*confirm*_____ he has yet another one.

7-8. The prisoners of war were kept in _____*seclusion*_____ for three months except for Christmas Day, when they were permitted to see others and to _____*transmit*_____ messages to their families over a radio.

9-10. The title of the magazine article—"Miracle Weight Loss"—was _____*deceptive*_____. It suggested there is a magical way to lose weight, but such a claim isn't _____*valid*_____—the facts show otherwise.

➤ Final Check: Chicken Pox

Here is a final opportunity for you to strengthen your knowledge of the ten words. First read the following passage carefully. Then fill in each blank with a word from the box at the top of this page. (Context clues will help you figure out which word goes in which blank.) Use each word once.

I remember the day my brother Danny dragged himself home from third grade and complained, "Mommy, I don't feel too good." My mother took one look at my usually (1)_____*vigorous*_____ brother, yelled "Aargh!" and flew up the stairs with him. The other eight of us ran after them, demanding to know what deadly disease he had. "Get away!" my mother cried. "It's chicken pox. He has to stay in (2)_____*seclusion*_____ until all his spots are gone."

Poor Danny had to (3)_____*submit*_____ to having his spots checked by all the other mothers in the neighborhood. "Spots can be (4)_____*deceptive*_____," one lady explained. "They might have been measles, but I have to (5)_____*confirm*_____ your mother's conclusion. These are definitely chicken pox."

After the women left, my mother said firmly, "None of you is to set foot in Danny's room for at least seven days. I don't want him to (6)_____*transmit*_____ this disease to you. I don't think I could survive having the other eight of you sick all at once." She walked away muttering something about how it might already be too late because people are (7)_____*susceptible*_____ to chicken pox germs even before the sick person gets spots.

Then I started thinking: if my mother's claim that Danny's spots would last at least a week was (8)_____*valid*_____, that meant he would get out of school for a week. I was filled with jealousy. Still, I didn't want to (9)_____*defy*_____ my mother, so I didn't go to Danny's room during the forbidden seven days. Instead, unable to (10)_____*restrain*_____ myself, I crawled into bed with him each night.

To this day, my mother says I purposely set out to destroy her sanity. But the situation wasn't all that bad. The eight of us didn't get sick all at once. The other seven got sick two weeks after me.

SCORES: Sentence Check 2 _____%   Final Check _____%

Enter your scores above and in the vocabulary performance chart on the inside back cover of the book.

Previewing the Words

Find out how many of the ten words in this chapter you already know. Try to complete each sentence with the most suitable word from the list below. Use each word once.

Leave a sentence blank rather than guessing at an answer. Your purpose here is just to get a sense of the ten words and what you may know about them.

accelerate	adverse	advocate	audible	coherent
comparable	competent	consecutive	conspicuous	deteriorate

1. Nan had a purple birthmark in a ___conspicuous___ spot—on her forehead.

2. When two products are of ___comparable___ quality, why not buy the cheaper one?

3. The bank teller was known for being very ___competent___—she did her job quickly and well.

4. When the microphone went dead, the lecturer's words were no longer ___audible___ at the back of the hall.

5. Because of the ___adverse___ conditions of their first Arctic winter, many settlers returned to the comforts of civilization.

6. The singer's voice had not ___deteriorate___d at all during the course of her career. It was as strong, steady, and rich as ever.

7. The reporters would work nights for two ___consecutive___ weeks, and then they'd work days for a month straight.

8. My physician is an ___advocate___ of using nicotine gum when quitting smoking. She says the gum makes it more likely the quitter won't start smoking again.

9. A good speech has a clear, ___coherent___ structure. That is, it is held together by logic and order.

10. Instead of slowing down at a yellow traffic light, Eric would ___accelerate___ so that he could speed through before the light changed to red.

Now check your answers by turning to page 166. Fix any mistakes and fill in any blank spaces by writing in the correct answers. By doing so, you will complete this introduction to the ten words.

You're now ready to strengthen your knowledge of the words you already know and to master the words you're only half sure of, or don't know at all. Turn to the next page.

Ten Words in Context

Figure out the meanings of the following ten words by looking *closely and carefully* at the context in which the words appear. Doing so will prepare you for the matching test and the practices on the two pages that follow.

1 **accelerate**
(ak-sel'-ə-rāt')
-verb

   a. The sleds began sliding down the hill slowly and then **accelerated** to flying speed.

   b. Doug's car **accelerated** rapidly, allowing him to catch up with the slowly moving ice-cream truck.

2 **adverse**
(ad-vûrs')
-adjective

   a. Mozart created musical masterpieces in spite of his **adverse** circumstances—illness and debt.

   b. The **adverse** newspaper review of the last Marlon Brando movie convinced many readers not to see it.

3 **advocate**
(ad'-və-kit)
-noun

   a. The two sisters are both strong **advocates** of reform. Lynn campaigns for wildlife protection, and Barbara for a national health-care plan.

   b. Our minister is a strong **advocate** of a drug-free America.

4 **audible**
(ô'-də-bəl)
-adjective

   a. Dogs, bats, and other animals can hear high-pitched sounds that are not **audible** to humans.

   b. The argument next door was barely **audible**. So I put a cup on the wall and my ear to the cup so I could hear better.

5 **coherent**
(kō-hîr'-ənt)
-adjective

   a. To be sure that your essay has a **coherent** organization, write an outline first.

   b. Organizing ideas in a **coherent** manner on paper also helps one to think in a more orderly and logical way.

6 **comparable**
(kom'-pər-ə-bəl)
-adjective

   a. The quality of some relatively new used cars is **comparable** to that of brand-new ones.

   b. Because the two jobs were **comparable** in challenge, interest, and salary, Roy had trouble deciding which to take.

7 **competent**
(kom'-pi-tənt)
-adjective

   a. Some secretaries are more **competent** than their bosses. They know more about the business, are better organizers, and are much more hard-working.

   b. To be a **competent** juggler takes a lot of practice.

8 **consecutive**
(kən-sek'-yə-tiv)
-adjective

   a. Franklin Delano Roosevelt served three **consecutive** full terms as President and died not long after beginning his fourth.

   b. First Vera had the flu. That was immediately followed by mono, which was followed by pneumonia. These **consecutive** illnesses kept her out of work for two months.

9 **conspicuous**
(kən-spik'-yo͞o-əs)
-adjective

   a. Becky's wide-brimmed red hat is so **conspicuous** that it's impossible not to notice her in a crowd.

   b. The new skyscraper stands fifty stories high, making it the tallest and thus the most **conspicuous** building in the city's skyline.

10 **deteriorate**
(di-tîr'-ē-ə-rāt')
-verb

   a. Over many years, the abandoned house had **deteriorated** until its walls crumbled and its floorboards rotted.

   b. Jenny's health continued to **deteriorate** until her classmates started to visit her regularly. Then she began to improve.

Matching Words and Definitions

Check your understanding of the ten words by matching each word with its definition. Look back at the sentences in "Ten Words in Context" as needed to decide on the meaning of each word.

_e_	1. accelerate	a.	able to be heard
_d_	2. adverse	b.	following one after the other
_h_	3. advocate	c.	similar
_a_	4. audible	d.	harmful; unfavorable
_g_	5. coherent	e.	to speed up
_c_	6. comparable	f.	obvious; easily noticed
_j_	7. competent	g.	connected in a logical and orderly way
_b_	8. consecutive	h.	a supporter; someone who argues for a cause
_f_	9. conspicuous	i.	to become worse; go down in quality or condition
_i_	10. deteriorate	j.	capable; well qualified

CAUTION: Do not go any further until you are sure the above answers are correct. If you have studied the "Ten Words in Context," you will know how to match each word. Then you can use the matches to help you in the following practices. Your goal is to reach a point where you don't need to check definitions at all.

➤ Sentence Check 1

Complete each sentence below with the most suitable word from the box. Use each word once.

accelerate	adverse	advocate	audible	coherent
comparable	competent	consecutive	conspicuous	deteriorate

1. Dee doesn't like to be _conspicuous_, so she sits in the back of the classroom, where few can see her.

2. Anyone can become a _competent_ cook, but few people develop into great ones.

3. The summer's heat seemed endless. Records were set nationwide for the number of _consecutive_ days above ninety degrees.

4. Since I hate pollution, I'm an _advocate_ of passing state laws to limit the amount of pollution in the air.

5. When the comedian sensed his audience was becoming bored, he _accelerate_d his pace to more jokes per minute.

6. At the movies, Tina put her arm around me and said in a barely _audible_ whisper, "I love you. Pass the popcorn."

7. Our relationship began to _deteriorate_ after we had a big fight over money.

8. People often bring their own children up in a manner _comparable_ to the way they were raised. Thus abused children may become abusing parents.

9. During her high fever, Celia loudly called out broken words and phrases. She seemed unable to speak in full, _coherent_ sentences.

10. The weather was bad, and two of the astronauts were sick. Because of these _adverse_ conditions, the shuttle flight was canceled.

Now check your answers to these questions by turning to page 166. Going over the answers carefully will help you prepare for the next two checks, for which answers are not given.

➤ *Sentence Check 2*

Complete each sentence below with two words from the following list. Use each word once.

accelerate	adverse	advocate	audible	coherent
comparable	competent	consecutive	conspicuous	deteriorate

1-2. "Has your marriage started to ____*deteriorate*____?" asked the radio announcer. "If so, you may benefit from the services of Dr. Louis Frank, one of the city's most ____*competent*____ marriage counselors."

3-4. Our neighbors have had parties this week on three ____*consecutive*____ nights—on Friday, Saturday, and Sunday. And they played their stereo so loudly that it was ____*audible*____ in our bedrooms.

5-6. The sun has an ____*adverse*____ effect on the skin. It ____*accelerate*____s the aging of the skin, resulting in more wrinkles at a younger age.

7-8. We had trouble assembling the bike because the instructions were not ____*coherent*____ and we had to figure out the assembly on our own. Including such poorly written instructions is ____*comparable*____ to including none at all.

9-10. After driving around a neighborhood for twenty minutes before finding the address I was looking for, I am an ____*advocate*____ of ____*conspicuous*____ house numbers.

➤ *Final Check:* Walking

Here is a final opportunity for you to strengthen your knowledge of the ten words. First read the following passage carefully. Then fill in each blank with a word from the box at the top of this page. (Context clues will help you figure out which word goes in which blank.) Use each word once.

I am a strong (1)____*advocate*____ of walking over jogging, two activities which are in no way (2)____*comparable*____. Walking is very relaxing and can be done during all but the most (3)____*adverse*____ outdoor conditions, such as icy sidewalks or a thunderstorm. Walking is also rather easy to learn; most people, in fact, are quite (4)____*competent*____ at it by their teens (but then they learn to drive, and the ability starts to (5)____*deteriorate*____). Walkers see the world at a leisurely rate. With each (6)____*consecutive*____ step, they take in another view of colorful flowers, beautiful trees, and collapsed joggers. In contrast, runners see the world as a blur of images jiggling up and down. Joggers bounce so much that their fronts or rears are bound to shake in a manner so (7)____*conspicuous*____ that passersby can't help but stare. Walkers, on the other hand, keep their pride. Unlike a runner, a walker needs to (8)____*accelerate*____ only if a growling dog appears nearby. Also, walkers can hold a conversation that is (9)____*coherent*____ enough to make sense. In contrast, the jogger's brain is too shaken to produce orderly sentences, and the voice is reduced to a barely (10)____*audible*____ gasp. Certainly, walking is in every way superior to jogging. In walking, you just pass by. In jogging, you also pass out.

SCORES:	Sentence Check 2 _____%	Final Check _____%	

Enter your scores above and in the vocabulary performance chart on the inside back cover of the book.

UNIT FIVE: Test 1

PART A
Choose the word that best completes each sentence and write it in the space provided.

1. **perceptive**
   susceptible
   profound
   infinite

   Bernard is ___susceptible___ to headaches. Whenever he has to study, his head

   starts to pound.

2. **defy**
   confirm
   lure
   disperse

   My sister made the mistake of letting a high salary ___lure___ her to a job that

   bores her.

3. **site**
   vocation
   sequence
   seclusion

   The land developer built a huge mall on the ___site___ where the racetrack

   had burned down.

4. **disperse**
   inflict
   subside
   restrain

   As his attacker was about to ___inflict___ serious injury, Robert broke free

   and ran away.

5. **data**
   severity
   nostalgia
   mania

   Sharon feels she now has enough ___data___ to begin writing her report on

   eating disorders.

6. **audible**
   comparable
   valid
   parallel

   I have trouble parking ___parallel___ to the curb. My car is always farther out

   in back than in front.

7. **morbid**
   susceptible
   adverse
   infinite

   To devote herself so fully to the poor, Mother Theresa must have a(n) ___infinite___

   amount of love for them.

8. **competent**
   theoretical
   deceptive
   conspicuous

   Instead of getting a ___competent___ typist, my boss hired someone who types

   with one finger and usually hits the wrong key.

9. **vigorous**
   treacherous
   perceptive
   competent

   The soap opera had many ___treacherous___ characters who thought nothing of

   cheating people they supposedly loved.

10. **consecutive**
    adverse
    comparable
    finite

    My English instructor has such high standards that a "B" from her is

    ___comparable___ to an "A" from most teachers.

11. **deteriorate**
     initiate
     dispense
     discriminate

     Doug bought orange socks instead of red because, in the store's poor lighting, he couldn't _*discriminate*_ between the two colors.

12. **sophisticated**
     inept
     dismal
     susceptible

     Because of her world travels, Jessie is more _*sophisticated*_ than her cousin Leona, who has never left their small hometown.

13. **accelerate**
     lament
     subside
     distort

     Most of us _*lament*_ the end of our first romance. I cried off and on for three whole weeks the first time I ended a relationship.

PART B
Circle **C** if the italicized word is used **correctly**. Circle **I** if the word is used **incorrectly**.

Ⓒ I 14. The boy let go of his balloon, and it quickly *ascended* to the ceiling of the shopping center.

C Ⓘ 15. I felt much worse when my muscle cramp *subsided*.

Ⓒ I 16. My brother had to *restrain* himself to keep from eating the entire cheesecake.

C Ⓘ 17. When the nuclear power plant exploded, its dangers became *theoretical*.

Ⓒ I 18. Gary wore a *conspicuous* red jacket so his blind date could spot him easily.

Ⓒ I 19. The prisoner was put in *seclusion* after causing several fights with other inmates.

C Ⓘ 20. Angela's pregnancy made her so *vigorous* that all she wanted to do was sleep.

Ⓒ I 21. I didn't realize the *severity* of Bill's injuries until I heard he was still in the hospital three months after his accident.

C Ⓘ 22. My apartment is *dismal*. Several large windows allow the sun to shine in on the cheerful yellow and white furnishings.

C Ⓘ 23. Paco is *inept* at checkers. He can win most games blindfolded.

Ⓒ I 24. Dad was going to tell the waiter the soup should be hotter but then decided the complaint was too *trivial*.

C Ⓘ 25. When asked to pay for the window he had broken, Larry was *obstinate*. He said "Gladly!" and paid for it immediately.

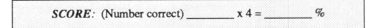

SCORE: (Number correct) _____ x 4 = _____ %

Enter your scores above and in the vocabulary performance chart on the inside back cover of the book.

UNIT FIVE: Test 2

PART A
Complete each sentence with a word from the box. Use each word once.

audible	deceptive	deduction	deteriorated
dimensions	dispense	disperse	intervene
mania	nostalgia	perceptive	transmitted
vocations			

1. The neighbors asked the police to _____*disperse*_____ the noisy group of teenagers gathered at the corner.

2. Certain servers at the school cafeteria _____*dispense*_____ larger portions than others.

3. One of her students _____*transmitted*_____ German measles to Melba while she was pregnant.

4. I rarely _____*intervene*_____ in fights between children. I believe they should work things out for themselves.

5. No one responded when the speaker asked, "Can you hear me?" because his words were too soft to be _____*audible*_____.

6. On Career Day, professionals came to the high school to tell the students about their _*vocations*_.

7. I was shocked to see how my old high school has _____*deteriorated*_____ since I moved away. It's in great need of repair.

8. The picture in the magazine ad is _____*deceptive*_____. It makes the doll look much larger than it really is.

9. My counselor is very _____*perceptive*_____. The other day she knew something was bothering me even though I said, "I'm fine."

10. Looking over his high school yearbook and remembering all the fun he had made Al feel great _____*nostalgia*_____ for his school days.

11. Since I didn't know the exact _____*dimensions*_____ of my bedroom windows, I had to guess which curtains to buy.

12. At first, Kim didn't know the correct answer on the multiple-choice test. But through _*deduction*_, she ruled out each of the wrong answers.

13. Henry Ford had a _____*mania*_____ for using soybeans. He once came to a meeting wearing clothing that, except for his shoes, was made of soybean products.

PART B
Circle **C** if the italicized word is used **correctly.** Circle **I** if the word is used **incorrectly.**

C (I) 14.   Of my parents, my father is the *dominant* one. He does almost anything my mother says.

(C) I 15.   Jed ran to *summon* the fire department when he saw smoke coming from his neighbor's window.

C (I) 16.   We all thought the senator's speech was quite *coherent.* It was too disorganized to follow.

(C) I 17.   Before my TV completely broke, it *distorted* the picture so that everything was stretched sideways.

C (I) 18.   Joyce's baby is more *sedate* than most. When he isn't climbing all over the furniture, he's screaming.

(C) I 19.   In January the school will *initiate* a stricter dress code. For the first time, cut-off jeans and short skirts will be forbidden.

C (I) 20.   Ruth is *morbid.* She always looks forward to a dance, a party, or dinner with a friend.

(C) I 21.   As an *advocate* of public transportation, I try to convince more voters to support the bus and train systems.

(C) I 22.   Eric usually works every other weekend. But when he filled in for Ann on his weekend off, he ended up working three *consecutive* weekends.

C (I) 23.   Since words and music can be combined in *finite* ways, there is no end to the number of songs that can be written.

C (I) 24.   The words of the song—"Yummy, yummy, yummy, I've got love in my tummy"—were so *profound* that I couldn't help laughing.

(C) I 25.   Post-it notes are based on a simple but *ingenious* idea: paper that sticks but can also be removed.

SCORE: (Number correct) _____ x 4 = _____ %

Enter your scores above and in the vocabulary performance chart on the inside back cover of the book.

UNIT FIVE: Test 3

PART A
Complete each sentence in a way that clearly shows you understand the meaning of the boldfaced word. Take a minute to plan your answer before you write.

    Example: A child might **defy** a parent by _____ *refusing to mow the lawn.* _____

1. A camper might experience such **adverse** conditions as _____ *(Answers will vary.)* _____

    _____

2. One **valid** reason for missing class is _____

    _____

3. I usually **accelerate** my car when _____

    _____

4. Ramon felt **dismal** because_____

    _____

5. There is a **controversy** in our country about _____

    _____

6. If it were **literally** "raining cats and dogs," then _____

    _____

7. You could **confirm** a date with a friend by_____

    _____

8. Babies have an **innate** ability to _____

    _____

9. If you were to **submit** to someone's demand for a loan, you would _____

    _____

10. The advertising was **deceptive** because it _____

    _____

PART B
After each boldfaced word are a *synonym* (a word that means the same as the boldfaced word), an *antonym* (a word that means the opposite of the boldfaced word), and a word that is neither. Mark the antonym with an *A*.

Example:	**inept**	_____common	_A_ skilled	_____ clumsy

11. **initiate**   _____ raise   _____ begin   _A_ end

12. **conspicuous**   _____ obvious   _A_ hidden   _____ greedy

13. **subside**   _____ examine   _____ lessen   _A_ increase

14. **trivial**   _A_ important   _____ gloomy   _____ minor

15. **defy**   _A_ obey   _____ challenge   _____ mislead

PART C
Use five of the following ten words in sentences. Make it clear that you know the meaning of the word you use. Feel free to use the past tense or plural form of a word.

audible	controversy	distort	inflict	intervene
mania	severity	sophisticated	vigorous	vocation

16. _____ *(Answers will vary.)* _____

_____

17. _____

_____

18. _____

_____

19. _____

_____

20. _____

SCORE: (Number correct) _____ x 5 = _____ %

Enter your scores above and in the vocabulary performance chart on the inside back cover of the book.

A. Limited Answer Key

An Important Note: Be sure to use this answer key as a learning tool only. You should not turn to this key until you have considered carefully the sentence in which a given word appears.

Used properly, the key will help you to learn words and to prepare for the activities and tests for which answers are not given. For ease of reference, the title of the "Final Check" passage in each chapter appears in parentheses.

Chapter 1 (Taking Exams)

Previewing the Words

1. drastic
2. anecdote
3. candid
4. comply
5. acknowledge
6. appropriate
7. alternative
8. compel
9. concise
10. avert

Sentence Check 1

1. candid
2. anecdotes
3. drastic
4. avert
5. concise
6. comply
7. compel
8. alternative
9. acknowledge
10. appropriate

Chapter 2 (Nate the Woodsman)

Previewing the Words

1. urban
2. erratic
3. fortify
4. reminisce
5. dialogue
6. extensive
7. forfeit
8. illuminate
9. isolate
10. refuge

Sentence Check 1

1. erratic
2. refuge
3. fortify
4. forfeit
5. isolate
6. reminisce
7. illuminate
8. dialogue
9. extensive
10. urban

Chapter 3 (Who's on Trial?)

Previewing the Words

1. legitimate
2. morale
3. menace
4. integrity
5. undermine
6. lenient
7. delete
8. naive
9. impartial
10. overt

Sentence Check

1. impartial
2. undermine
3. menace
4. morale
5. legitimate
6. naive
7. delete
8. overt
9. lenient
10. integrity

Chapter 4 (Students and Politics)

Previewing the Words

1. prospects
2. bland
3. antidote
4. radical
5. propaganda
6. reinforce
7. agenda
8. ruthless
9. relevant
10. apathy

Sentence Check 1

1. ruthless
2. bland
3. relevant
4. reinforce
5. prospects
6. antidote
7. agenda
8. radical
9. apathy
10. propaganda

Chapter 5 (Night Nurse)

Previewing the Words

1. illusion
2. erode
3. novice
4. hypocrite
5. gruesome
6. obstacle
7. idealistic
8. endorse
9. impact
10. imply

Sentence Check 1

1. gruesome
2. erode
3. imply
4. novice
5. idealistic
6. hypocrite
7. endorse
8. impact
9. obstacle
10. illusion

Chapter 6 (Theo's Perfect Car)

Sentence Check 1

1. rebuilt
2. visible
3. supermarkets
4. prejudge
5. restful
6. unicorn
7. extract
8. autobiography
9. multipurpose
10. unlucky

Chapter 7 (Relating to Parents)

Previewing the Words

1. contrary
2. concede
3. transition
4. superficial
5. conservative
6. sustain
7. denounce
8. deter
9. disclose
10. scapegoat

Sentence Check 1

1. scapegoat
2. sustain
3. denounce
4. concede
5. deter
6. superficial
7. disclose
8. transition
9. contrary
10. conservative

Chapter 8 (Job Choices)

Previewing the Words

1. surpass
2. tentative
3. inhibit
4. compensate
5. derive
6. supplement
7. moderate
8. verify
9. conceive
10. diversity

Sentence Check 1

1. derive
2. verify
3. moderate
4. tentative
5. surpass
6. supplement
7. inhibit
8. conceive
9. diversity
10. compensate

Chapter 9 (No Joking)

Previewing the Words

1. blunt
2. pretense
3. optimist
4. remorse
5. chronological
6. alter
7. chronic
8. prolong
9. refrain
10. ample

Sentence Check 1

1. refrain
2. optimist
3. alter
4. prolong
5. ample
6. remorse
7. blunt
8. chronological
9. chronic
10. pretense

Chapter 10 (Museum Pet)

Previewing the Words

1. prominent
2. prudent
3. donor
4. acute
5. recipient
6. anonymous
7. bestow
8. arrogant
9. apprehensive
10. phobia

Sentence Check 1

1. phobia
2. anonymous
3. acute
4. arrogant
5. recipient
6. bestow
7. prudent
8. apprehensive
9. donor
10. prominent

Chapter 11 (Unacceptable Boyfriends)

Previewing the Words

1. adhere
2. dogmatic
3. assess
4. defect
5. alienate
6. doctrine
7. contempt
8. absurd
9. compile
10. affluent

Sentence Check 1

1. assess
2. affluent
3. alienate
4. contempt
5. compile
6. doctrine
7. adhere
8. defect
9. dogmatic
10. absurd

Chapter 12 (Coping with Snow)

Sentence Check 1

1. spectacular
2. phonetics
3. interrupt
4. enclosing
5. autobiography
6. antisocial
7. binoculars
8. cordless
9. Postnatal
10. submerge

Chapter 13 (My Headstrong Baby)

Previewing the Words

1. rational
2. accessible
3. compatible
4. prevail
5. retrieve
6. awe
7. exempt
8. retort
9. cite
10. propel

Sentence Check 1

1. prevail
2. propel
3. retrieve
4. exempt
5. awe
6. accessible
7. compatible
8. cite
9. rational
10. retort

Chapter 14 (Mr. Perfect?)

Previewing the Words

1. fictitious
2. pessimist
3. dubious
4. liable
5. miserly
6. ecstatic
7. gullible
8. encounter
9. fallacy
10. evolve

Sentence Check 1

1. miserly
2. liable
3. fictitious
4. dubious
5. encounter
6. ecstatic
7. pessimist
8. fallacy
9. gullible
10. evolve

Chapter 15 (A Narrow Escape)

Previewing the Words

1. obsession	6. harass
2. fluent	7. elapse
3. ordeal	8. evasive
4. futile	9. persistent
5. infer	10. lethal

Sentence Check 1

1. fluent	6. lethal
2. harass	7. ordeal
3. obsession	8. futile
4. evasive	9. persistent
5. elapse	10. infer

Chapter 16 (The Power of Advertising)

Previewing the Words

1. delusion	6. convey
2. versatile	7. stimulate
3. subtle	8. universal
4. savor	9. devise
5. vivid	10. unique

Sentence Check 1

1. devise	6. stimulate
2. universal	7. convey
3. savor	8. delusion
4. subtle	9. unique
5. vivid	10. versatile

Chapter 17 (Waiter)

Previewing the Words

1. equate	6. defer
2. malicious	7. inevitable
3. endeavor	8. impose
4. patron	9. indignant
5. option	10. passive

Sentence Check 1

1. inevitable	6. malicious
2. options	7. impose
3. equate	8. indignant
4. passive	9. defer
5. patron	10. endeavor

Chapter 18 (Black Widow Spiders)

Sentence Check 1

1. dictating	6. conform
2. pedals	7. disarm
3. tripod	8. microscope
4. transplant	9. Scriptures
5. penmanship	10. televised

Chapter 19 (Adjusting to a New Culture)

Previewing the Words

1. retain	6. gesture
2. reciprocate	7. refuted
3. dismay	8. exile
4. recede	9. adapt
5. ritual	10. revert

Sentence Check 1

1. dismay	6. revert
2. recede	7. adapt
3. refute	8. exile
4. gesture	9. reciprocate
5. retain	10. ritual

Chapter 20 (A Dream About Wealth)

Previewing the Words

1. frugal	6. notable
2. elaborate	7. impulsive
3. mediocre	8. exotic
4. emerge	9. indifferent
5. indulgent	10. liberal

Sentence Check 1

1. mediocre	6. elaborate
2. indulgent	7. frugal
3. emerge	8. indifferent
4. notable	9. impulsive
5. liberal	10. exotic

Chapter 21 (Children and Drugs)

Previewing the Words

1. alleged	6. affirm
2. coerce	7. sadistic
3. query	8. elite
4. impair	9. allude
5. essence	10. immunity

Sentence Check 1

1. coerce	6. affirm
2. sadistic	7. alleged
3. impair	8. elite
4. essence	9. query
5. immunity	10. allude

Chapter 22 (Party House)

Previewing the Words

1. revoke	6. reprimand
2. recur	7. shrewd
3. tactic	8. plausible
4. skeptical	9. stereotype
5. provoke	10. ridicule

Sentence Check 1

1. ridicule	6. tactic
2. stereotype	7. skeptical
3. plausible	8. reprimand
4. shrewd	9. provoke
5. recur	10. revoke

Chapter 23 (Procrastinator)

Previewing the Words

1. vital
2. simultaneous
3. consequence
4. procrastinate
5. strategy
6. detain
7. transaction
8. destiny
9. diminish
10. Tedious

Sentence Check 1

1. transaction
2. diminish
3. procrastinate
4. consequence
5. simultaneous
6. strategy
7. destiny
8. vital
9. detain
10. tedious

Chapter 24 (King of Cats)

Sentence Check 1

1. malnutrition
2. centimeters
3. Criminology
4. monorail
5. memorize
6. manual
7. inadequate
8. laughable
9. thermogram
10. imported

Chapter 25 (Changes in View)

Previewing the Words

1. vocation
2. severity
3. subside
4. theoretical
5. summon
6. site
7. profound
8. dispense
9. discriminate
10. dismal

Sentence Check 1

1. discriminate
2. profound
3. subside
4. summon
5. vocation
6. dismal
7. dispense
8. severity
9. theoretical
10. site

Chapter 26 (Balloon Flight)

Previewing the Words

1. ingenious
2. infinite
3. ascend
4. inflict
5. initiate
6. lure
7. mania
8. literally
9. finite
10. nostalgia

Sentence Check 1

1. initiate
2. finite
3. inflict
4. nostalgia
5. lure
6. mania
7. ascend
8. infinite
9. ingenious
10. literally

Chapter 27 (Family Differences)

Previewing the Words

1. obstinate
2. inept
3. lament
4. perceptive
5. data
6. morbid
7. intervene
8. innate
9. parallel
10. sedate

Sentence Check 1

1. data
2. inept
3. morbid
4. sedate
5. perceptive
6. parallel
7. intervene
8. obstinate
9. lament
10. innate

Chapter 28 (Murder Mystery)

Previewing the Words

1. distort
2. sequence
3. trivial
4. dimensions
5. treacherous
6. disperse
7. sophisticated
8. controversy
9. dominant
10. deduction

Sentence Check 1

1. disperse
2. deduction
3. controversy
4. dominant
5. distort
6. trivial
7. dimensions
8. treacherous
9. sophisticated
10. sequence

Chapter 29 (Chicken Pox)

Previewing the Words

1. valid
2. transmit
3. confirm
4. defy
5. submit
6. susceptible
7. restrain
8. seclusion
9. deceptive
10. vigorous

Sentence Check 1

1. vigorous
2. valid
3. susceptible
4. confirm
5. submit
6. seclusion
7. restrain
8. deceptive
9. transmit
10. defy

Chapter 30 (Walking)

Previewing the Words

1. conspicuous
2. comparable
3. competent
4. audible
5. adverse
6. deteriorate
7. consecutive
8. advocate
9. coherent
10. accelerate

Sentence Check 1

1. conspicuous
2. competent
3. consecutive
4. advocate
5. accelerate
6. audible
7. deteriorate
8. comparable
9. coherent
10. adverse

B. Dictionary Use

It isn't always possible to figure out the meaning of a word from its context, and that's where a dictionary comes in. Following is some basic information to help you use a dictionary.

HOW TO FIND A WORD

A dictionary contains so many words that it can take a while to find the one you're looking for. But if you know how to use guide words, you can find a word rather quickly. *Guide words* are the two words at the top of each dictionary page. The first guide word tells what the first word is on the page. The second guide word tells what the last word is on that page. The other words on a page fall alphabetically between the two guide words. So when you look up a word, find the two guide words that alphabetically surround the word you're looking for.

• Which of the following pair of guide words would be on a page with the word *skirmish?*

   (skimp/ skyscraper)   skyward / slave   sixty / skimming

The answer to this question and the ones that follow are given on the next page.

HOW TO USE A DICTIONARY LISTING

A dictionary listing includes many pieces of information. For example, here is a listing from the *Random House College Dictionary*, Paperback Edition. Note that it includes much more than just a definition.

driz•zle (driz'əl), *v.,* **-zled, -zling,** *n.* —*v.* **1.** to rain gently and steadily in fine drops. — *n.* **2.** a very light rain. —**driz'zly,** *adj.*

Key parts of a dictionary entry are listed and explained below.

Syllables. Dots separate dictionary entry words into syllables. Note that *drizzle* has one dot, which breaks the word into two syllables.

• To practice seeing the syllable breakdown in a dictionary entry, write the number of syllables in each word below.

   gla•mour *2*   **mic•ro•wave** *3*   **in•de•scrib•a•ble** *5*

Pronunciation guide. The information within parentheses after the entry word shows how to pronounce the entry word. This pronunciation guide includes two types of symbols: pronunciation symbols and accent marks.

Pronunciation symbols represent the consonant and vowel sounds in a word. The consonant sounds are probably very familiar to you, but you may find it helpful to review some of the sounds of the vowels—*a, e, i, o,* and *u.* Every dictionary has a key explaining the sounds of its pronunciation symbols, including the long and short sounds of vowels.

Long vowels have the sound of their own names. For example, the *a* in *pay* and the *o* in *no* both have long vowel sounds. Long vowel sounds are shown by a line above the vowel.

In the *Random House College Dictionary*, the *short vowels* are shown by the use of the vowel itself, with no other markings. Thus the *i* in the first syllable of *drizzle* is a short *i.* What do the short vowels sound like? Below are words from the *RHCD* pronunciation key which illustrate the *short vowel* sounds.

   a bat   **e** set   **i** big   **o** box   **u** up

This key means, for example, that the *a* in *bat* has the short-*a* sound.

- Which of the words below has a short vowel sound? Which has a long vowel sound?

    drug _short_   **night** _long_   **sand** _short_

   Another pronunciation symbol is the *schwa*, which looks like an upside-down *e*. It stands for certain rapidly spoken, unaccented vowel sounds, such as the *a* in *above*, the *e* in *item*, the *i* in *easily*, the *o* in *gallop*, and the *u* in *circus*. More generally, it has an "uh" sound, like the "uh" a speaker makes when hesitating in speech. Here are three words that include the schwa sound:

     in·fant (in'fənt)   **bum·ble** (bum'bəl)   **de·liv·er** (di-liv'ər)

- Which syllable in *drizzle* contains the schwa sound, the first or the second? _second_

   Accent marks are small black marks that tell you which syllable to emphasize, or stress, as you say a word. An accent mark follows *driz* in the pronunciation guide for *drizzle*, which tells you to stress the first syllable of *drizzle*. Syllables with no accent mark are not stressed. Some syllables are in between, and they are marked with a lighter accent mark.

- Which syllable has the stronger accent in *sentimental*?   _third_

     sen·ti·men·tal (sen'tə-men'tl)

Parts of Speech.   After the pronunciation key and before each set of definitions, the entry word's parts of speech are given. The parts of speech are abbreviated as follows:

     noun—*n.*   pronoun—*pron.*   adjective—*adj.*   adverb—*adv.*   verb—*v.*

- The listing for *drizzle* shows it has two parts of speech. Write them below:

     _____ _noun_ _____   _____ _verb_ _____

Definitions.   Words often have more than one meaning. When they do, each meaning is usually numbered in the dictionary. You can tell which definition of a word fits a given sentence by the meaning of the sentence. For example, the word *charge* has several definitions, including these two: **1.** to ask as a price. **2.** to accuse or blame.

- Show with a check which definition applies in each sentence below:

     The store charged me less for the blouse because it was missing a button.   1 _√_   2 ___

     My neighbor has been charged with shoplifting.   1 ___   2 _√_

Other Information.   After the definitions in a listing in a hardbound dictionary, you may get information about the *origin* of a word. Such information about origins, also known as *etymology,* is usually given in brackets. And you may sometimes be given one or more synonyms or antonyms for the entry word. *Synonyms* are words that are similar in meaning to the entry word; *antonyms* are words that are opposite in meaning.

WHICH DICTIONARIES TO OWN

   You will find it useful to own two recent dictionaries: a small paperback dictionary to carry to class and a hardbound dictionary, which contains more information than a small paperback one. Among the good dictionaries strongly recommended are both the paperback and hardcover editions of the following:

   The Random House College Dictionary
   The American Heritage Dictionary
   Webster's New World Dictionary

ANSWERS TO THE DICTIONARY QUESTIONS
   Guide words: *skimp/skyscraper*
   Number of syllables: 2, 3, 5
   Vowels: *drug, sand* (short); *night* (long)
   Schwa: second syllable of *drizzle*

Accent: stronger accent on third syllable
Parts of speech: noun and verb
Definition: 1; 2

C. List of Words and Word Parts

able, 121
absurd, 53
accelerate, 153
accessible, 69
acknowledge, 5
acute, 49
adapt, 101
adhere, 53
adverse, 153
advocate, 153
affirm, 109
affluent, 53
agenda, 17
alienate, 53
alleged, 109
allude, 109
alter, 45
alternative, 5
ample, 45
anecdote, 5
anonymous, 49
anti, 57
antidote, 17
apathy, 17
apprehensive, 49
appropriate, 5
arrogant, 49
ascend, 137
assess, 53
audible, 153
auto, 25
avert, 5
awe, 69
bestow, 49
bi, 57
bland, 17
blunt, 45
candid, 5
cent, centi, 121
chronic, 45
chronological, 45
cite, 69
coerce, 109
coherent, 153
comparable, 153
compatible, 69
compel, 5
compensate, 41

competent, 153
compile, 53
comply, 5
con, 89
concede, 37
conceive, 41
concise, 5
confirm, 149
consecutive, 153
consequence, 117
conservative, 37
conspicuous, 153
contempt, 53
contrary, 37
controversy, 145
convey, 81
data, 141
deceptive, 149
deduction, 145
defect, 53
defer, 85
defy, 149
delete, 13
delusion, 81
denounce, 37
derive, 41
destiny, 117
detain, 117
deter, 37
deteriorate, 153
devise, 81
dialogue, 9
dict, 89
dimensions, 145
diminish, 117
dis, 89
disclose, 37
discriminate, 133
dismal, 133
dismay, 101
dispense, 133
disperse, 145
distort, 145
diversity, 41
doctrine, 53
dogmatic, 53
dominant, 145
donor, 49

drastic, 5
dubious, 73
ecstatic, 73
elaborate, 105
elapse, 77
elite, 109
emerge, 105
en, em, 57
encounter, 73
endeavor, 85
endorse, 21
equate, 85
erode, 21
erratic, 9
essence, 109
evasive, 77
evolve, 73
ex, 25
exempt, 69
exile, 101
exotic, 105
extensive, 9
fallacy, 73
fictitious, 73
finite, 137
fluent, 77
forfeit, 9
fortify, 9
frugal, 105
ful, 25
futile, 77
gesture, 101
graph, gram, 57
gruesome, 21
gullible, 73
harass, 77
hypocrite, 21
idealistic, 21
illuminate, 9
illusion, 21
immunity, 109
impact, 21
impair, 109
impartial, 13
imply, 21
impose, 25
impulsive, 105
in, 121